France a

France and the Nazis

MEMORY, LIES
AND THE
SECOND WORLD WAR

Adam Nossiter

Methuen

This paperback edition first published in 2003 by Methuen

1 3 5 7 9 10 8 6 4 2

Copyright © 2001 by Adam Nossiter

Originally published in Great Britain in 2001 by Methuen as
The Algeria Hotel: France, Memory and the Second World War

First published in 2001 by Houghton Mifflin, New York

Methuen Publishing Ltd
215 Vauxhall Bridge Rd, London SW1V 1EJ

Methuen Publishing Limited Reg. No. 3543167

A CIP catalogue record for this book is
available from the British Library.

ISBN 0 413 75970 9

Typeset by Deltatype Ltd, Birkenhead, Merseyside

Printed and bound in Great Britain by
Cox and Wyman Ltd, Reading, Berkshire

To Sharon and Franklin

Contents

PART THREE

Tulle: Living Memory

Maps

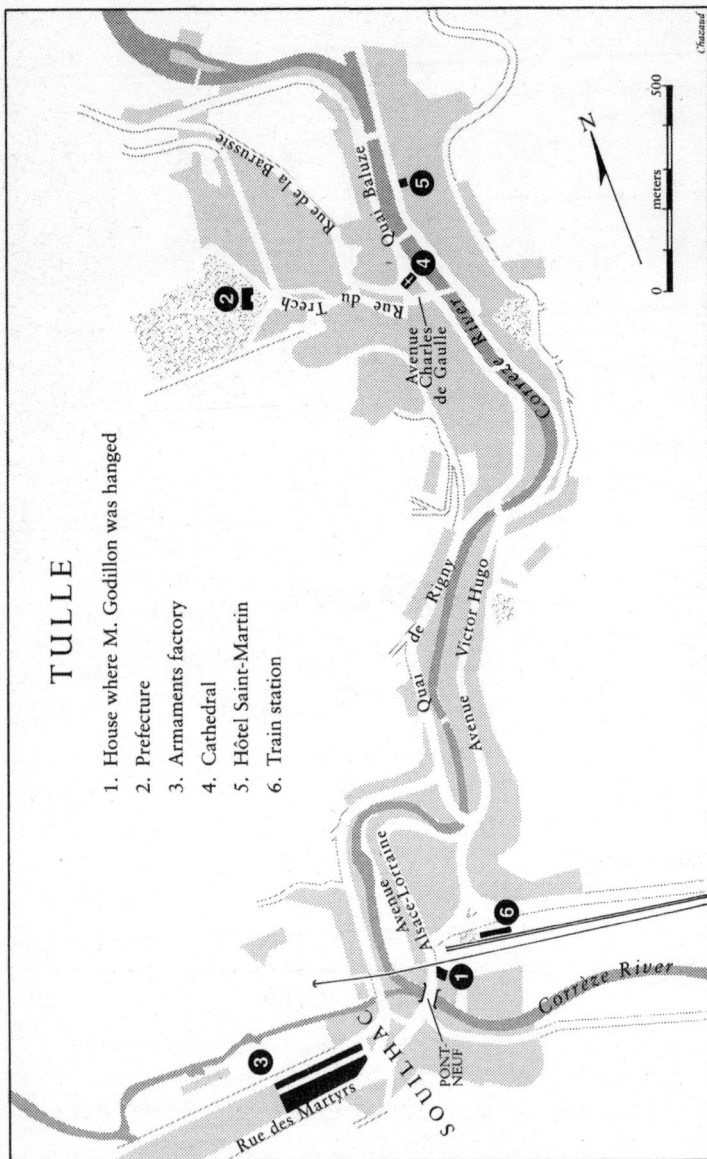

TULLE

1. House where M. Godillon was hanged

2. Prefecture

3. Armaments factory

4. Cathedral

5. Hôtel Saint-Martin

6. Train station

Corrèze River

Rue de la Barussie

Rue du Trech

Quai Baluze

Avenue Charles de Gaulle

Quai de Rigny

Avenue Victor Hugo

Avenue Alsace-Lorraine

SOUILHAC

Rue des Martyrs

PONT NEUF

Corrèze River

N

0   meters   500

Chazaud

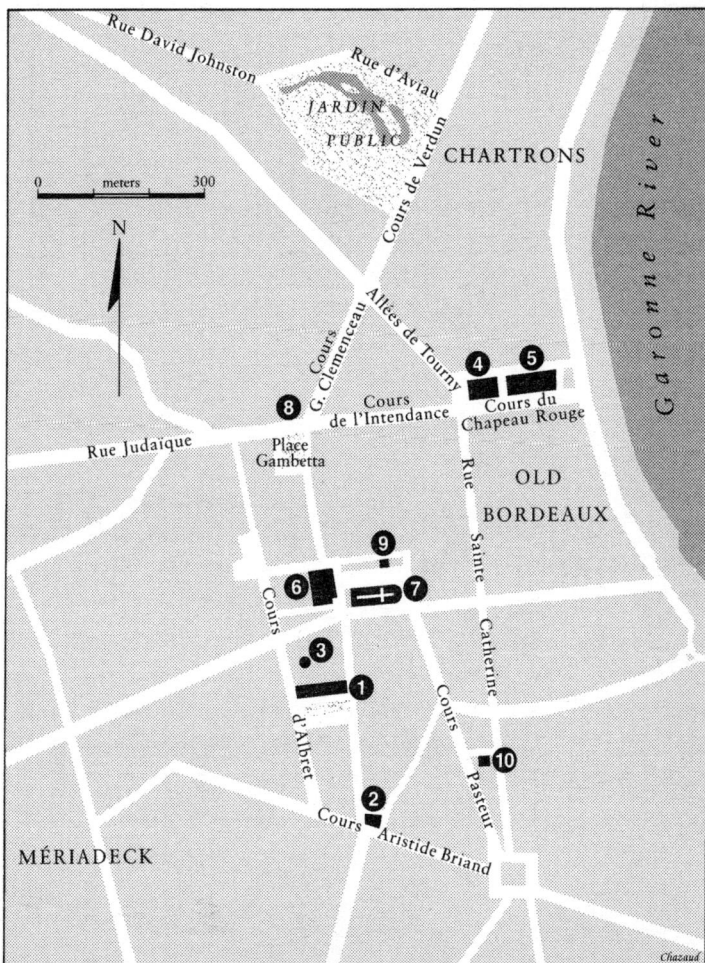

Rue David Johnston

Rue d'Aviau

JARDIN
PUBLIC

CHARTRONS

Cours de Verdun

Garonne River

0 meters 300

N

Allées de Tourny

Cours
G. Clemenceau

4 **5**

Cours
de l'Intendance

Cours du
Chapeau Rouge

8

Rue Judaïque

Place
Gambetta

Rue Sainte

OLD

BORDEAUX

9

Cours

6 **7**

Rue Sainte Catherine

3

1

d'Albret

Cours

10

Pasteur

2

MÉRIADECK

Cours Aristide Briand

Chazaud

BORDEAUX

1. Palais de Justice
2. Bourse du Travail
3. Fort du Hâ
4. Grand Théâtre

5. Hôtel de Saige
   (Old Prefecture)
6. Hôtel de Ville
   (City Hall)

7. Saint André Cathedral
8. Café Régent
9. M. Naquet's apartment
10. Synagogue

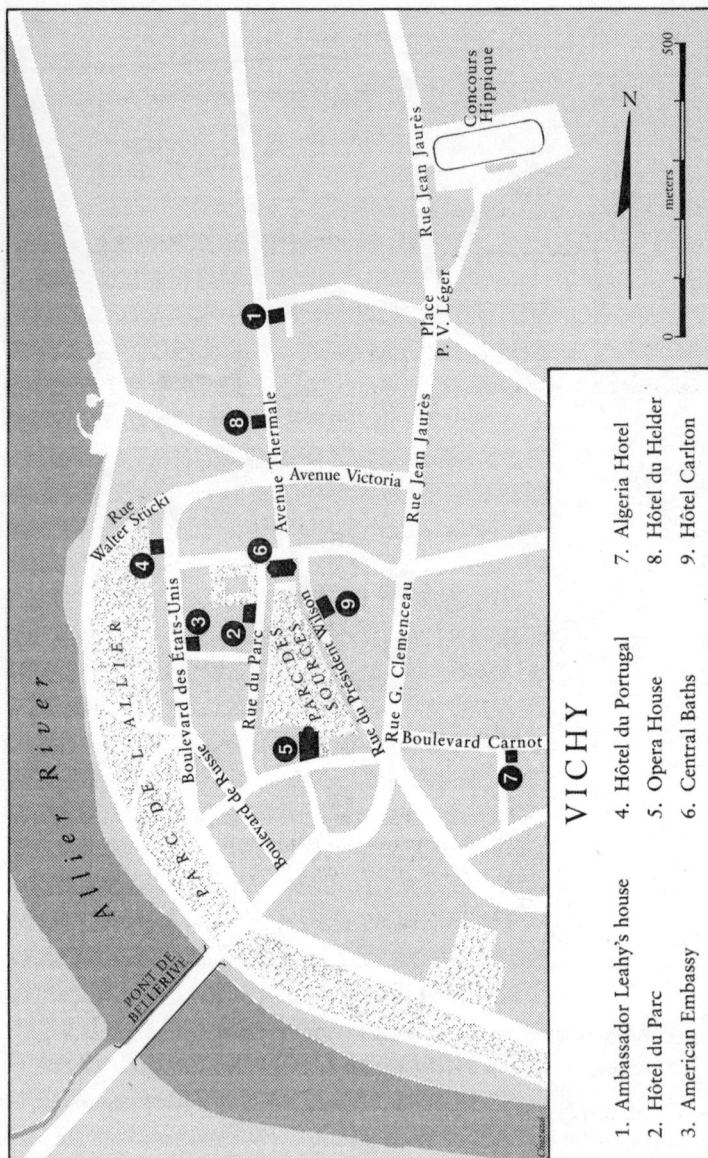

Concours
Hippique

Rue Jean Jaurès

Place
P. V. Léger

N

500

meters

0

Rue Jean Jaurès

Avenue Thermale

Avenue Victoria

Rue
Walter Stucki

Boulevard des États-Unis

Rue du Parc

Rue du Président Wilson

Rue G. Clemenceau

Boulevard de la Rasse

PARC DE L'ALLIER

Allier River

PARC DES SOURCES

Boulevard Carnot

PONT DE
BELLERIVE

VICHY

1. Ambassador Leahy's house	4. Hôtel du Portugal
2. Hôtel du Parc	5. Opera House
3. American Embassy	6. Central Baths

7. Algeria Hotel
8. Hôtel du Helder
9. Hôtel Carlton

Chartrand

FRANCE
UNDER THE OCCUPATION

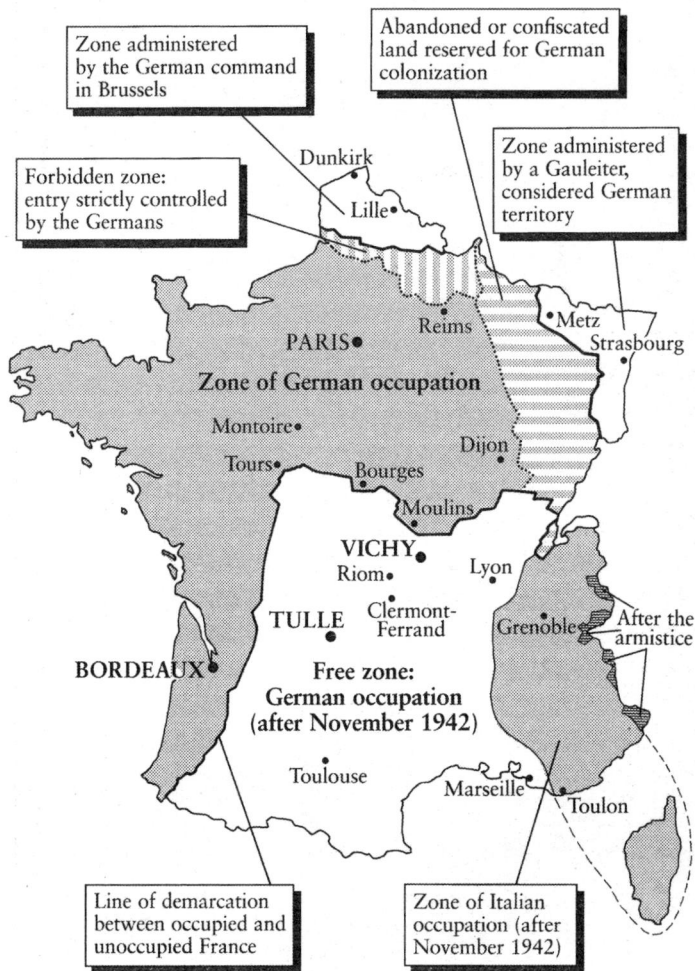

Zone administered
by the German command
in Brussels

Abandoned or confiscated
land reserved for German
colonization

Forbidden zone:
entry strictly controlled
by the Germans

Zone administered
by a Gauleiter,
considered German
territory

Dunkirk

Lille•

•Metz

Reims

Strasbourg

PARIS•

Zone of German occupation

Montoire•

Tours•

Dijon

Bourges

•Moulins

VICHY•

Riom•

Lyon

TULLE
•

Clermont-
Ferrand

Grenoble

After the
armistice

BORDEAUX•

Free zone:
German occupation
(after November 1942)

Toulouse
•

Marseille

•Toulon

Line of demarcation
between occupied and
unoccupied France

Zone of Italian
occupation (after
November 1942)

Chazaud

Introduction:
The Sewing Room

WHEN I WAS A small child, living in a gloomy old house at the edge of Paris, there was a room on the first floor I avoided entering. It was not a big room, just large enough for an ironing board, a Singer sewing machine and a bed. The room was called, in my family, the sewing room. There was nothing forbidding about the little room; it had plenty of light, its colours were pale, and it looked out on the street, a solid bourgeois street of nineteenth-century houses at the unfashionable end of a fashionable district. Some time after we moved to 18 rue Weber, which is near the Porte Maillot in the Sixteenth Arrondissement, the room took on a fearful association. In this room, my parents said, a man – the owner of the house – had killed himself. They provided an explanation, impressive and immeasurably big, or so it seemed to me. The man had committed suicide, I was told, the day the Germans marched into Paris. He had been a famous doctor, and he had gone into the room to put a gun to his head (this last part turned out to be incorrect).

It had happened in the past. When? Not the distant past, apparently. It was not recited as a kind of gruesome curiosity, as when I was given a lesson out of a guidebook in front of some European monument. This was serious: the tone was solemn. It was something that affected the tellers. My parents had not read about it in a book. The information had come nearly firsthand, or at least from somebody who had a connection to it.

My parents had not known this doctor. There was no reason why his action, undoubtedly distressing, should have had any special impact on them. Yet there was something else that gave it force: the history behind it. And so the explanation itself became at least as fearsome a fact as the doctor's death. The man killed himself because the Germans marched into Paris. For a six-year-old child, born in the United States in 1960, far in time and space from whatever sinister occurrences might have been behind the death of the man, that explanation immediately assumed troubling overtones. This was all the more true because it was associated with a clear image: I thought I knew what 'marched' meant. It couldn't have been good.

When I grew older, I tended to dismiss the story. It seemed to be an example of parental exaggeration, even a far-fetched projection of certain inner fears and animosities that themselves might have been legitimate but were unlikely to have had such an intimate link to our mundane family life. There was no use putting oneself into a story not one's own, or so I thought.

It wasn't until years later that I began coming across references to the suicide of Dr Thierry de Martel in June 1940. Many books describing the defeat of France in that year mention this notorious death. The historians evoke it as a singular gesture, exemplary in some respects, though there were at least fifteen suicides in Paris that day. Thierry de Martel was a society doctor, an aristocrat who had had a brilliant career, a pioneer of brain surgery in France and the director of the American Hospital of Paris. As a young man he had been an ardent anti-Dreyfusard, and before the war he had joined anti-parliamentary, anti-Semitic organisations like Action Française and Faisceau (Fasces). He was a fervent nationalist and a decorated World War I veteran who had lost his son in that war. Thierry de Martel had always told friends that he wouldn't be able to bear the idea of German troops in Paris. On June 13 he wrote to his friend William Bullitt, the American ambassador: 'I made you the promise that I wouldn't leave Paris. I didn't say whether I would stay in Paris alive or dead. Alive, I give the enemy a blank cheque; dead, an uncovered one.'

On Friday, June 14, 1940, a brilliant sunny day, troops of the Wehrmacht entered the city. They marched up to the Arc de Triomphe and down the Champs-Élysées, Thierry de Martel had arisen early, shaved and dressed with his usual care. He heard the troops and their tanks. He went to his study on the first floor, stretched out on the divan, and injected himself with strychnine. His housekeeper found him several hours later, a copy of Victor Hugo's play *Hernani*, open to the line 'Since one must be tall to die, I arise,' by his side. A letter warned against any possible attempt to revive him. Six weeks later the far-right newspaper *Candide* paid tribute to the memory of 'our faithful colleague'.[1]

Not long ago, I looked up Thierry de Martel's name in the Paris telephone book for 1939. At the top of page 889, above an advertisement for a neighbourhood confectioner that still exists, I saw 'Martel, (Dr T. de), 18, rue Weber (16ᵉ)'.

A few historians have used the example of the doctor's suicide to open or close their accounts, a desperate act foreshadowing the period to follow or epitomizing the one just ending.[2] For me (and I realized this long after my family had left France), the story also may have been a kind of beginning. It was an ongoing problem to be solved, one that had entered the mind of a small child, survived adolescent scepticism, and been revived in the light of an adult's greater knowledge and puzzlement. For a long time I was obliged to be reminded of it every day, whenever I walked past that little room. Around it our family life continued, but so did the fact of the doctor's death. The paradox was this: something old yet bad had happened in there. It had happened a long time ago, yet it continued to be bad. And it had happened because 'the Germans marched into Paris.'

These intruding facts would have seemed striking to me, all the more so in that they coexisted with a familial atmosphere of confidence. Several years ago, watching portions of a French newsreel from 1965, I glimpsed a trace of this atmosphere. In the newsreel, President Charles de Gaulle gives a press conference under the crystal chandeliers of the Élysée Palace. Visible for an instant among the reporters, standing out because of his height, is a man with dark hair and horn-rimmed glasses. This was my father, then a member of the *Washington Post*'s Paris office.

Assembled amid all this gilt and velvet, my father and his colleagues have a deferential air about them. De Gaulle was God in those years. Some of my earliest childhood memories are infused with his image. On Bastille Day in 1966, I was taken to an outdoor fireworks display, a wondrous occasion culminating logically in the representation of the General himself, his huge nose and peaked French military hat floating in the ether. When I was a small child, de Gaulle seemed to be the reason for my father's employment, if not his existence. His name was part of the furniture at 18 rue Weber. Unlike some of the American reporters, my father admired him, seeing as constructive the grandiose ambitions others found absurd. 'On balance, the world is deeply in debt to this strange man,' he wrote in 1966. Sometimes I would hear the General's emphatic voice pridefully booming out of our black-and-white television. My father shared this mid-1960s confidence. 'The central feature of present-day Europe, both east and west of what used to be called the Iron Curtain, is its comparative affluence,' he wrote from Paris. The article, entitled 'Notes on the New Europe', is accompanied by a photograph of him sitting at a café on the Champs-Élysées, peering at the newspaper *Le Monde*.[3]

The late war continued to exist in this optimistic world, but only as a kind of negative foil. The country was moving forward; de Gaulle, as everybody knew, had triumphed in those war years, incarnating the essence of France with his refusal to collaborate. His version of the war's aftermath – nothing of the country's murky collaborationist regime subsisted, and France had been reborn – was the accepted one. 'After war, he wiped out most vestiges of the Vichy dictatorship and restored France's democratic institutions,' my father wrote in 1966. Our admired family doctor, like many others, had 'been in the Resistance,' a phrase I remember as being nearly as common as *'bonjour'*. The Marais, the old Jewish quarter, meant Sunday trips to Goldenberg's restaurant, not roundups of Jews twenty-odd years before. The disciplinarian French schoolteachers who terrorized us were 'Nazis', to be successfully resisted by brave parents. Of course, no one in my family had any inkling of Thierry de Martel's political allegiances.[4]

There would have been a relative lack of interest corresponding, for other reasons, to an attitude that prevailed in France during those years. The country's official public relation to the war was still untroubled. Paradoxically, the war was both closer in time – I remember buildings fitted in ancient coats of soot, just as they are in the haunting photographs of occupied Paris – yet further away than it was to become. In that era, the war was simply a part of history, safely resolved. The French historian Henry Rousso has written that it was in 1964, the year of my family's arrival in France, that 'this new version of the Occupation – a version most comforting to French sensibilities – achieved its definitive form: France was now cast as a nation that "forever and always resists the invader," whatever uniform he might wear, be it the grey-green of the German army or the paraphernalia of the Roman legion.'[5]

Against this background there was the interior world of the

house and the aura of what had happened in the sewing room. What made that event linger? It was not a question I would have asked myself at the age of six. Yet long after most definite memories of that time and place had disappeared, long after I left that house, the doctor's story stayed in my mind. It stayed even through years in which France was far from my thoughts. Recently I went back to the neighbourhood around the rue Weber for the first time in more than thirty years. Something much less precise than a memory, but palpable nonetheless, had persisted: the scale of the buildings and the angles at which the streets met each other were oddly familiar. It amounted to no more than a vague feeling. Yet the vagueness of this persistence put into sharper relief the memory of the sewing room.

A woman I met several years ago in the town of Vichy, where I was living while writing this book, asked with some bewilderment what could have motivated me, an American, to take on the messy subject of France and its war. I mumbled something about old ties to the country, and the conversation moved on, away from the particular subjects that had brought me back. She began talking about a mutual acquaintance in the town, a bluff, friendly man with whom I had cordial relations. The woman began talking about his parents. She slyly suggested that their role during the Occupation had been less than honourable. She said their relations with the Germans had been perhaps a little too close. The woman did not make this observation because she was a student of history. In fact, as a subject of reflection, she couldn't have been less interested in the period of the war.

She made the remark to cast discredit on the man's parents and, by association, the man himself. Something about this gambit was familiar to me. It was unpleasant enough – I was fond of the person in question – to make me think about it afterward, and familiar enough not to have surprised me at all.

It had that deep familiarity of something that may have been implanted a long time ago, a way of thinking I might have lived with half consciously for years. The woman was reaching back into a past that was, in some sense, still alive for her, even though she professed disdain for its more everyday manifestations – for instance, the books about the war and the Occupation that crowded bookshop shelves, even in Vichy.

A recurring story about France in the American press over the last several decades was that memories of the Occupation had unexpectedly come back to haunt the country. Whenever scandalous revelations surfaced about the half-hidden wartime record of some official, the point would be made: France was newly haunted by its past. This seemed to me unprovable, inasmuch as it concerned 'France'. I met many people there who appeared genuinely indifferent to what had happened a half-century before and whose lives showed no sign of being influenced by it.

Yet it also seemed clear, just on the surface, that in certain times and places, this phenomenon of being concerned with the past, sometimes to the point of obsession, did exist. The mere fact that old men, some of them quite respectable, were being accused of misdeeds long afterward appeared to be evidence. Clearly, some long-finished events still had the power to move people, or infuriate them.

The notion of a continuing past couldn't have seemed ridiculous to me. Early on, there had been the story of Dr Martel, and later, awareness of the recent Jewish past. This sequence was not coincidental. Discussions about the Holocaust were infrequent in my family. My father, a secularized Jew from the Upper West Side of New York City, was nineteen when the war ended. He turned to the study of economics, a tool to remake the world, and toyed with the idea of joining Israel's fight for independence. Unqualified admiration for the Israelis didn't survive reporting trips to the Middle East, but he was more likely to be preoccupied by their struggles than by, say, the Warsaw Ghetto (though, as a young reporter in 1954, he wrote movingly about a pair of ghetto survivors who had settled in New York).[6] I told him once that I had been reading Primo Levi. 'Who is that?' he asked. The Holocaust museum project in Washington, DC, disturbed him – evidence of morbid obsession, or so he thought. It wasn't that he was uninterested in what had happened to the Jews; far from it. But it was not a subject of continuing interrogation. It seemed more important to understand the world from outside that prism.

This imperative didn't apply to me. The Holocaust imposes itself, its shock waves felt all the more strongly in my generation's adulthood for having been muted earlier on. These reverberations made the shiftings in public conscious-ness that had occurred in France easier to comprehend for someone like me, born long after the war. Indeed, the phenomenon of a previously half-acknowledged, now renas-cent history was not unfamiliar.

If the past had resurfaced for the French, it had done so largely through the portal of the Jewish experience. The wartime crime for which President Jacques Chirac accepted national responsibility, in his landmark speech of 1995, was the persecution of the Jews and not, say, French assistance to the Germans on the eastern front. The reasons were bound up with the complicated reckoning that had taken place in the country, itself related to the larger, international change of perspective on the continuing significance of the Holocaust.

In the years after the war, certain facts had not been dwelt on – French officials had helped the Nazis deport Jews, and the Vichy government's policy of bureaucratic anti-Semitism was not innocent in the genocide. French Jews themselves had not been eager to focus on these facts. A quarter of the country's prewar Jewish population of 300,000 had been deported. Those Jews who remained wanted to regain their place in France – a place Vichy had denied them – not demand justice that might mark them out once again. Their fellow citizens needed no encouragement to accommodate this reticence. Through the 1950s and 1960s, years in which my family lived there, the question of French persecution of the Jews was not 'simply marginal, it was totally hidden,' the historian Henry Rousso has said.[7]

Then de Gaulle died, in 1970. The next year an innovative documentary film about the memory of the Occupation, *Le Chagrin et la pitié* (The Sorrow and the Pity), put on the screen persecutors and persecuted for the first time. It was banned from French television for twelve years, but crowds flocked to showings in a small Paris theatre. In the years that followed, the old facts that hadn't exactly gone away came to seem indigestible.

It was true that in the wave of anger against collaborators immediately after the war, some 10,000 had been shot, legally and otherwise, around 40,000 were jailed and perhaps another 45,000 were deprived of civic rights. But in no other occupied country in Western Europe did a smaller percentage of the population receive prison terms – 12 per 10,000. And, minor exceptions aside, the genocide of the Jews was never a focus in this account-settling. So, decades later, there was a feeling that the reckoning with the past had failed and that it was necessary to revisit that time. 'The Purge was botched,' the melancholy director of a provincial archives said before unexpectedly turning over quantities of records to me. And even those who hadn't been particularly interested in the fate of the Jews were now forced to think about the war again.[8]

Along with the film, one man, an American scholar, had helped create the mental landscape in which this new perspective could arise. Nearly thirty years after the appearance of *Vichy France: Old Guard and New Order*, his history of the Vichy government, the scholar's name still arouses passions in France.

'Have you seen this? It refutes Paxton!' a man in late middle age said triumphantly, brandishing a book at me, in a country house outside Vichy one afternoon. I met people who contemptuously mispronounced the historian's name, and an elderly woman in Paris who said fiercely that she had kept his book on her bedside table for almost three decades. In Bordeaux in the autumn of 1997, Robert Paxton had been called on to testify in the trial of Maurice Papon, the retired functionary prosecuted for helping in the wartime deportation of the town's Jews. Stepping out of the courthouse, the modest Columbia University historian was mobbed by a horde of reporters, fans and curiosity seekers. The large crowd that showed up to hear his testimony was rapt; the young man sitting next to me said, reverentially, 'It's so strong, isn't it?'

Back in his hotel room, in a semichaotic atmosphere with the phone constantly ringing, Paxton and his wife formulated an elaborate plan to avoid the reporters dogging his steps. He was unused to this kind of attention; in his own country he remains obscure. With mild distaste he asked, 'Did you see it the other day?' adding, without waiting for my reply, 'It was like a school of bluefish, a feeding frenzy.' He had the reserve you would expect of someone whose pastimes are harpsichord playing and bird watching. With a schoolboy's bewilderment, Paxton said, 'It's almost like a cargo cult. Somehow, I'm coming from afar with some kind of medicine.'

Paxton's book had established truths about what happened in France during the war which have not yet been shaken. He destroyed myths that originated partly in the propaganda of Marshal Pétain's Vichy regime, and which, for the most part, the Gaullist government had seen advantageous to maintain. The most important of these truths had to do with an innocuous word that even today cannot be used casually in France: collaboration. In the late 1960s Paxton, using German documents that French scholars had never consulted (he was mocked for this exploit by one prominent critic, still active in the pages of France's second newspaper, *Le Figaro*),[9] found that 'collaboration', far from being a policy pressed on weak French officials by overbearing Nazis, in fact had been just the opposite: a goal in which the Germans were only mildly interested, but one ardently pursued nonetheless by leaders of the Vichy government, Pétain foremost among them.

The second of Paxton's truths had to do with the nature of this government. Under the armistice signed with the Germans in June 1940, the French had been allowed to maintain their government; it established itself in the spa town of Vichy, while the former capital and the most prosperous three-fifths of the country – the north and the coast – were occupied by the German military, a situation that persisted until November 1942, when the Germans moved into the south as well, following the Allied invasion of North Africa. France north and south continued to be administered mostly by French civil servants, under the intermittently watchful eyes of the Germans. Paxton's analysis showed that the Vichy government was not a stopgap affair simply reacting to the German presence – the received wisdom. Instead, it had far-reaching goals for an authoritarian reorganisation of society. 'Vichy was not a Band-Aid,' Paxton wrote. 'It was deep surgery.'[10] It was driven by a right-wing ideology with deep roots in French culture. Marshal Henri Philippe Pétain, the hero of World War I, and his subordinates were going to take advantage of France's defeat to establish a reactionary new order, rolling back seventy-odd years of parliamentary democracy.

The viewpoint of the American historian was disquieting. It suggested that 'Vichy' had been more than merely a disagreeable but illegitimate pause, which was the Gaullist orthodoxy for many years. His book was received respectfully in the United States in 1972, but it was turned down by the major French publisher Gallimard the following year before being accepted by a smaller publishing house.

The country's historical establishment greeted it coolly. Paxton himself was puzzled by the poor reception he received from the Institut d'Études Politiques, France's leading political-science institution. But the popular press, for the most part, was intrigued by what he had written.[11] There is a quiet outrage in the historian's impeccably documented pages, and it touched a chord with a new generation in the years that followed. 'The more I studied the Vichy regime, the angrier I got,' Paxton said when I asked what had motivated him. Modestly, he disclaimed the title of ground-breaker, pointing to the German historian Eberhard Jaeckel and to Marcel Ophüls's *The Sorrow and the Pity*. But the 1968 publication of Jaeckel's book went largely unnoticed and has been long out of print, and in France *Le Chagrin et la pitié* is not even available on video.

Paxton's work is what provincial schoolteachers know, and his book is the one universally available in France. His influence is still felt. At a symposium in his honour at Columbia in 1997, Henry Rousso defined the unique position the American had come to occupy in the intellectual life of France. He compared Paxton to a 'site of memory', almost like one of France's historic monuments: 'Robert Paxton has thus become a character in the national novel of France. He is the messenger, come from afar to deliver the unpleasant news to a country that was steeped in its past and, until that point, proud of it . . . His word has served almost as a kind of gospel for an entire generation.'[12]

He had helped create a new, different consciousness, one that eventually brought into the open a more complete picture of the country's wartime experience. There were judicial proceedings against old men like Maurice Papon, waves of activity by French and foreign scholars, and newspaper headlines that added nuance to the notion that de Gaulle had 'wiped out most vestiges of the Vichy dictatorship', as my father had put it back in 1966. For one thing, the country's president from 1981 to 1995, François Mitterrand, turned out to have been, in his youth, a more enthusiastic participant in that authoritarian experiment than anyone had suspected.

These public manifestations seemed to be signs of something that had never actually gone away: a familiar relationship with the recent past. They created the possibility that you could perhaps get a glimpse of this relationship. It might be the last such opportunity, a moment at the point of its disappearance. The war has been over for nearly sixty years. The obituary pages of French newspapers these days record, at least once a week (or so it seems), the death of a famous *résistant*.

For three years, I lived and worked in three towns in France trying to find out what it means to coexist with the past. I took it as a given that in the places I went to, certain people – more than just a few, perhaps not enough to impress a pollster – were obliged to think about the past. Did this mean that they lived with it? Did the past manifest itself through the words they spoke? Could the ongoing effect of the past be measured? Did past events – the events of the war – continue to exist in any objective sense? What might be the relationship between a preoccupation with the past and expressions of this preoccupation? I started with a prejudice: memories – in other words, that which had survived the passage of time – should be taken seriously. Memory's distortions, if I could identify them, would be precious indications of how people lived with the past today.

I chose the three towns in order to examine different phases of intensity in the relationship with the past. These phases of intensity would increase from town to town – each had had a different degree of closeness to the events of the war. This would allow me, or so I hoped, to get as close as possible to the question of what it might mean to live with the past. I wasn't interested in what could be considered the artificial transmission of the past – that which took place, say, in the classroom. Rather, I wanted to find manifestations, even random ones, that could be considered echoes of lived experience.

First I installed myself in Bordeaux, in the autumn of 1997, for what would probably be the last trial in France having to do with the war. Maurice Papon, who had been an official in the government's local administration in those years, now found himself accused of complicity in crimes against humanity, a number of compromising documents with his signature having been accidentally discovered sixteen years before. The old port of Bordeaux was associated with an ancient, proud commerce, not the war, though it had been the largest city outside Paris in the occupied zone, the area occupied by the German military. I wanted to see how the inhabitants reacted to this unprecedented confrontation with the past. Unexpectedly, the trial lasted six months, giving me plenty of opportunity to observe. The judicial proceeding itself, in all its strangeness – a man in his late eighties being examined over events more than a half-century old – offered a controlled opportunity to measure the late twentieth century's relationship to those events. Maurice Papon was the first high French civil servant ever to be tried for taking part in the genocide of the Jews, though not the first of the nation's officials. There had been long delays in his case, some engineered by him, some due to judicial sluggishness. In 1994 Paul Touvier, a former member of Vichy's paramilitary political police, the Milice, was convicted of crimes against humanity for the murder of seven Jews fifty years before. But the significance of Touvier's trial was limited by the defendant's loutishness and insincerity.

After Bordeaux, I moved to Vichy, the resort in the centre of France chosen almost by accident, after the armistice with the Germans, to be the seat of the French government. The world has known this government ever since as the Vichy government; the town is indelibly associated with a regime long since condemned to opprobrium. The inhabitants would thus be forced to think, regularly and in all likelihood unwillingly, about the past.

Finally I looked at Tulle, a provincial capital in the south-central region, where German troops carried out a terrible massacre one hot afternoon in June 1944. The killing had been so public, and so awful in its means, that the inhabitants couldn't have failed to have been marked by it, probably down to the present.

In an earlier book about the persistence of the past, I looked at the legacy of an unpunished civil rights murder in one corner of the American south. For years the dominant culture there, the whites, had been able to tell itself that the story was settled. This was part of the fabric of everyday life – an element that, in its small way, helped ensure the smooth dovetailing of one day with the next. But the story was not settled. For the African Americans in Mississippi, it was one of a thousand irritants, at times symbolizing all of them, with the potential to sour ordinary existence. It summoned up memories of a past – segregation – that echoed enough into the present to make the unresolved murder all the more vivid. Whites could scornfully dismiss it as just 'history', but in the episode I wrote about, they discovered that they too had been living with the old story, albeit negatively. The vehement professed indifference that greeted the presumed murderer's reindictment after thirty years offered a clue about the story's real place in the thinking of those I interviewed.

You could see that in Mississippi 'history' might actually be present, a past lived with to an unsuspected degree. Whether or not the particular 'history' in question was fully part of lived experience might not necessarily be important; the imagination was capable of filling in what was missing. It seemed to be a characteristic of memory that the smallest detail had the potential to expand, in the individual, into a story that might appear overwhelming. And then reasonably contented living would not go forward until there was some resolution, or until many more years had gone by than a past that could be measured simply in decades.

This knowledge helped me undertake a similar exploration

of the relationship between past and present in France. Some aspects of memory would not change, across continents and vastly differing circumstances.

Still, the point has been made many times: an American writing about France during the war should do so with some circumspection. The United States has never been conquered, never been occupied. The phenomenon of an old event, a past, that continues to be bad is something a white American like myself might hope to understand, but only at a distance. All the more reason why I never intended, in undertaking this book, to confront another question often encountered in recent writings about France: whether or not the country had 'come to grips' with its past – presumably, whether or not it had fully explored, and honestly judged, the way its leaders and significant numbers of its citizens had thought and acted in that period. It seemed evident to me that it had not. But to a greater or lesser degree, no national entity has 'come to grips' with its past. All relationships with the past are a continuing dialogue, more or less honest according to circumstances, culture and tradition. This is not to say that it was possible for me to approach portions of the research for this book in a spirit of perfect neutrality. Nobody whose writing touches on France during the war can fail to wonder at what is 'in one special sense, a mystery', as the historian Tony Judt put it – the mystery of what happened in the country with claims on universal civilization.[13]

The French wonder about it too. Their deep involvement with their own recent history is, in one sense, an exotic phenomenon to an American. Our country is not used to collectively looking back in this impassioned way. But in another sense this phenomenon is instructive. The experience of the French, or so it seemed to me, could offer lessons about living with searing history – ambiguous choices, painful humiliation – years into the future.

I

• • • •

BORDEAUX, PAPON AND
THE EXIGENCIES OF MEMORY

The Stain on the Stone

THE STONE OF Bordeaux is covered by a thin blanket of grime. The city's classical buildings look oddly derelict, like certain proud bag ladies in the fancier quarters of Paris or New York. For miles and miles along the Garonne River, the longest sweep of Louis XV façades in the world stretches black and dingy, coated with soot. The golden limestone of Bordeaux is stained. By the time a building is cleaned, top to bottom, the process must start again. 'Our stone is very porous,' people will tell you apologetically, having just lauded their city's eighteenth-century perfection. The dirt on the luminous stone is an irritant. It mocks the urban landscape's harmony.

It is a city of incipient soot. On Bordeaux's most elegant avenue, one of the purest of the eighteenth-century structures is just beginning to turn colour, from golden to a dusky ochre. Number 28 Allées de Tourny is an immaculate, austere rectangle, ornamented only by one of the city's famous grinning stone masks, a Bacchus, its ironic features now darkening slightly. It is one of only two buildings unaltered during the nineteenth-century transformation of the Allées, the centre of Enlightenment Bordeaux. The most respectable people in Bordeaux, snug in their loden coats and furs, pass it every day. One day during the trial of Maurice Papon, I went inside this privileged spot, now an upscale mortgage bank, to see if its present occupants had any notion of the rich man who had owned it many years before. Did they know that M.

Papon's secretary once, a long time ago, had occasion neatly to type their address on a document of impeccable formality? 'The parts belonging to Mmes Bouchara and Guerini, partners in the building at twenty-eight, Allées de Tourny in Bordeaux, and to M. Naquet, Joë, principal owner, are declared under predominantly Jewish influence, in accordance with the German ordinance of 18 October 1940.' These words meant the building was to be seized immediately and turned over to 'Aryan' administrators, by signed order of Maurice Papon, secretary-general of the Gironde prefecture.

'M. Naquet? Ah, no. No. Never heard of him.' The receptionist smiled. I showed her the document.[1] She looked uneasy. 'You'll have to talk to the estate agent' – the man who managed the property. I went next door to a fancy chocolates store, all marble and polished mirrors, unchanged from its founding in the 1840s. The chocolates had been there when number 28 was owned by M. Naquet, and long before. When I walked in the proprietor was wearing an apron, smeared brown from making his sweets. He stared at the paper and the 'État Français, Service des Questions Juives' (French State, Jewish Affairs Office) on the letterhead. His face displayed mild consternation. He glanced around to see if anybody else was in his store. Then he saw that the paper had nothing to do with him. 'This Papon thing, it's all coming too late, much too late,' he said. 'There are more important things to worry about.' There was a thin smile. 'I mean, not more important, but more ... ' He seemed relieved when I turned to go. The next day I called the estate agent. Did he know anything about M. Naquet's one-time ownership of the building? 'I can't give you any information whatsoever,' he said coldly. 'Nothing at all.' He hung up.

Of course it was preposterous. I had irritated these people, and they had a right to be angry. What difference should a half-century-old story make to them, whether or not it involved an injustice or something even more sinister? There was no reason to think they were connected with what had happened so long ago. They were legitimately implanted on the Allées, which remained a high spot of French civilization. This spacious avenue bears the name of the eighteenth-century governor who transformed Bordeaux, making it a city of broad and noble vistas, in contrast with the medieval warren of earlier centuries. The Allées, so peaceful and soothing when a warm breeze rustles through the elms on a summer Saturday, was the centrepiece of the enlightened governor's project. 'I don't know of a more beautiful place in France,' Stendahl said of it in the 1830s.

Who wouldn't partake of the feeling of stability imparted by this thoroughfare? During the Occupation, Wehrmacht officers had a private dining room at the Brasserie Dubern, at 44 Allées de Tourny. (Its current *patronne*, taking me on a tour, proudly showed me the eighteenth-century panelling that had so delighted the Germans.) The Waffen SS established its regional recruiting office at number 25. It was no accident that M. Naquet, the richest Jew in Bordeaux before the war, the owner of twelve buildings in the city, all in the choicest spots, put some of his considerable fortune in a house on the Allées. He was there because of everything the street symbolized in the life of his city. The story of M. Naquet was henceforth intimately entwined with that of the Allées – more so than, say, an ordinary property owner's story would have been. And in due time, the French authorities came to appropriate his properties, the most conspicuous of any of those belonging to the Bordeaux Jews. They seized his vast apartment in the imposing stone mansion across from the Bordeaux cathedral, bustling with governesses and servants before the war. At the trial, a subordinate of Papon's remembered seeing it inexplicably 'all shuttered up' one day in 1943. The authorities took the building on the Allées. That detail of the Occupation, one of the thousands Maurice Papon later complained had inundated him in those years, also became part of the avenue's history.

M. Naquet was an unpleasant little man on several accounts, fond of his possessions and not much else. He was also practical and hard-headed. Unlike the poorer Jews whose relatives later put Maurice Papon in the dock – the trial's civil plaintiffs – he had not waited around for the police to knock. He had the money to flee, and in 1943 he left for Nice, where he was duly rounded up and deported to Auschwitz with his wife and two daughters (the eldest was a lively, 'bold' girl, Papon's subordinate remembered with bemusement).

I didn't tell his latter-day neighbours the end of M. Naquet's story, but I did not need to. In a general sense they might have known it already, just as they were dimly aware of the knowledge I had brought them. This awareness was obvious: they were not shocked, for instance, by the document with the État Français letterhead, unmistakably war era, the only time in nearly 130 years that official papers did not carry the word 'République'. They had not exhibited the reaction of people surprised by a new fact – had not, in any sense, wanted to engage me in conversation about it. The most eagerly awaited witnesses, early in Maurice Papon's trial, were the veteran historians, those who had exposed Vichy's myths. As it turned out, however, their testimony was already common knowledge, so the reporters in the sauna-like press gallery fell asleep in waves. In the same way, the people on the Allées knew enough in general – Jews had been deported from France, their property had been expropriated – to be made immediately uneasy by the paper in my hand.

And now they might suspect that the warm stone of their 'magnificent' avenue, as Stendhal called it, had been stained by that unpleasant history. They were connected to it, willingly or not. The history of M. Naquet was embedded in the Allées de Tourny, just as the disfiguring grime kept appearing on the golden stone.

1

Papon's Wager

The Settled Past

MOST PEOPLE in Bordeaux would have scoffed at the idea of a latter-day connection to such old stories. And it was certainly possible to walk into the fancy mortgage bank every day for a lifetime and never be troubled by them. Maurice Papon was counting on this sentiment. He was counting on the well-dressed middle-aged man who, hurrying away from the looming neoclassical Palais de Justice, the courthouse, one day with his wife, muttered to me, 'I'm irritated, profoundly irritated.' There were plenty of others like him. Over the course of Papon's six-month trial for complicity in crimes against humanity, the logic of the old man's defence found a grateful echo in the town he had left behind many years before. I was to hear it often, at dinners, on the street, among the reporters covering the trial. In Papon's estimation, the past had no claim, because it was unknowable. It was too late, far too late, to be reopening these accounts.

His lawyer, holding forth in the echoing great hall of the Palais de Justice to a crowd of reporters one day, put it this way: Maurice Papon was an unwilling participant in a 'surrealist spectacle'.

In other words, the particular reality the court was determined to conjure up had nothing to do with the actual reality Maurice Papon had known. This tack insisted on the old man's radical isolation. For the court, there had been eight trains from Bordeaux, with 1560 Jews on them, between July 1942 and May 1944, during which time the accused had overseen the Service des Questions Juives. (In fact there had been ten trains, but from two of them no relatives had come forward to accuse Papon and French judicial officials had failed, through negligence, to step into the breach.) The Service des Questions Juives, a modest office within the Gironde prefecture, had organised the roundups and deportations demanded by the Germans. To the local police it gave the lists of Jews, it hired the buses to pick them up, and it made sure the necessary trains would be waiting. At the end, after the Jews were gone, on the desk of the director of the Service des Questions Juives would be found the keys to the now empty apartments.

For Papon, numbers and organisational charts were beside the point. Only he was the possessor of that particular past now in question. An impenetrable screen exists between our time and that time; he himself could see through it, but with difficulty: 'These are events which took place in a fog,' he said one day. He knew the strange anti-logic of those years. But how could we? 'It's a mistake to look for logic in an illogical time,' he said once, dismissing pointed questioning. That world – of German orders and uniforms, of trains full of Jews, of laconic meetings in the Hôtel de Saige, the warren-like prefectural building downtown (a sumptuous eighteenth-century palace, now shabby and abandoned this past quarter-century) – had vanished forever. Only he, Maurice Papon, former subprefect, prefect and minister of the Republic, could judge it. 'I have had the sad privilege of living through several generations,' he said, seized by one of his habitual fits of melancholy toward the end of an autumn afternoon. Looking out at his questioners, and evidently thinking of them, he added, 'The human spirit is incapable of undertaking the sad gymnastics of living in a wholly other epoch.'

It was absurd to try him, Papon would suggest, since he was one of the last contemporaries of the events in question.

Sometimes he would denounce the immense pile of documents on which the case against him was based (the 'dossier' filled an entire small room in one of the lawyers' offices). 'A piece of paper is a piece of paper,' Papon said angrily from his little glassed-in box one day. 'It will never reconstitute the tragic times we lived through.' Projected over his head was a yellowing sheet on which a certain Jew had been 'invited to present himself' to the prefecture for failing to wear the prescribed cloth star. The Jew dutifully complied, was arrested, deported and never heard from again.

Once, Papon said that the very words in the documents no longer had their meaning of fifty years ago. 'The words don't have the same sense,' he said. So it was useless to be taken aback by what his deputy at the Service des Questions Juives wrote in 1942, after the French police had conducted the first roundup of Bordeaux Jews: 'It seems that those interned, and the Jewish community, understood perfectly the reason for the operation, and appreciated that it was carried out by French police.' There were gasps when these words were read out in court. But Maurice Papon insisted, 'After a half-century, it is true that the meaning of the words has changed.'

He could conjure up no more radical separation between past and present in a country where the line between speech and action is fine (the word '*verbe*' means not only 'verb', the part of speech denoting action, but language itself). If the language was different, then the whole code of morals might have changed too. Papon might have been talking, say, about the Roman Empire – a defunct civilization speaking a defunct language. You might as well judge Nero.

If Maurice Papon was right, then the whole improbable exercise – the bringing to justice of an eighty-seven-year-old man for things that had happened more than fifty years ago – was not just doomed to failure, it was absurd. The wager was considerable. More was at stake than just the trial. There were the millions of individual memories, hidden away in every French family throughout the country. Under Papon's logic, these would have about the same moral weight as old family photographs in an attic. If he was right, the country's prodigious three-decade exercise in understanding the wartime past would be undermined, as would President Chirac's apology for Vichy's crimes and the work of the historians and the film-makers who had laboriously constructed new visions of those years. All of this effort was reinforced by a single notion: the moral continuity of past and present.

If Papon was right, that past had been settled many years ago, and there could be no question of judging it anew. This promiscuous moving back and forth between generations was repugnant to the ex-minister and his monarchist lawyer. In Paris, the conservative politicians were finding it equally distasteful. Within two weeks of the trial's opening, one of their leaders wrote, in a sympathetic newspaper, 'Enough, enough, enough!' At the trial, the distinguished old men who vouched for Papon, the living monuments from the Académie Française and the Gaullist ministries, were clear on at least this one point: all the latter-day effort had been wasted time.

He had posed a question that went beyond the simple matter of his conviction or whether or not nine jurors could be persuaded to send him to jail. It was nothing less than the question of whether or not his trial mattered – of whether or not it had any resonance at all for the larger population.

There was room for doubt. It wasn't just the old man's argument that was persuasive, but his persona. Here was a former minister who had a distinguished career behind him, perfect mastery of the subjunctive, a taste for Château Margaux, and amiable friendships among the *académiciens*. He had the economical gestures of somebody accustomed to making points without strain. The poised way he opened his briefcase inside the little glass box betrayed years of punctual attendance at important meetings. Papon's courtroom demeanour, his head always turned slightly away from the civil plaintiffs, demonstrated an innate sense of hierarchy.

Then, the procedure's practical difficulties only reinforced the notion of its strangeness: critical witnesses who were dead, so sick they couldn't make it to court, or so feeble they literally hobbled to the witness stand; memories with gaping holes; an accused whose lapses into illness caused delays for weeks at a time; jurors whose parents even were too young to have experienced the war. 'This is a hospital for witnesses,' Papon's lawyer remarked early on, reading off a list of medical excuses. He wasn't entirely wrong. 'No, it's a cemetery for witnesses,' he corrected himself a little later, having come across a clump that had recently died. Papon's superiors, notably the former regional prefect Maurice Sabatier, had died; most of his subordinates had died; Germans and ex-*résistants* had died.

The country's judicial apparatus was obviously stumped. After the trial had officially started, it took nearly two months of floundering, from a juridical point of view, before the first facts against Maurice Papon were presented.

Reminders of how strange the exercise was came in every one of the meandering sessions inside the Palais de Justice. Here was an enclosed, artificially lit universe that, for five or six hours each day, revolved only around the obsessive events of a half-century ago. The epic length of the trial, the longest criminal trial in the history of France, created a kind of double life for six months, half in the bland present and half in that period of searing grimness. After each session, you would step back out into the daylight, hear the city buses roar down the Cours d'Albret, see the housewives fetching their loaves from the bakery, and blink at the sudden rush forward of time. There were constant reminders of this enormous gap, as on the day when I spotted two tiny men, ancient *résistants*, bundled up in green felt and wool, stepping gingerly out of a taxi to proffer the day's testimony. They looked like children's-book elves; they had come from another world. Their presence at a real trial was improbable.

In fact, the whole notion of retribution against an eighty-seven-year-old seemed suspect. How much time would he realistically spend in prison? It disturbed the accused that the outcome of this trial, whether or not he was convicted, would be far from the neat little judicial bundle ideally obtained. He was being tried under a law – the Crimes Against Humanity Law, created by the Allies for the Nuremberg trials – that was not even a part of French jurisprudence until 1964. Papon, the loyal servant of whatever regime happened to be dominant, was not disingenuous when he indignantly asserted his belief in republican institutions – like balanced trials, for instance. He had reason to be grateful to the French Republic: it had been good to him, like the Vichy regime that preceded it. Vichy had offered him four promotions in less than two years (he prudently turned down the last three, coming as they did in 1943 and 1944), but the Republic was hardly less generous. In the years after the war he was top assistant to secretaries of state in Paris, departmental and regional prefect (positions roughly akin to state governorships, only more powerful; vast areas in Algeria with millions of inhabitants were under his firm control), and in the late 1950s de Gaulle made him prefect of police in Paris, a sensitive position he occupied for ten years, distinguishing it with violent repressions of Algerians demonstrating for independence (at least forty-eight of whom were found drowned in the Seine after one demonstration, a number not officially acknowledged until 1999). His career ended at the summit, with his own ministry.

Long before that, the Gaullists who inherited the nation from Vichy had bestowed the blessing that permitted what followed: they carried him unscathed through the intermittent rigours of the postwar purge. In this he was both typical and lucky – typical because, though former ministers were jailed, prefects dismissed and members of the Milice (Vichy's paramilitary political police) shot, civil servants like Papon who quietly did their jobs were mostly left undisturbed. Out of approximately 1.5 million functionaries, only some 28,000 incurred penalties after the Liberation,[1] and no one at Papon's level was troubled solely over what he might have done, or not done, with respect to the Jews.

But Papon was lucky, too, because even then his destiny had been marked out as exceptional: late in the trial it emerged that he was the only high-level bureaucrat in all of France to have been *promoted* within his own prefecture at the Liberation. 'He was my most precious and trustworthy assistant,' de Gaulle's representative in Bordeaux had gratefully written, thinking back to the chaos of the months straddling Occupation and Liberation in that city.[2] Even Papon's skilful boss and patron Maurice Sabatier, though escaping any unpleasantness, had been moved far from the city. Sabatier died in 1989, six months after himself being charged with complicity in crimes against humanity; long after the trial ended, I saw his name on a 1941 US State Department list of officials considered particularly collaborationist, one of only two in the Ministry of the Interior.[3] Sabatier, thought of as a gentleman by his colleagues, had had the good grace to accept all responsibility for his younger protégé before his death.

This personal history, with which Papon was deeply imbued, made his position now, barely a mile from where he had sat fifty-three years before, all the more inconceivable. By his own rigorous standards, the France of 1997 had no business trying to reenter, through the necessarily narrow portal of his memory, the years of the *Militarbefelshaber Frankreich*, the *Feldtkommandantur*, and the *Sicherheitsdienst*. In the 1920s, he had attended the finest French educational institutions, the Lycée Louis-le-Grand and the Institut d'Études Politiques. He had been trained in the three-part exposition, taught to present a set of facts, analyse it and issue a conclusion. In the present circumstances – the extraordinary time lapse, the lacunae, the emotional weight of the charges – it was not rational to expect a balanced conclusion. The former minister of the budget had a right to expect that others would be obeisant to this strict model.

There were plenty who wanted to. At a dinner party one night, a vivacious, well-spoken woman sitting near me exclaimed: 'It's ridiculous, fifty years later. What benefit can it possibly bring? It's too late.' Or, one grey Sunday afternoon, in the living room of neighbours across the street: 'I've never understood what this was all about. He had to obey orders, right?' This came with an edge of annoyance from a middle-aged man sunk into an armchair at the far end of the room. He had been sucking on a small cigar and eyeing me curiously. As for the Jews, 'at first they were sent to ghettos, right? And that's what people thought?' There was nothing wrong with this, he said, because the ghetto was a perfectly normal place for a Jew. 'And in the nineteenth century the Jews lived in ghettos, no?' He got up to go to work, at the Rothschild family's wine business. 'Well, I'm off to the Jews!' he said heartily.

The Papon matter was doubly irritating, and doubly negligible, because it was an affair willed by 'the Jews'. It was not, strictly speaking, a matter between French people. 'The Jews, they stick together just unbelievably. They help each other out,' the cheerful *patronne* of a Bordeaux restaurant explained to me the night before the trial opened. 'They really are very conservative, you know, much more than we are. They're always going to their mosque, oh, I mean, you know what I mean. Do you know,' she said gaily, 'they're so bitter about Papon. Some of them have lived their whole lives for this moment.'

One morning I encountered my upstairs neighbour in the stairwell. He was a friendly, melancholy retired sales representative who occupied himself tracing his lineage back to Philip Augustus and the twelfth century.

He looked disgusted, almost nauseated.

'What on earth is the matter?' I asked.

He had just come from the trial. 'What nonsense!' he hissed. He could hardly talk. 'Besides, you know, even before the war, the government tried to remove Jews from certain government positions. There were just too many occupying government posts. They had to do it. The Jews, you know, they stick together too much. And why do the Jews always manage to make people hate them?'

I whispered a protest.

'Ah, you're Jewish?' he said. 'Well, I didn't know.'

My host that grey Sunday had said anxiously, 'It's true that a lot of people have a bad reaction when you bring up the Papon trial.' It was a remark that, four months into the affair, seemed so obvious I hardly noticed it. At lunch in a restaurant one day, a fashionable lawyer swept past our table. He was a friend of the Bordeaux newspaperman I was with, but had ostentatiously declined to greet us. The newspaperman was irritated at this snub directed at me. He explained: the lawyer resented the injustice being done to the old man. He resented it so much he had (unsuccessfully) volunteered his services to the sophisticated Parisian defence team. He certainly wasn't going to waste his time with an American who had insinuated himself into the scandalous exercise.

The consensus seemed clear: that past was settled. The old man could have his lock on memory.

Tenuous Certainties

'YOU WON'T LEARN much from those young people,' a woman said to me one day outside the Palais de Justice. She had seen me chatting with some earnest high school students in the bright sunshine. She was a retired tax inspector, neat and proper in a wool skirt, her hair well coiffed.

The students, disappointed at the day's dull testimony, were still hungry for talk of the war. They were from Mérignac, the working-class suburb where the Jews had been interned before being shipped off. It was the rich people in Bordeaux who collaborated, they said; their own families had hated the Germans. They evoked the experiences of grandparents for me, passed-on memories of privations and children with foreign names suddenly missing from schoolrooms.

The woman was provoked by this. When the teenagers left she began a monologue. 'Young people tell me they would have refused to sign. Ha! And what could he have done? If you are in the administration, you follow orders. This trial is a waste of time. There's no point to it. You know, I was astonished at that number, sixteen hundred. But then, when I saw the names . . . These were all foreign names, from Poland, Russia, wherever. Stopnicki, and so on. These were little people, they lived badly. In Mériadeck. The people we knew – you know, names like Lopez and Salazar, the Spanish – they were all there at the end of the war.'

She smiled. 'Are the Americans really interested in all this? And you, are you an Israelite?'

She was a jolly, amiable woman, and she had understandably tried to put some distance between herself and the freight trains packed with Jews. After all, those who died were unimportant because they were poor immigrants; the important Jews, from the Sephardic families established for centuries in Bordeaux, survived. Perhaps I had a distorting special interest as a Jew? She had softened this insinuation, delicately using the polite term common in the prewar years, 'Israelite'. During the war, some of the Vichy enthusiasts tried to ban it from official discourse.

But it all seemed too easy an escape, too obvious, apart from being inaccurate: 'the Spanish' or 'the Portuguese', as the Bordelais have called them for generations – the Sephardic Jews – did not all avoid being deported. Was she making herself feel better? Had she been only 'astonished' by the number sixteen hundred, brought up with no prompting from me?

'Besides, we didn't really see any Jews during the war,' she added, inconsequently.

Her tone changed. A memory came back. During the Occupation she had a playmate, a little girl she felt close to. She pictured the two of them walking to school together on the empty wartime pavements, past some of the grandiose buildings downtown, like the Grand Théâtre – just the two of them in the shadow of the immense eighteenth-century colonnade. One day the little girl had appeared wearing the yellow star. This was puzzling. But her mother had told her not to concern herself with it, and she stopped asking questions. Then, she lost touch with the little girl. She wasn't certain what had happened to her. But she knew that after the war, she had not seen her again.

The monologue moved on to the horrors of the Liberation, including a naked young woman with a shaved head being dragged through the streets, a 'horizontal collaborator', glimpsed from the family balcony. The retired tax inspector shuddered. This was a preferred theme among those who scoffed at what was going on inside the Palais. I recalled the snorting sound with which a woman I knew, standing beneath a distinguished oil painting in her salon, pronounced the initials FFI, the Forces Françaises de l'Intérieur: 'Eff Eff Fee!' The ragged FFI were often the de facto authority at the Liberation; they were said to have ordered the ritual shaving of women accused of sleeping with Germans. In the Gironde region, a favourite practice had been to tie women naked to the balconies of town halls; in Libourne, at the edge of Bordeaux, a woman was shaved, stripped and forced to stand on the pedestal of a statue the Germans had melted down.[4]

The retired tax inspector resumed her thread. Well, the trial of Papon was a 'waste of time', no doubt about that.

Was it? The conviction had not stopped her from waiting

two hours in the spectators' line to get in, and spending the whole afternoon in the Palais de Justice. And it had led her straight to the disquieting memory of the little girl queerly marked out, then gone. She wanted to be indifferent to the trial, and she wanted the past to be settled. But it didn't altogether work.

Perhaps there was something else besides scorn for the trial. These people weren't as free to leave Maurice Papon alone as they may have liked. You could sense a kind of buried consciousness waiting to be stirred up, hidden beneath tenuous certainties. There were apparently two levels of understanding. There was the past that served for everyday use, and then there was another past, informed by memory and conscience, more difficult to acknowledge.

The retired tax inspector was reluctant, but something had forced her to remember. So it seemed that the individual did not always have the upper hand in this tussle with memory.

Unbroken Connection

I WANTED TO find out what form the memories took and to see what triggered them. Did the process generate discernible energy? Could it be seen, heard, or felt? And was Maurice Papon's wager a safe one? Was the past safely interred? I would have to traverse the grey stone streets, past the mean two-storey houses and the solemn bourgeois apartment buildings, across physical and social space, to find out. A clever Paris intellectual I met mocked Bordeaux's somnolence, describing with glee the two little old ladies who always fell asleep at her readings in the city's big downtown bookstore. But the trial of Papon was prodding Bordeaux into a kind of wakefulness, however grudging. Indeed, for most people there, my very reason for being in their presence was a provocation. And yet, as an American, I had *laissez-passer* to make this traversal, an instant credibility that was somewhat embarrassing to me. Sometimes I found myself the object of surprising confidences. Why? An elderly woman, a retired domestic with clear half-century-old memories of the German police, suggested the reason on a park bench one day: 'If it wasn't for you, they would still be here.'

So it was easier for me than for a native to penetrate this ambient layer of unease, which thickened as you moved up the social scale. It was almost like a phenomenon of the weather – like the fog that rolls over the city's disused docks on early winter evenings. If you were, say, a Bordelais with clear-cut views about Papon and the Occupation, like the grizzled café owner I met on the Quai des Chartrons – 'No excuses, he signed' – you had to negotiate your way around this dense matter, usually by avoiding it altogether. 'The clientele, ha, no, I never discuss it,' he said. He had his reasons. The Chartrons is the historic heartland of the Bordeaux wine aristocracy, the people François Mauriac mocked for their masterful palates and empty heads. During the war, their cellars had been open to the invader. Once, I asked Gérard Boulanger, the leading local lawyer in the case, what the wine barons thought of his sixteen-year crusade against Papon. He laughed. 'How on earth should I know? They'll certainly never invite me to dinner. I'm not too worried about it. You eat very badly in those houses.'

To the café owner, Papon was a bastard. But that was not something you would catch him saying, because of the response it might provoke. 'I might not like what I hear,' he said reluctantly, grunting between cigarette puffs. If anything, Papon's presence in the glass box thickened the fog. 'The Bordelais is hard to talk to about it,' a cobbler in old Bordeaux said on the day the trial opened. His mother had married a man who had 'done some resistance' and spoke often of the war's privations, and he himself was talkative. But of all topics he avoided this one. He didn't want to risk an argument. A

bank employee I knew, not a native of Bordeaux, curtly
dismissed the idea that the city might still have a hangover
from the war. Then he began talking about a certain stratum,
compromised long ago. He didn't elaborate. He looked around
the bank, smiled, and stopped talking.

There were others in Bordeaux like those three, whose
consciousness of the war years, whether directly or indirectly
nourished by memory, was unproblematic. 'There's nothing
complicated about it, at all,' the café owner had said gruffly.
The case of Maurice Papon was straightforward. 'It's perfectly
clear.' He, for one, had no difficulty recalling how his mother
shepherded two Jewish children, friends of the family, into the
unoccupied zone.

At the trial, there were the sympathetic spectators, the hardy
regulars who kept coming long after the curiosity-seekers of
the early days had given up. One day, a photo-booth picture of
a woman wearing a stylish 1930s hat and posing with her baby
daughter is projected in court. One spectator wipes away tears,
someone sitting nearby bows her head and others in the
audience look stricken. Standing by the screen is the stout
woman, in late middle age, who has just finished testifying; the
smiling woman in the picture is her mother, deported a half-
century ago, and she tells us this is the only photograph she has
of the two of them. On another day, there is calm and bitter
testimony about a similar separation in early childhood: a
dignified man in his sixties evokes a young boy on a railway
platform in southwestern France in the summer of 1942. He
looks down the platform and sees his mother, turning to him
for the last time as she is put on the train. The audience is
leaning forward, and in row after row hand is set to chin in
concentration. These were people like the friendly sad-eyed
woman who came most days because she grew up in
Mériadeck, the crowded working-class district where the
Bordeaux Jews were rounded up. She was not a Jew, but she
and her husband couldn't forget the hours spent with long-

missing schoolmates at the Mériadeck school, a grim thirties-modern building that is one of the few surviving structures from the old neighbourhood.

These people were like the Jews. They had difficulty forgetting, not remembering. Maurice Papon had already lost his wager with them. But among those I encountered they were in a small minority – and they were probably in a minority in Bordeaux too. (In France, a poll taken during the last month of the trial showed 52 per cent judging it not to have been 'useful', a figure that might have understated general dissatisfaction, given the other results: 82 per cent felt that they had learned 'little new' about the Occupation from it, and 62 per cent declared themselves still somewhat mystified about Papon's role, even after six months of court.)[5] The people who had no difficulty remembering, mostly in the working classes, believed in the moral continuity of past and present. They had never broken with the past. It wasn't with them that I would discover whether or not Maurice Papon was right. Instead, I would have to find those who had inherited the city, those who might have reasons for not remembering. This was the class that, as one of the civil plaintiffs said to me grimly, had been primarily interested in saving its furniture.

2

The Missing Context

Bordeaux

SO THE PERSPECTIVE of the elegant saleswoman in the antique furniture store seemed worth registering. 'There are plenty of people here who go to church with a perfectly good conscience, rail on about the Papon trial and didn't lift a finger during the Occupation,' she said to me. I was startled. This harsh judgement emerged from the Louis XVI marquetry through which she had been manoeuvering. Until that moment, the woman, with her carefully tied foulard, and the furniture with its elaborate inlay, had seemed of a piece. The bitterness of her tone made me suspect something was missing. It was easy enough to imagine that her clients railed against the Papon trial, and that these men and women emanated from families immobile fifty-five years before. But the mere fact of being provoked suggested consciences not quite as immaculate as she claimed.

A sophisticated Paris journalist I knew sneered at the headlines proclaiming 'Bordeaux, Capital of Collaboration' in the trial's opening days. He claimed that privilege for the real capital. Most weekends he took the train home to the metropolis, so he would have had more difficulty noticing what began to seem evident to me: unease over the public history of Bordeaux. And that, in turn, helped explain, at least in part, the private unease that I encountered. If the common history was embarrassing and therefore hidden, there was no context in which people could situate their own actions.

Perhaps the city's passage through those years offered uncommonly small cover. Maybe Papon, the young secretary-general at the prefecture, might not look so bad at all in this context, might in fact have to be defended.

Bordeaux's wartime history appeared to be missing. The 'history of Bordeaux during the Occupation' does not exist. In the popular French imagination, Bordeaux during the war has a vague odour of collaboration. But the actual history has not been written down and acknowledged – like, say, the general history of Vichy France, set down by the American historian Robert Paxton a quarter-century ago, copied and modified since but essentially the same. There was one easily available narrative, the one that treats Bordeaux as the 'tragic' capital of defeat, the city that briefly sheltered threatened or defeated French governments in 1870, 1914 and 1940. This is Bordeaux as spectator to hapless victimhood, and a coffee-table book on just this theme was prominently displayed in local bookshops throughout the trial.

But for the years after 1940, the few books by local historians are more than charitable to their city. The single volume with pretensions to scholarliness, on the history of the wine dynasties, published in 1991, devotes less than a page to the Occupation, and contents itself with modestly remarking that 'some establishments were able to maintain, even augment, their business, because the German market was able to provision itself under exceptionally favourable conditions.'[1] The standard general work on Bordeaux's history, a comprehensive effort by a collective of local academics, published in 1990, has one paragraph on collaboration and does not mention the wine milieu in connection with it. It asserts that '204 Israelites' were deported from Bordeaux – less than one-eighth the actual number.

A recent book by the son of a local *résistant*, *Bordeaux 1940–1944*, has four paragraphs on the city's economic elite, and notes that the head of the wine brokers' association was forced to resign in 1945 for favouring sales to the Germans, but does not name him. The book has a chapter called 'The Jewish Question in Bordeaux' (taking up the Nazi-Vichy terminology) and quotes the parliamentarian Robert Lazuryck's remark, about the terrible last days of the Third Republic in the city, that 'never, in all my life, was I called a "dirty Jew" as often or as openly as in Bordeaux in 1940.' The author goes on to write, apparently in extenuation, 'It must be said' that numerous well-off Jewish merchants were then passing through Bordeaux, 'whose affluence quickly became unpopular' with the Bordelais.[2]

I found suggestions of this void in consciousness all over town. Four days before the trial opened I met the historian who knows most about those years in Bordeaux, Michel Bergès. A stout, voluble man, a professor at the local university, he was spluttering with indignation over what was about to take place, though he could be considered directly responsible for it. One day in February 1981 he had been crouching in a dark attic at the Gironde departmental archives on the rue d'Aviau. With the director of the archives he was looking through old files from the Occupation. In a worn orange folder they found a document from the summer of 1942 concerning a roundup of local Jews. The two men saw a name at the bottom: Maurice Papon. 'But it's the minister!' the director of the archives said, nearly shouting.[3]

In recent years Bergès had switched sides, becoming one of Papon's principal defenders. He had evolved what he called a 'theory of signatures' according to which the signatures of Papon were without great significance, while those of his boss Sabatier were. Since the original discovery, many more documents had surfaced, all of them important but not all of them carrying Papon's signature, the professor suggested in interviews. 'It seems to me Papon was not the supreme decider,' Bergès was to say during his testimony, exculpating the defendant in a role nobody had ever attributed to him. 'I've learned moderation,' the professor said in a torrent of words filling two afternoons and punctuated by the word 'uncertainty'. (Some, attempting to explain his about-face, suggested he had been insulted when the investigating magistrates failed to consult him in the 1980s; others, that he resented the publication of numerous books about Papon, none written by him.) His change had earned him the hatred of Bordeaux's Jews and ostracism from old allies in the fight against Papon. When I met him, he called the lead plaintiff a 'mediatized crook', said Papon was a scapegoat and accused the prosecution of ignoring the probative labours of historians like himself. I asked him when his own analysis of the period would be available. 'Soon, very soon,' he said, getting up from the café where we were seated. Bergès has been conducting research on Bordeaux for nearly two decades.

Other historians in Bordeaux were sure he held keys to the city's past. By his own admission he had obtained, years earlier, several critical documents with the help of a sympathetic archivist. But Bergès wasn't budging. 'You see, I have a programme,' he said cryptically.

One day I went into the imposing marbled mansion that houses the archives of the Gironde. I asked to see the files on wartime economic collaboration in Bordeaux. 'Oh, I very much doubt it,' the prim woman at the front desk said, smiling superciliously. I submitted a formal demand. It took eight months and approval from a ministry in Paris for permission to see the fifty-five-year-old files. When they were finally handed over, the archivist had carefully removed virtually every incriminating document, every name of every implicated Bordelais. What was left could not have been more innocuous. 'The honour of the families has to be protected,' she said. The files mentioned an explosive newspaper article that had appeared in a Liberation-era newspaper: a leaker on the local purge committee had named names. Mysteriously, the newspaper had disappeared from every public holding in the city.

The collections of the municipal historical institute (its official designation is 'The Memory of Bordeaux') begin only in the year 1946. A single item from the Occupation years is available by special request, a jerky silent home movie shot by a German officer in 1940. He dutifully recorded the landmarks in the strangely empty city. This short film, which should be so anodyne, is actually rather painful to watch. The German has posed a winsome Bordelaise in front of most of these monuments, and she stares out uneasily at the camera. There is the promise of future submission and compromise in these grainy scenes.

And there is Mériadeck, site of the nighttime roundups a half-century ago. With its laundry hanging in the streets and its small, dilapidated houses, it was equally despised by the Nazis, the wartime municipality and its Gaullist inheritor. Bordeaux has long since vacuumed this district clean. In the 1960s old Mériadeck was levelled and replaced with a frigid forest of concrete high-rises interspersed with barren esplanades now favoured by petty criminals. The Bordelais still hate the area, but for different reasons. The aura of uncompromising sterility is rivalled, in my experience, only by Ceausescu's Bucharest. There are no reminders of the Jews who once lived here, though there are several memorials to de Gaulle and the Resistance.

Two long blocks from the Palais de Justice, I would sometimes pass a hulking three-storey edifice reminiscent of Mussolini's civic buildings in central Rome, only shabbier. This is the Bordeaux Union Hall, built in the late 1930s, the grandiose architectural legacy of Mayor Adrien Marquet, mockingly characterized as 'the apprentice *Duce*' by a great local liberal of that era.[4] It is one of the few physical reminders of a time when the mayor of Bordeaux could set a thousand fellow citizens in motion, marching through the city's nighttime streets in custom grey shirts, red ties and armbands stamped with the Greek letter gamma, all shouting his name in unison, as in some Gallic Nuremberg rally: 'Long live Marquet!' Many years later, one of Marquet's deputies was to remember that the intertwined horns of the gamma, the zodiacal symbol of the ram, of springtime, of renewal and force, 'marked out a kind of swastika'.[5] During the war Vichy's Milice, the brutal paramilitary police, was to adopt Marquet's gamma.

The former mayor's Union Hall is now a forlorn but imposing shipwreck on the city block it occupies. Running nearly the length of its massive, dirty concrete façade are outsize pilasters underneath a high colonnade, and to the side of them is a grotesquely elongated, three-storey art deco bas-relief with an allegorical representation of Bordeaux among the city's riches. Inside, a vibrant mural covers the walls of a vast second-storey auditorium, fantastic giant white antelopes dancing next to a recumbent hermaphroditic nymph, all of it overtopped by a thrusting Mercury, the god of commerce. The building is Marquet's temple to labour, symbol of the one-time Socialist's wooing of the working class. It was designed by his personal master builder, an architect who admired the Mussolinian style and read the fascistic *Action Française*.[6] He spent huge sums recruiting well-known contemporary artists, among them several winners of the prestigious Prix de Rome. At the building's dedication on May Day 1938, Mayor Marquet said, 'Labour has the right to benefit from some of the splendour it has spread throughout the world.'[7]

Bordeaux has not been proud of this building for years. Guidebooks don't give it a mention. Great chunks are missing from the façade, and ugly prefabricated dividers obscure the murals. Here and there linoleum covers the floor. It has the neglected feeling of a dreary welfare bureau in some southern US state capital. In a wilful effacement of Marquet's progenitorship, the steps of the sweeping double staircase have been stickered with the names of union members martyred by the Germans and Vichy during the war. I told a harassed union official in one of the dingy cubicles that I admired the structure.

He sneered in disbelief. 'You actually like this Stalino-Nazi pile?'

Marquet has been studiously forgotten. Not a single street, square, or building is named after the man who dominated politics in the city for nearly a quarter-century and led it through its most trying time. It is as if New York had erased La Guardia from its history. Here was a man who, after all, had founded a national political movement and served as Vichy's first interior minister. The *New York Times* of July 9, 1940, three weeks after the collapse, had put him on its front page, calling Marquet, inaccurately as it turned out, the third member of a 'triumvirate' that was to rule the new 'fascist state' of France.

Bordeaux's workers, embarrassed by the turn of their former champion, have long since consigned Marquet to oblivion. A yellowing artistic guide to the Union Hall, published in the 1980s by the Confédération Générale du Travail, the country's biggest labour group, does not even mention the mayor, though it notes the visit of a Rosenberg son. 'Marquet's star was fading, so he tried to harness the workers,' an ancient union official who had attended the building's inaugural in 1938 grumbled, with more feeling than accuracy.

Of course, Bordeaux had no choice. The city's imperative in striking Marquet from the collective memory was no less pressing than, say, Stalin's in eliminating certain commissars from official photographs. And the same dictates governed the absence of a widely accepted narrative of the wine aristocracy's wartime conduct. As soon as the war was over, these men had commenced the construction of a brand-new narrative, gratefully entrusting Bordeaux's fortunes to a dashing young Resistance general with no local connections but strong ambitions. Jacques Chaban-Delmas, the future prime minister, was to remain mayor for the next fifty years. And Bordeaux, the city without its own Resistance, went on to name more of its streets for Resistance heroes than any town of its size in France.

There was a reason. Paris may have had more, and more flamboyant, collaborators. And Bordeaux may simply have given free rein to normal expressions of the ambient Jew hatred, albeit with some distinctive vigour: for instance, the sign proclaiming 'No Dogs, No Jews' outside the elegant Café Régent, still the most agreeable in Bordeaux ('during the war it was forbidden to Jews and maybe to dogs,' the Bordeaux poet Bernard Delvaille wrote gaily in his whimsical book about the city);[8] the large attendance, sixty-one thousand in little over a month, at the German-sponsored exhibition of 1941, 'The Jews and France', a bigger crowd than anywhere but Paris; and Bordeaux's early lead over the capital in establishing the first Institute for Jewish Questions in April 1941, with the professed goal of 'eliminating, within the limits of our possibilities, the Jewish influence'.[9] You could find the notices for 'Jewish holdings to be sold' in the city's leading wartime newspaper, *La Petite Gironde*, between the ads for Lux, 'a marvellous product that dectuples the life of your fabrics,' and Pamprel, 'the natural drink'. If you had glanced at the front page on July 9, 1943, you would have seen the headline 'The Jewing-Out of the United States'.

The Bordelais saw no reason to feel any particular hangover from these manifestations of what had, after all, been a national tendency. So it was understandable that France's leading contemporary novelist, Philippe Sollers, who grew up there during the war, could blandly declare to an American interviewer in the late 1970s, 'Bordeaux was a city where anti-Semitic propaganda was hardly successful.'[10]

Still, it would have been hard to find another major city in France where the elites, political and economic, were so firmly engaged with the invader. In the late summer of 1944, four men had shared nearby cells in the dank fifteenth-century Fort du Hâ in Bordeaux. Each represented a constituent part of the local governing class. There was Marquet the ex-mayor; Louis Eschenauer, the jolly 'emperor' of the wine milieu; the *abbé* Bergey, a fire-breathing priest, former deputy and 'idol' of the region's clergy; and Louis Boucoiran, the prefect and representative of Vichy. (At the trial there were suggestions that the slow-witted Boucoiran had taken the fall for his more clever nominal subordinate, Papon.)[11]

Adrien Marquet: Difficult Burden

BORDEAUX IS FORGETFUL, and it is also forgiving. 'People like Marquet, at least they tried to save the furniture. If everyone had left, well, the Germans would have taken everything,' a distinguished personage in the wine aristocracy said, sitting in an eighteenth-century armchair. 'Adrien Marquet, now there was an eminent personality. He was a man of a great deal of authority,' one of Marquet's last surviving collaborators, a cultivated Frenchman who had served as the mayor's interpreter with the Germans, said to me.[12]

Late in June 1940, with the Germans now installed in Bordeaux, Marquet set out the new reality for his fellow municipal officials. 'The hour of truth has arrived. There is only one: a new order is being born in Europe, and France must integrate itself within it,' he told the city council.[13] As mayor, he was to make a sincere effort, donating the city art gallery for the anti-Jewish exhibit and even giving the inaugural speech ('France is so, well, Jewed out,' his old interpreter remarked to me more than a half-century later. 'The banks, businesses, the political circles.') The mayor created a think tank, the French Propaganda Centre for a New Europe. He rubbed shoulders with Wehrmacht dignitaries at openings, telling the crowd at an exhibition, 'Germany Today', in May 1941: 'This exhibit allows visitors to take the measure of National Socialism in Germany. It is good for France that, in looking at what your great nation has accomplished. Frenchmen will reflect on what they must do to become again a great nation, determined to participate according to our national spirit in the European Reconstruction.' After the war, the Bordeaux police commissioner Bernard Poinsot, later executed for his savage repression of *résistants*, told investigators: 'I knew, like everybody else, that he played host to, and was hosted by, ranking officers, in the restaurants.'[14] The Germans, as grateful as Marquet's own flock, allowed the mayor to fly the French flag over city hall, a rare privilege.

Marquet would have been a difficult burden, had Bordeaux chosen to assume him. During the Papon trial, some local historians complained about the unfairness of branding the city collaborationist simply because the mayor had been a collaborator, Bordeaux was not political, one of them said; Bordeaux didn't know the extent of Marquet's collaboration, said another.

Yet what was distinctive about the combined trajectory of Marquet and Bordeaux was its consistency. Mutual devotion had been unflagging, right up until the undefined point at which Bordeaux prudently decided to consider the former mayor – unconsciously adapting the Gaullist formula about Vichy – null and void.

This point would have occurred long after the war. It certainly occurred well after Marquet was sentenced to ten years' loss of civil liberties for his service to Vichy, after he was released from jail, after forty months, in 1948, and after he scored a surprise political comeback in municipal elections in 1953. It must have occurred considerably after his death in 1955 – his funeral was crowded – because even as late as 1957 a local *Who's Who* carried a brilliant panegyric for the former mayor: 'The entire population of Bordeaux will keep a grateful memory of the great and honest administrator that he was.'[15]

In other words, for a very long time Bordeaux was either oblivious or indifferent to what de Gaulle had concluded about it: 'a city whose mayor, Marquet, was a notorious collabora-tor'.[16] And even if Bordeaux did not know of all of Marquet's dealings with the Germans (and the mayor had aided this ignorance by burning his records at the Liberation), it must have known as much as de Gaulle.

The city had faithfully followed the political mutations of the well-tailored dentist with the short black moustache. It elected him as a Socialist and tribune of the working classes in 1925, reelected him in 1929, and put him back in office in 1935, two years after he had veered decisively toward a muscled brand of socialist nationalism that was then the trademark of certain well-known foreign leaders. Above all, Bordeaux was thankful for a spectacular building programme that included not just the Union Hall but a new sports stadium with a daring cantilevered roof, new university buildings, municipal slaughter houses, hospital facilities, sewers, street lighting and more.

By the time of this last reelection, Marquet had provoked one of the earliest, most celebrated premonitions of the impending disaster. 'I confess that I am appalled,' the great socialist leader Léon Blum had said after hearing the mayor-deputy launch his strutting formula for a new socialism, 'Order, Authority, Nation', at a Socialist Party congress. Marquet the 'stuntman', the 'provincial dandy', formed his own party, the Neo-Socialists, and took to surrounding himself with bully boys at speeches.[17] Communists and Jews were targets. Léon Blum 'was pushing us to war for the Soviet Union and Jewry', he said in 1938. Bordeaux, in short, had equipped itself with a leader who was as close to fascism as Frenchmen got in those years.

In June 1940, with the shattered government cowering in his city, Marquet militated for a deal with the Germans ('the climate in Bordeaux had become abominable,' the future prime minister Pierre Mendès-France was to remember many years later) and was rewarded with a ministry in the new regime's first government, headed by his friend Pierre Laval.[18] On June 28, he welcomed the new German military governor, von Faber du Faur, with fresh flowers, new drapery and a new carpet at what had been the French army's Bordeaux command.[19]

By July he was secretly complaining to the SS that Vichy was full of Jews, and pressing them for a private meeting with Hitler. The entreaties were ignored. But as interior minister he did his best to make up for the new government's softness, firing thirty-five prefects of doubtful allegiance, locking up the deputies who had fled to North Africa to continue fighting and hunting down, for the Germans, foreign political refugees in France. 'Everybody is afraid of the Minister of the Interior, Adrien Marquet,' a prominent citizen of the town of Vichy noted in his journal on August 19, 1940. 'But as far as I am concerned, I will not accept that this mayor of Bordeaux, who always accepted luncheon invitations from Ellisen in his famous chateau in the environs of Bordeaux, now not only pretends not to know him, but aggravates the measures taken against him, and threatens the dispossession of his holdings – susceptible to being considered "Jewish holdings".'[20] The Ellisens were a Protestant-Jewish family of 'Portuguese' origin, later forced to flee by the Germans.

In September, dismissed from the government (along with the other parliamentary deputies remaining in it), he returned to Bordeaux. But he maintained his contacts with the Germans, going to Paris once a week. With the fascistic Marcel Déat he organized a lunch for German dignitaries at Maxim's in February 1942, to complain that collaborators like themselves weren't being taken seriously. 'For the first time in eighteen months there is a radical disagreement between us,' Ernst Achenbach, the councillor at the Reich's embassy, said when Marquet refused a new Vichy posting despite German entreaties.[21]

'How many times did one not hear him say, discussing the occupying forces, "Those people don't understand anything,"' his biographer, the distinguished Bordeaux lawyer Robert Dufourg, wrote in his defence in 1948. So it was only a problem of German incomprehension, of not understanding. Otherwise, there was common ground.[22]

If there were rough spots in the mayor's relations with the Germans, the same was not true of his ties to the Bordelais. 'The entire city of Bordeaux understood and accepted this man,' one of his lawyers said at his trial in December 1947. 'Not for one minute was it mistaken about his acts and his attitudes.' How could it have been, when these attitudes were obvious even before the war, and for the first two years of it, and had been on display every week in *Le Progrès de Bordeaux*, a weekly newspaper sympathetic to collaboration, directed by Marquet. Like 108 other Vichy ministers and high officials, he was ordered to stand trial for treason in front of a specially constituted High Court of Justice in Paris. Marquet appeared at the trial in an elegant dark grey suit lightly flecked with white, sombre but erect. He defended himself with dignity, called Papon an 'authentic *résistant*', and declared: 'When I think of the Jews who didn't wear the yellow star at Bordeaux, when I think of the hostages who weren't shot, who were only deported and came back alive, I tell myself that I was wrong for me, but right for them.'[23]

Notable citizens of Bordeaux, one after another, took the stand to testify that the 'mayor of Bordeaux defended the interests of the people of Bordeaux,' as Léon Beziat, a restaurant owner and self-described member of the Resistance, put it. Walking to the Bordeaux law courts, 'I hear the voice of the common people,' another lawyer, the esteemed Bordelais barrister Chalès, told the court. 'Whatever their political opinion, they ask, "When are you going to get our mayor liberated?"'[24] At the trial, Marquet had merely to account for his brief service at Vichy. Besides, the judges were sympathetic, only the Communist Maurice Kriegel-Valrimont registering ironic astonishment at the tactics of 'a certain Bordelais Resistance that maintained ties with the Hun'.[25]

He escaped a prison sentence, like the majority of those who appeared before the High Court; his one-time friend and former patron Laval was one of only three who were executed. Marquet was back in Bordeaux a month after the end of his trial. Burning to recapture his old position but still deprived of civic rights – a sympathetic public works firm employed him as a consultant – he harnessed a surrogate to combat Chaban-Delmas in the 1953 city elections. The old Neo-Socialist was not about to renounce a lifetime's political habits. What had worked in the 1930s would work still. In speeches to crowded halls he denounced the 'Parisian' interloper, while his faithful followers circulated the rumour that Chaban's real name was Cohen. The tactic united his old constituents of the tiny Bordelais houses known as *échoppes*, or 'stalls', with the right-thinking bourgeois of the grand buildings, and the Resistance hero Chaban lost his absolute majority.[26] Marquet was preparing a final assault when, in April 1955, he suffered a heart attack at a public debate. He was seventy-one, and he had mounted the only serious political challenge Chaban was ever to face.

He had been 'the most collaborationist mayor in France', the fascist writer Lucien Rebatet wrote in his memoirs. His funeral at the church of St Bruno was packed with mourning Bordelais, ex-deputies, and personalities from the wine milieu, including its erstwhile 'emperor', Louis Eschenauer.

Louis Eschenauer: Doing Business

'WINE IS SUCH a very fine profession,' a woman in the wine milieu said to me once, expressing the self-image common in Bordeaux. She and others in the business radiated the quiet sense that what they did was ennobling. It was hardly a business at all, more a kind of lucrative adjunct to an aristocratic life of pleasure or culture, or both. In her case, she enjoyed a reputation for youthful dissipation that had nothing to do with her actual age. At dinner one night with a young and successful personage in the trade, the inheritor of a great Bordeaux name, there was casual talk of obscure 1930s writers, of great conductors, of violinists and composers. The present did not intrude (a few disparaging remarks about the Papon trial aside), and commerce hardly at all. 'These people want to see themselves as civilised,' a young man on the fringes of the business said to me bitterly.

The wine families maintained a certain way of living, usually running toward the sporting rather than the aesthetic. Sailing at Arcachon, tennis at the Primrose Club, hunting on horseback in the moors south of Bordeaux – engrossing pursuits, consecrated by standing in the Chartrons hierarchy. Intermarrying relentlessly over two centuries – Lawtons with Cruses, with Schlers, with de Luzes, with Kressmans, with Bartons and Guestiers – they guaranteed themselves a homogeneity of tastes. 'It is certain that the Chartrons, the Intendance, or the Rousselle [other aristocratic neighbourhoods] gave itself over only very modestly to the pleasures of letters, and that the model of the wine merchant who collected art could seem limited to only a few exceptional personalities,' one sympathetic historian wrote about the caste in the nineteenth century. 'By contrast, the taste for horses was very widespread.'[27] A son of the Chartrons who had fled to Paris was vituperative about his Bordeaux contemporaries: 'They are so stupid and ignorant. They aren't like you and me. If they saw a book lying on a table, they would ignore it.' Of an earlier generation, Mauriac had written: 'During tennis season at the Primrose, one wouldn't find a single family of the bourgeoisie where anyone would have the effrontery to talk about anything else.'

Louis Eschenauer, a man of suavity and charm, the most successful dealer in the Chartrons, had not seen the war as a reason to give up his style of life. Before, he had gratified a passion for horses, wintered in Egypt and taken his mistress on frequent trips to the Basque coast.[28] One year he lost so much money at the track that, his wine fortune notwithstanding, he had serious money problems. With the war, travelling became more difficult, but he continued to frequent his adored racetrack, though now with different companions: his new business partners, the Germans.

To a younger colleague who had known 'Uncle Louis' at the end of his life, this was 'a bad mistake', surely his worst. He had 'shown himself in public with German officers', said Jean-Henri Schÿler. He had not, like the family of M. Schÿler, confined himself to entertaining a German officer, a 'charming man', distantly related, in the privacy of their Médoc wine estate.

Eschenauer, for one, had seen reason to be grateful rather than discreet. He did superb business with the Germans, selling nearly 10 million francs' worth of wine during the war – a decent sum for one man, considering that in 1941, the entire French state made forced payments of 144 million francs to the German Reich.[29] Nearly every day the German naval captain who commanded Bordeaux's port dined in style at the mansion of 'Uncle Louis'. As with others of German descent in the Chartrons, the new masters were not altogether alien to him. 'For us, these people weren't like the Russians,' said M. Schÿler. 'The ones that one passed in the street, these were people who were extremely correct.'

By November of 1940 Eschenauer had already gone into business with them. With Heinz Böhmers, a wine merchant from Bremen who was now the Reich's special emissary for wine purchasing, he formed a company, Great Wines of France. It proposed to begin its greatness at the estates of an expropriated Jewish family.[30] Not that he had any more animus against Jews than was normal: 'Decidedly the Jew Rosie is remarkable, here he is, more than taken care of!'

Eschenauer wrote about successful English competitors, the Rosenheims, in 1907.[31]

'He was a remarkable businessman, but business for him didn't have national boundaries,' M. Schÿler said. 'And it was based, above all, on friendships.' Eschenauer's friendship with Böhmers, the man who supplied export vouchers to the Chartrons, was unflagging, despite all the evil that befell him as a result. It survived the war, his imprisonment and trial, and the loss of part of his fortune, as he himself told Böhmers's young son long after. The German wine man would doubtless have understood that 'Uncle Louis', at his trial in 1945, was obliged to characterise him as a 'vulture'.[32]

This fondness for the benefactor from the Reich was shared by a number of the great Chartrons families. It was their misfortune that Böhmers's secretary, at the Liberation, remembered the particular 'warmth' of one important wine broker, the keen interest of another in discussing music and literature with her boss, the 'ceaseless' invitations from a third (accompanied by menus and guest lists), and the deferential bowing of yet another.[33] Thanks to Frau Kircher's indiscretions, many of the wine men wound up in the grim wooden barracks of the Mérignac detention camp outside Bordeaux, where the Jews had been kept before being shipped off to Auschwitz. ('Ridiculous!' Marquet's old interpreter, Jean-Philippe Larrose, a fellow inmate, exclaimed – though he made contacts in the barracks allowing him to embark on his new career in wine.) In all, forty-three wine establishments were found to have had dealings with Böhmers, eleven were fined more than five million francs, and two men, including Eschenauer, were jailed.[34]

One day in 1950, Böhmers's son returned to Bordeaux, taking up the family business for his late father. That evening, his mailbox at the Hôtel Splendide was stuffed with invitations from the Chartrons. In the meantime, 'Uncle Louis' had swept by and taken young Böhmers to the races.[35] Now in his eighties, he had stoically resigned himself to the humiliation of his (much reduced) punishment, confinement to the Gironde for five years.

'The immense goodness of the man,' M. Schÿler said, musing. 'He is deeply missed by all his colleagues. He left us all with very profound memories.'

3

The Exigencies of Memory

IT HAD BEEN a balmy late winter day filled with hazy sunshine, and the dry, bare Médoc looked surprisingly meridional. The little whitewashed towns were warm and empty, like outposts of Spain stuck several hundred miles north. There wasn't a soul in the empty vineyards. The country was at rest. M. Schÿler was in a sunny mood. He beamed happily in the parlour of his family's eighteenth-century mansion, its walls covered in buoyant allegorical frescoes. There was nothing in his version of Louis Eschenauer's story to disturb his benign outlook. If the older man had committed an error in being seen with the Germans, it was 'a superficial one', M. Schÿler said. 'He didn't betray a soul. But, he was seen.' At his trial, he had been subjected to 'unjust insults'. As I left, M. Schÿler showed me Eschenauer's self-published account of how he had saved Bordeaux from destruction as the Germans fled in August 1944. He urged me to read it.

So Eschenauer's only collaboration was that others saw him at the racetrack. Had he not been seen, it would not have existed. His real identity was that of heroic saviour of his city. Certain details – the partnership with Böhmers, the hefty profits thanks to the Germans – were not important enough to mention.

I walked back down the gravel path, past M. Schÿler's smiling workers and his warehouses, feeling oddly disoriented. The customary moral centre – reproval – had been missing. I had been treated to a kind of weightless refocusing of the past. Silence was part of the narrative. The usual framework for describing those years, the one I expected as a matter of course, in which at least lip service is paid, say, to notions of the invader's barbarism, was missing. 'In general these were people who were perfectly proper,' M. Schÿler had said.

Such were the demands of Bordeaux's reconstructed story. What had happened was either forgotten or given a high gloss, or both. The bluster of memory offered excellent potential cover. That at least was the hope. Yet if the city's collective history could be uneasily disposed of in this way, it seemed less tenable as a strategy for individuals. In personal relations with the past, it seemed, it wasn't as simple to construct a new story, one with unpleasant edges smoothed out. Manipulation and forgetting might not be an option. In other words, this struggle with memory might not be a strictly voluntary phenomenon. Perhaps there were other exigencies besides those of the will. How did these imperatives show themselves?

Agitation and Reminiscence

THE MERE APPEARANCE of Eschenauer's old streets suggested that finding out would present difficulties. François Mauriac, the caustic native son, had pictured the city's elite lifelessly immured behind its limestone walls. They were penetrable only at great moral cost. In his memoir from the 1920s, after he had escaped, he wrote: 'Bordeaux is without depth. It stretches out, an immense façade, as if all of its houses longed to gaze out on the other river bank.' The unease of several people I had encountered early on – the café owner, the cobbler, the banker – over what others were thinking echoed Mauriac's observation. Their own city presented itself as an impenetrable façade, the thinking of the bourgeois as unyielding as the streets of grey stone. 'There are entire streets overcome by a strange stupor,' wrote Mauriac's biographer, the Bordeaux writer

Michel Suffran, 'rows of façades tightly sealed, as closed off as mortuary masks.'[1] In Mauriac's novel *Préséances* (*Precedences*) the most redoubtable fortress of the upper bourgeoisie is the solid phalanx of houses facing the Jardin Public, so close the prim city park might be its private back yard. For the novel's melancholy hero the park is the essential but temporary refuge from the snobbery within these nineteenth-century mansions.

From the street, they yield nothing. No light penetrates the shutters, and no doors ever seem to open. The neighbourhood looks abandoned, though it is hardly that. I never saw anybody leave or go into one of the houses on the rue d'Aviau. They adhere strictly to an inexorable rule of French urbanism: the more lifeless the neighbourhood, the more respectable it is. They are the most respectable addresses in Bordeaux.

One morning during the Papon trial I got a call from one of these houses. There was anger on the other end of the line. 'I'm horrified by this trial!' the voice said, nearly shouting. 'I am a Frenchwoman, a Catholic, and I will not accept this!'

It was nearly dark when I got to the rue d'Aviau. The grey stone houses blended into the grey light. There wasn't a soul on the street. A uniformed maid showed me into the high-ceilinged parlour, an oasis of light in this gloom. A fire was blazing in here, and eighteenth-century tapestries and bad oil paintings hung on the wall. Sitting on a plush sofa was Mme Dignac, the daughter of a prominent prewar politician, a deputy and minister who had denounced, in the 1930s, France's feeble air forces. Mme Dignac had married comfortably into the wine establishment. In a corner, sunk into an armchair, was M. Calvet, whose family had been one of the pillars of the Bordeaux wine trade for almost two hundred years.

'I never would have called you. I don't speak to journalists,' Mme Dignac said. 'My children warned me not to.' But since she belonged to the Daughters of the American Revolution, by virtue of an eighteenth-century ancestor, I was exempted from the ban.

M. Calvet worked his hands; Mme Dignac was leaning forward on the sofa. There was a tension in the room. Something was waiting to be unleashed, a feeling not readily yielded up, evidently, beyond the neighbourhood. Mme Dignac said several times, 'I can't stand it!' and M. Calvet repeated, 'It's appalling!'

Events were slipping out of control. The Papon trial was on the front pages of newspapers, and Pétain's picture was re-appearing on the covers of news magazines. The Catholic Church, their own spiritual leader, had apologised publicly for passivity during the wartime persecutions. It was time to take a stand. The words came with energy and passion. 'We will never accept that a president drags us through the mud, saying that we were guilty of something,' Mme Dignac said, referring to President Chirac's several apologies for the crimes of Vichy. 'I won't accept that the French are accused of being co-administrators of the Final Solution! It's monstrous. What are you doing to the future generations?' M. Calvet said: 'We have the feeling of not being heard. This is destroying the unity of our country. It's horrible. It makes me want to vomit.'

Something was awry in perceptions of the war. They were not the Occupation's guilty ones, but its victims. How could this have been forgotten? It came back to them in a memory even more haunting than hunger and fear, banal concerns that affected all Frenchmen. They had lived the war as teenagers in families of substance. So they had been forced into unwanted intimacy with the invader.

It was the first recollection they enunciated, the sharpest point of their remembrance. 'It's a terrible memory, terrible, to have had the Germans in your own house.' M. Calvet wrinkled his face. He was not speaking figuratively. Like other families of the city's *haute bourgeoisie*, theirs had billeted German officers. Sometimes, M. Calvet said with disgust, the officer would descend for his morning coffee wearing a helmet. For four years, another officer of the Reich had trudged the stone stairs I could just now glimpse, right off the very room in which we were sitting so comfortably. The teenage Mme Dignac had avoided speaking to him. But in the collapse at the end, when the Resistance guerrillas came calling, she warned him to get out, fast. Months later, at the end of the Papon trial, Mme Dignac's first words at a party were, 'Ah look, I know what the Germans were like! They were in my house!'

The Occupation had reached them where they were most sensitive: the family establishment, the inherited building that, more than just a dwelling place, was the repository of sacred possessions and the bulwark of status. (As an American, I was to be considered especially susceptible to this. Later, Mme Dignac's son was at pains to plant me in front of an enormous dull seventeenth-century Dutch still life, to serve me wine from his stepfather's production and to describe his family as 'leading'.)

They were victims like other Frenchmen, perhaps even more so. The memory of those years when the Germans were in the parlour melded into a reminiscence of the Liberation, more immediately menacing still. Accounts were settled, friends and relatives punished, and the cowardly ruffians of the Resistance were riding high. This was a time of 'social revolution', Mme Dignac said, a reversal of the natural order. 'It was horrible, frightful, that settling of scores,' M. Calvet said.

They were not guilty, not guilty, not guilty – three times she had repeated it. Why, her father, the deputy, had grabbed the arm of the lawyer Daninos, the most prominent Jewish attorney in prewar Bordeaux, and warned him to get out of town (after the lawyer fled, Maurice Papon directed the liquidation of Daninos's office, in accordance with the new laws on the Jews). M. Calvet, for his part, remembered the Jew in the family orbit, a M. Weil, a 'most elegant' man, a longtime employee who was 'practically a friend of the family'. One day he didn't come to work; it wasn't clear why. 'The way he was, I wonder, he must have suffered,' M. Calvet said tonelessly. His father had been for Pétain, but the Marshal, after all, had 'saved so many Jews', and besides had done 'good work for morality and the organisation of youth'.

'What I don't understand is, why is all this being stirred up now?' Mme Dignac asked. 'This period marked us, it tore us apart. You *can't* stir it up. You have to go on,' M. Calvet said.

'The one who started all this is a Communist, Ilinsky, Silinsky,' said Mme Dignac, mangling the name of one of the most visible figures in Bordeaux, Michel Slitinsky, the deported immigrant's son who launched the case against Papon in 1981. He was mentioned in the local newspaper nearly every day and was frequently on television. 'You know, that person with white hair.' Shuddering slightly, she added, 'M. Guillotine is well entrenched.'

She moved on to a lament over the execution of Louis XVI. Confounded, I struggled to be sympathetic. This wasn't a joke. I mumbled something about the continuities of French history. Mme Dignac went on, oblivious. 'I'll never understand how a people can cut off the head of its sovereign,' she said. But the same spirit was abroad now. Papon, the elegant man in the fine grey suit, was another martyr to the lower orders. 'The mob is always dangerous,' M. Calvet threw in.

Potential sources of malaise were outside and in, as close as the pantry (her own maid, Mme Dignac said, was related to the Papon trial's civil plaintiffs), maybe closer. 'I'm suffering, as a Bordelaise, I'm suffering,' Mme Dignac said.

It was time to go. They were as angry as when I arrived. The room was suddenly claustrophobic, hemmed in by a lifetime's resentments.

On the street, I pondered the violence of these sentiments. Why, if they were victims along with other Frenchmen, were the old feelings so painful? A few weeks later, Mme Dignac's middle-aged son, Denis, received me, in red velvet bedroom slippers, in the panelled study. 'As a Frenchman, I'm not particularly proud of that period,' he said.

He shut the door. His mother was in a different part of the vast house, and he filled in a few details she had left out. Her father, his grandfather, had been among the 560 deputies who voted dictatorial powers to Marshal Pétain after France's defeat. On a sheet of paper, Denis had carefully drawn up an elaborate family tree, showing what happened to old M. Dignac after that fateful vote of July 1940: the grateful Marshal named him to Vichy's National Council; at the Liberation he had been placed under house arrest; he wasn't rehabilitated until 1951. A letter of September 1944 from the Liberation Committee of the Gironde, preserved in the National Archives, describes Pierre Dignac as a 'notorious Collaborator'.[2] I hadn't heard a word of this from Denis's mother.

The Vichy citizen who had commented so acerbically on Adrien Marquet in August 1940 encountered Pierre Dignac a few days later: 'Pierre Dignac is fairly well satisfied with the attitude of the German occupation troops in his region: it's a more or less general sentiment in the Southwest.'[3]

Some time after my meeting with Denis Dignac, I ran into the lawyer Daninos's niece at the Palais de Justice. What about the escape of her uncle, a man known for tough-minded independence? 'Pierre Dignac had nothing to do with it,' she said firmly.

Mme Dignac had said, 'These feelings of guilt, well, I don't have them.' But she had neglected to mention her father's Pétainism, she had presented a 'saved Jew' story (the outline of these tales was becoming familiar to me) of questionable veracity, and the first words out of her mouth when I was seated had been 'All my family were patriots.' M. Calvet, like others in the wine milieu, had quickly mentioned that selling wine to the Germans had been unavoidable; he was more eager to tell me of his arrest by the Germans for crossing the line of demarcation, on a visit home from school.

There was unease over the unadorned family narrative, as if it weren't quite acceptable. And there was the memory of the Occupation right in their living rooms, of humiliation that denied full-fledged victimhood. Their teenage years had been violated. These sentiments were all unwanted. Hence the search for an occult explanation: the 'Communist' Slitinsky and others with foreign-sounding names. Where was the malaise really located? Somewhere between mistrust of the present and a remembered past that was unresolved. It would be better, on the whole, to let the past go. But this wasn't possible. There was, at least at that moment, a national mood of remembrance that wouldn't allow it. And then, they would be reminded with every glance around the room, every innocuous plunge into interior reminiscence. They were chained to the past. So agitation would fill up the parlour like stifling smoke.

The Past's Bad Taste

THERE WERE MILIEUX with less complicated histories. Not every family included a Pétainist deputy. I went down to the docks a few days later to find another Bordeaux, one more turned toward the world. By the Garonne River there is a hint of the sea, the stage of Bordeaux's prosperity in past centuries. Among the Protestant wine brokers who alighted here in the seventeenth and eighteenth centuries, there were not only Germans but English and Irish. They were forced to establish themselves in this then-distant section of town, far from the Catholic elites into whose families they later married. A few of their descendants carried on their trade, and their manner, by the river.

The city opens up here, the wide vistas over the Garonne's muddy water giving a sense of space. If there was immunity from the old stain anywhere, it would be in these more open precincts. As Mauriac promises, Bordeaux becomes just a thin crescent of façades stretched out along the Garonne's curve. When the river mattered, these buildings were the city's most important; at the end of the eighteenth century the American consul dispatched by George Washington had his mansion built along the curve, with a queer little pavilion on the roof to better observe the new republic's ships coming up the Garonne.

Today you can look over from the river and see nothing but a mass of undifferentiated black, the stone façades covered in grime. It is broken up by the flashing signs of seedy cafés, video outlets and convenience stores. The road along the Garonne is the city's major artery, a highway clogged with traffic and clouded in fumes. But at intervals along the quay, there are discreet hints that the dark façades conceal a different world. Affixed to some of these blackened buildings are gleaming brass plaques, announcing in a flowing incised script the ancient wine broker within.

I rang the bell at number 110, crossed a vast, silent covered eighteenth-century courtyard, and ascended a sweeping stone staircase in the far corner. At the top a solid broad-faced man with curly grey hair was waiting. M. Hugues Lawton, a retired wine exporter, was the seventh generation of a family that had been intimately associated with the commercial efflorescence of Bordeaux for some 250 years. He had been described to me in the wine milieu as an irreproachable person, someone who had fought with the Free French as a teenager near the end of the war. This service was rare enough in Bordeaux that it was the subject of general knowledge. The family's position in the hierarchy was unassailable. M. Lawton's grandfather had founded the Primrose Club, still a bastion of exclusivity in Bordeaux more than one hundred years later.

His forebears, recent and distant, hung on the whitewashed walls: a painting of a bewigged Anglo-Irish gentleman who had come from Ireland in the 1730s to trade wines, the founder of the dynasty, and a large photograph of a top-hatted man spitting a stream of dark liquid, M. Lawton's father at a 1950s tasting. Between the two, the family had never strayed from the wine business.

M. Lawton was seated behind a long folding card table in a bare room filled with bright sunlight. Behind him were stacks of cardboard boxes for his wine. Otherwise the room was as uncluttered as what I now listened to: the war had been over for fifty years, the Papon trial was immensely foolish, the world thought France was crazy as a result, de Gaulle's myth of a resistant nation had always exasperated him, France was at Vichy not London during the war, and it had been freed thanks to England and America. Right away, he wanted me to know two things: exactly how much he admired my country (very much), and his precise estimation of the deportation of the Jews ('I tell you, it was an infamy'). He spoke in a self-deprecating low monotone, an undemonstrative Churchillian growl. It was a surprise to hear the words coming out in French, not English.

Apparently, he had attained a kind of frank equanimity about the war. This was new to me. If there was agitation, it was beneth the surface. M. Lawton didn't waste time worrying about such a distant past. Nor did he give it a Pétainist sugar-coating, like M. Calvet. He was courteous but impatient. After an hour I started to leave.

'Do you think about the war much these days?' I asked, half knowing the answer.

'I speak with my brother every morning,' he said, 'and every morning we talk about the war.'

I was taken aback. His war appeared to have been settled many years ago. It seemed to have no more claim on him than, say, some inferior vintage. So what provoked him to return to it, as he apparently did, day after day?

'These are memories that are very fresh, very fresh,' M.

Lawton said. But why? He wasn't particularly interested in revealing more. 'I was marked by the disaster,' he said. How had he been marked? M. Lawton remained abstract. 'France passed from the first to the second rank, rapidly,' he murmured. He shook my hand distractedly. The interview was over.

Mauriac, a resentful child of one of the more dilapidated downriver sections of old Bordeaux, had mocked the Anglo-Saxon mannerisms of his city's uptown wine aristocracy, the men who bought their suits on Savile Row, sent their sons to Eton or lesser schools, even frequented English dentists. But M. Lawton's circumspection didn't seem like an affectation.

And yet he had dropped a few hints. I thought about them as I walked back along the dingy riverfront. He had mentioned some disquieting memories and talked unhappily about becoming 'used to things'. There was a routine trip with his parents to Paris, for instance, in the summer of 1942. They had gone to the Marais to visit the Musée Carnavalet, the delightful history museum, just like any tourists taking their leisure. Except that in the summer of 1942 the narrow streets of the Jewish neighbourhood had become a quiet staging ground for the trip to Auschwitz. It wasn't possible for M. Lawton or his family to be altogether oblivious. He had seen the yellow star then for the first time, and he was 'bowled over'.

He was to see the telltale patch of cloth again, though not with the same effect. 'Alas, one gets used to things,' M. Lawton had said. And then he had talked about the indignity of passing German officers in the street. So had he been forced to rub up against the field-grey uniforms often during those years? Oh yes. 'Alas, one gets used to things,' he had said again.

This phrase came out a little despairingly. It was the only time he lapsed from his understated equanimity. He wasn't proud that these scenes, one much like another, had stopped shocking him. He had had to accommodate himself to them, and he realized it.

His self-analysis was surprisingly accurate, though M. Lawton, as it turned out, was only half aware of its plausibility.

'He had a perfectly dignified attitude during the war,' M. Lawton said about Adrien Marquet. This was manifestly untrue, as was his next statement: 'He was a man of great integrity.' With no disapproval he said that his father had sent Marquet packages of provisions in jail at the Liberation. Louis Eschenauer was only a 'little simple'. M. Lawton, like Mme Dignac, had trouble remembering Michel Slitinsky's name. 'Stinsky, or whatever his name is,' M. Lawton said. He had not made the connection between his own disquieting memory of the yellow star and why, for instance, Slitinsky had spent sixteen years agitating for the trial of Maurice Papon.

M. Lawton was a decent man. He had taken it on himself to raise the children of his cousin, killed in a car accident after the Liberation, as well as his own. In Bordeaux he had a kind of sanctity because of his comportment during the war. A young man I knew on the fringes of the wine trade, well outside the 'aristocracy of the cork', was able to tell me, reverentially, the unit M. Lawton had served in and the general he served under. M. Lawton's son, a cultivated Anglophile wine broker, proud of his London club, had absorbed these combat exploits in childhood. This was all he apparently knew of his father's war. Like his father, he was disdainful of his countrymen's wartime conduct.

Listening to M. Lawton's frank declarations in the light-filled room, I had been prepared to believe what a colleague in the wine trade had told me, only half ironically: M. Lawton was the 'conscience of Bordeaux'. But back down on the riverfront, amid the fumes and blackened buildings, I wasn't so sure.

His picture of the war was clouded. He was bothered by something more tangible than a distant memory: the unpleasant sensation of having been implicated, in spite of himself.

Here was what remained most vivid about the memories themselves. 'Alas, one gets used to things,' he had repeated. This feeling had required distance in order to be recognised, perhaps years of travelling the world selling wine. The events themselves had to be over and done with. It remained a sentiment difficult to assimilate and only partly acknowledged. He had had a lifetime to brood over what seemed at the time like minor adjustments.

Living with the Past

THESE PEOPLE HAD wanted me to believe it was farcical to extract any sort of meaning from the fifty-year reaching back, particularly coming as it did at the expense of a distinguished man. Yet they had revealed precise agitations welling up from that same past Papon had lived. Maybe the trial was not quite as far-fetched as it seemed.

'It wasn't that glorious a period,' M. Manciet, a quiet old Bordeaux functionary, had said to me the week before I saw M. Lawton, stating what was obvious. But this rare ancient survivor had the means – the memories – to be more explicit than M Lawton and the others, mere teenagers at the time. He could explain, if he chose, what it meant to rub up against the invader day after day, and what that contact had meant for the thousands of days since the end of the war.

During the Occupation M. Manciet had kept the city's central file of ration cards, in a long room in what is now Bordeaux's fine arts museum. It was an important job. The German police liked to linger here, riffling through the long metal boxes. Jews could be ferreted out this way, and Resistance members. M. Manciet remembered the visits well. Hanging his head slightly, he said, 'We didn't know what they were looking for.'

It was a puzzle. What was the purpose now, so many years later, of maintaining this fiction, since he had been more or less blameless? After all, he couldn't have stopped the Germans. But he was not interested in explaining. He did not want to continue the conversation, then or later. He regretted agreeing to see me.

There were only a few people left in Bordeaux who could suggest an answer – who could convey, unmediated, not the texture of life fifty-five years ago, but what sort of persisting residue may have been deposited from it into the present.

The Papon trial was stretching on into the winter, settling into the life of the city, ceasing to provoke quick and revelatory reactions from people who otherwise might have no reason to look back. By December, after two months, the crowds had long since thinned, giving way to fitfully attentive school groups. So others, the ones who unabashedly lived in the past, would have to be approached.

One day, I climbed into a tiny elevator and rode to the top of a marbled mansion at the city centre's edge. The lower floors hummed with a busy law firm's activity, but there was quiet as the elevator ascended. In a darkened corridor, a corpulent man in a bathrobe and slippers was waiting. He wore enormous oval glasses with thick black frames, and a handsome green button-up sweater was pulled over his thrusting belly. This was *maître* Robert Ducos-Ader, seventy-six, a lawyer who had defended Adrien Marquet at the Liberation. He was one of the last people left who had had any close contact with Marquet. During the Occupation he had written literary reviews for the mayor's collaborationist news-paper. After it, he had taken on Marquet's case, along with those of dozens of the region's collaborators, and even German officers.

He was a solidly respectable figure in the Bordeaux bar, though the lawyers in the Papon case considered him unsa-voury and made scurrilous remarks about him. His law firm, located on the Place des Martyrs-de-la-Résistance, had been a local powerhouse for years, the direction of it passing from the father to the son, who now busily occupied the ground floors.

A heart ailment was eating away at *maître* Ducos-Ader. Shuffling with the help of a cane, he ushered me into his office, encrusted with the memorabilia of half a century. Curious Byzantine-style crucifixes lined the shelves above his law books, along with bronze statuettes of various fauna. In the corners I spotted a death mask or two of notable persons. There was a case crammed with medals. He proudly showed me a junky copper medallion with the arms of Bordeaux on it, the sort of thing a provincial politico keeps handy in large quantities. It had been a gift from Adrien Marquet.

The air was stale and the light was bad; the place was like a mausoleum. I could clearly see the old lawyer's head, but the rest of his large bulk was swallowed up behind an outsize desk.

Maître Ducos-Ader thought he was in court. Without waiting for a question, he launched into what he called a 'few explanations' of Bordeaux during the Occupation. These turned out to be not explanations at all but a series of little scenes: Germans entering Bordeaux in their sidecars in June 1940, 'great big young men, very impressive'; Germans raising the Nazi flag and playing military music on Sundays by the Grand Théâtre, also 'very impressive', especially to the 'lower orders'; Bordeaux's Gestapo chief, 'not a bloodthirsty fellow at all', in fact 'a bit of a dreamer'; the city's leading journalists, meeting convivially at German propaganda headquarters; Eschenauer the wine king, 'Uncle Louis', lunching every week with the German navy's port *Kommandant*.

He said, 'I defended more collaborators than any other lawyer I know. Here and all over the region.'

'Was it difficult?'

He snorted at my naïveté. 'You know, I've defended plenty of child murderers.'

So many had been compromised with the Germans that individual cases no longer stood out. But it was possible, through yellowing newspaper clippings from the Liberation, to retrace the early rise of Ducos-Ader. All through the spring and summer of 1945, not yet twenty-five years old, he had ardently defended the small fry of the Bordeaux collaboration.

There was Claude Béchian, twenty-three, a construction worker who had denounced two colleagues for stealing a melon and cheese from a grocery store, leading to their arrest for distributing Communist tracts. 'The case of the accused was aggravated by the testimony of a mother in tears whose Jewish son was deported – curious coincidence, only a few days after the two young men had quarrelled,' *La Gironde Populaire* reported on May 12, 1945. In a 'moving summation', Ducos-Ader asked the jury to be indulgent. The *Nouvelle République*, reporting the same case, noted that the young lawyer's talent was 'asserting itself every day'. His client was released.

In June, with 'youthful ardour', he defended an imprudent bus company employee who had joined the Gestapo to earn extra cash exactly one year before, as the Allies were fighting through Normandy. In July he took up the case of a barber who, after joining a French unit fighting for the Germans, returned home to denounce his wife and brother-in-law for listening to the BBC. In August he represented Jeanne Gilbert, a fifty-year-old nurse from the coastal town of Arcachon. She had left her husband in 1941 because, the newspaper *Sud-Ouest* explained, he was an 'Israelite' and she wanted to 'avoid sharing the dangers inherent in his condition'. Mme Gilbert became the mistress of a German officer, to whom she provided valuable tips. Numerous local Resistance members were arrested and deported as a result. This time, despite a 'fine closing argument', Ducos-Ader's client received a sentence of twenty years.[4]

In the yellowed clippings, no other lawyer in Bordeaux is mentioned as frequently or as enthusiastically that summer.

'The young and already celebrated attorney Ducos-Ader,' *La Nouvelle République* called him on September 20, 1945.

Still, in his old age, he was modest. He didn't bring up any of these tributes to his skill in courtroom work that many of his contemporaries had shunned. Instead, amused, he recalled the hostile crowds that greeted him on court day in the small provincial towns. 'I even defended the officer in charge of the hangings at Tulle,' he said, referring to one of the worst German atrocities on French soil.

Then he interrupted himself. A pleasant memory was coming back. 'Now at Vichy, young man, the atmosphere was relatively relaxed. It was relatively happy, you understand,' he said in a raspy growl. 'There were all sorts of nightclubs.' He smiled. 'There was a sumptuous brothel, and I was taken to it. It was the one the high clergy went to, and all the diplomats.' Well, the Occupation had not been all hardship.

Maître Ducos-Ader was tired. He showed me out, past a lavishly equipped bathroom. There was a shower, shaving utensils, an array of toiletries. The *maître* obviously did a good bit of living up here among his memories. In the hallway, he pointed to a crude sketch on the wall. It was a courtroom scene in which a young man with a crewcut stood in the box of the accused. He had a look of innocence, anger and desperation. This was one of his clients, a member of the Vichy Milice, and he gave Ducos-Ader the sketch a few weeks before being executed. The old lawyer found this juxtaposition amusing. He produced a short laugh.

I began to understand. The young man's fate had not been at all tragic. Nor had it been particularly deserved. So there were no conclusions to be drawn, no theories or interpretations. There was only a series of stories, and everybody was compromised. Or if there was guilt, at least there was always a redemptory corner of innocence. 'Marquet was a good mayor. He was fascistic without being Nazi.' During his imprisonment 'he was very courageous.' As for Pétain's *révolution nationale*, the homegrown answer to national socialism, it had not been alien. 'Part of it corresponded closely to my Catholic education.' And the Germans? 'There was a German officer billeted with a family I knew well, near the train station. It began with distrust. Then he became an intimate in the family circle. 'Evoking this intimacy posed no problem for the *maître*. It did not embarrass him. The fate of the Jews was not a troublesome issue. 'I don't remember ever talking about the Jews during the war.'

I went back to the law firm on the Place des Martyrs-de-la-Résistance to see Benoît, his son, a few weeks later. I wanted to talk about the old man's work after the war. The subject had not seemed to interest Benoît. For several weeks he put me off. He was a busy man, a high-powered criminal defence attorney with the kind of provincial flash – longish grey hair, well-tailored clothes, spacious office with plate-glass windows – I used to see in successful lawyers in, say, Florida. He had once had the thankless task of defending Basque terrorists, an experience he apparently relished. Two months after the end of the Papon trial he was in court representing the family of a Jewish car dealer who had been kidnapped and murdered by right-wing extremists.

Benoît confessed to only the mildest interest in the war. He was waiting for my questions about his father and the collaborators. 'It was a way to get known, to practise his trade,' Benoît said. 'A lawyer has to understand his client and explain his actions.' These phrases were pronounced quickly. There was no lingering on the topic and certainly no magnifying of its importance. 'The lawyer's role actually amounted to very little in these cases,' he said. 'There was so little time. You had only two days for a case.'

Benoît had the rapid, down-to-earth manner of an American trial lawyer. He was long, lean and saturnine in contrast to his father's corpulence. He had relegated the old man's work to the realm of lawyerly professionalism. It had occurred in a distant, unrecoverable past. 'Like a lot of people in my generation, this didn't interest me particularly. It was like something prehistoric, when my parents talked about it.'

With some unease, he said as I left: 'They think this trial is opening up new divisions. They thought of themselves as completely blended into French society. This trial bothers them.' He said this about Jewish lawyers in Bordeaux – who had not previously entered into our conversation. It sounded as though he was talking about himself.

Three floors above, his father had not been uneasy. In the obscurity of his dark offices he had acknowledged some truths that others were shy of broaching. He was the guardian of Adrien Marquet's junky copper medallions, and he was not reticent about it. 'Here, look at this one,' he had said, chuckling. 'M. Marquet gave it to me.'

4

The Judgement of Papon: History's Revenge

The Strength of His Case

I WOULD OFTEN see Benoît Ducos-Ader striding across the great hall of the Palais de Justice during breaks in the Papon trial, busy with his work, too busy to drop into the courtroom. One day during the trial's terminal phase I ran into him in the midst of a jostling mob of reporters, lawyers and spectators. Curiosity about the outcome and spring weather had brought back the crowds.

Benoît eyed me uneasily. I was interested in an aspect of family history he was not keen on. This was an encounter he would rather have avoided. But it had been four months since my visit to the old man. I asked Benoît about his health. 'Monsieur, my father is dead,' he said.

He had died four days before Christmas. A large crowd had filled the ancient church of St Seurin for the service, according to the obituary in the local newspaper. The paper noted *maître* Ducos-Ader's prestigious teaching assignments, his appointment as a consultant to the Council of Europe, and his authorship of many law books. It did not mention his articles in the pro-German newspaper *Le Progrès de Bordeaux* or his defence of Marquet or of other collaborators.

The old lawyer might have found these omissions amusing. He had seen no reason to be pained by his past. His life before, during and after the Occupation had been a seamless whole. Maurice Papon, by contrast, had gambled on the idea of a radical separation from the past, and plenty of people in Bordeaux were willing to go along, at least on the surface. 'Those things happened so very, very long ago,' a smiling baker's wife said to me one day. 'And you know, we weren't touched, in my family, by the war.' Others, like the Lawtons, Calvets and Dignacs, wanted to go along with Papon but were not quite free to do so.

But the *maître* had integrated past and present, perhaps because he knew he couldn't avoid doing so. Who was right, Maurice Papon or Robert Ducos-Ader? Papon had staked out his position on what our relationship should be to the past. He was suggesting that merely to pose the problem of his guilt or innocence was almost indecent. Would he get away with it? The long unfolding of his trial, filling up two seasons and more in the grimy town, presented itself as a struggle over these questions.

For much of it, Papon had the upper hand. At the beginning, anything less than a conviction would have seemed unimaginable, if only because of the years spent bringing him to court and the moral weight of the charges. But in the trial's second half, a slow panic overtook the civil plaintiffs' lawyers. The former secretary-general's acquittal began to seem possible, even likely. The documents directly implicating him had been few, and virtually all the witnesses irrelevant. There were doddering retired bureaucrats who hadn't known Papon, *résistants* who hadn't known him and ex-deportees who hadn't known him. Not a single one was able to offer testimony specifying his role in the roundups.

The lawyers themselves had wasted huge amounts of time, launching quixotic diatribes against Papon that were full of vitriol and short on fact. Gérard Boulanger, the righteous Bordeaux attorney who had powered his sixteen-year crusade with a nervous energy that became familiar to the regulars, deeply marred his own cause. Convicting Papon had become his life's work. But, determined to re-create the entire history of Vichy, he lost himself during the trial on long historical excursions that left the rigid judge tense with impatience. 'So when did the Americans take on General Giraud?' Boulanger asked one endless afternoon, apropos of nothing. One day he said Papon and Klaus Barbie were the same, a comparison that in no way illuminated the character of either the cool French bureaucrat or the Nazi torturer.

The worst of the lawyers was the narcissistic son of the celebrated Nazi hunters Serge and Beate Klarsfeld, a young man with a long black mane who skated to the Palais de Justice on rollerblades, trailing television cameras and groupies behind him. 'I've got his cell-phone number!' I heard a woman reporter boasting. Arno Klarsfeld's speciality was stagy confrontations with the defendant. 'Is it my Jewish side or my German side that bothers you the most, Maurice Papon?' he thundered one day.

Judge Jean-Louis Castagnède, a straight-backed, intense man with a rolling southwestern accent, sharply interrogated the accused, paying close attention to his language. The judge honed in on particular words, looking for authentic insight into Papon's mental universe during the war. Once, he caught Papon using the word '*refoulement*' to describe his conception of German intentions in regard to the Jews: they were simply to be transferred from one part of France to another. But '*refoulement*' has the sense of 'expulsion', suggesting that he knew even then, despite protestations to the contrary fifty-five years later, that the Jews were headed outside France. Several weeks later the judge tripped up the defendant on the critical word '*déportation*'. 'Maurice Papon, you are slightly in retreat from yesterday, when you said that after a meeting with Sabatier, early in 1942, you understood the sense of "*deportation*",' he began. 'Today you're saying it wasn't until the end of August.' Papon could only agree, weakly. But the chronology was important, because the first train had left Bordeaux in July 1942.

The judge seemed one of the trial's few uncompromised actors until Arno Klarsfeld revealed, to everyone's amazement, that Castagnède was distantly related to one of the victims.

By the fourth month, three incriminating pieces of paper signed by the defendant had emerged. But two of them – a request for police to accompany the February 2, 1943, convoy of Jews to the Drancy concentration camp, and a demand for the arrest of four Jews the next month, in what came to be known as the 'Hungarian Jews' document at the trial – were useless for the purposes of the prosecution. Neither had been included in the indictment. The lapse was due solely to the negligence of the French Justice Ministry.

It wasn't just the slimness of the paper trail that made the lawyers nervous. There was Maurice Papon's pugnacity, manifested in a rhetorical verve that made his opponents seem leaden. The performance would have been unusual for someone much younger; for a man of eighty-seven it was extraordinary. 'I couldn't possibly agree with you, because at every moment you fabricate the reality that is convenient,' he snarled to one of the lawyers. An elderly man sitting behind me chuckled appreciatively; later he told me he was firmly convinced of Papon's guilt. 'Look, it would have been better simply not to have lost the war of 1940,' Papon snapped sarcastically to another lawyer, who was hectoring him about the fate of the Bordeaux Jews.

The attempts to demonise him failed. He was more unsettling than any demon. Parrying the heavy-handed lawyer who accused him of cowardice, he plausibly told the court that he had been a young man during the Occupation, and afraid. When he spoke of the German boot, complained of the pressure, shouted that the field-grey was omnipresent and that we couldn't possibly understand this, he made disturbing sense.

Mostly, it had become clear that Papon was not the zealous Jew-chaser depicted for years by Boulanger and the civil plaintiffs. 'I feel like I've been had,' an American reporter said to me one day. Indeed, the strongest evidence against Maurice Papon appeared to be nothing more than his position in the hierarchy, directing the Gironde prefecture's Service des Questions Juives.

Under him were the younger, career-minded men who ran that small office. Understanding its duties became critical to an assessment of Papon's own responsibility. Among its routine tasks was applying some of the French government's new laws: keeping the register of Jews up to date and administering the takeover of Jewish property. But as the Germans began pressing for roundups in the summer of 1942, the office took on more onerous duties. Papon presented it in these new circumstances as, alternatively, a protective agency for the Jews or the helpless transmitter of orders from the Occupation authorities.

As to the first claim, the evidence pointed in the opposite direction. The second turned out to be an overly modest estimate of the agency's functions. In the old documents, it appeared as the efficient executor of the Germans' surprising new demands. The Service des Questions Juives approached its task in all seriousness. Pierre Garat, the young man who headed the office for most of Papon's tenure, reported to his boss before the July 1942 roundup: 'The execution of these measures, in the period of time specified, is difficult but possible.' (The former secretary-general said in court, 'This phrase shocked me.') Two weeks later, on July 16, 1942, with the roundup successfully completed that day, Garat noted that the Germans 'will be able to see for themselves that every measure was taken for the operation to be carried out with the best possible results. In this respect, the roadblock units carried out the orders given them smoothly and efficiently.' (The defendant commented, 'I would have composed this phrase with more consideration and nuance.') The train with 171

Jews on board left Bordeaux's St Jean station at 8:53 A.M. on July 18, 1942, bound for Drancy.

If you had had business at the Service des Questions Juives during the war – if you were, say, a 'provisional administrator' of one of the newly Aryanized properties – you would have entered the Hôtel de Saige, the imposing prefecture, on the side facing the Rue de l'Esprit des Lois. You would have come through the courtyard, ascended a sweeping staircase of light-coloured local stone, proceeded down a long corridor, passed the prefect's and secretary-general's offices, and watched for an arrow pointing to a narrow flight of stairs. At the top, you would find yourself at what looked and sounded like any small government agency in a big provincial town, according to the testimony of the old secretaries – a sign on the door, two desks when you walked in, busy typing sounds, neat file box on the table. Except – and the stocky old ladies remembered this part a bit anxiously – there wasn't much joky conversation in the office, and when you were with the other young women at the prefecture, during lunch break, you didn't really feel like talking about what exactly you did, or even where exactly you worked.

Garat was either 'secretive' or increasingly 'pale' and 'withdrawn', according to which ex-secretary you believed. Yet whatever the burdens of the Service des Questions Juives, they were apparently not unconducive to the development of affectionate ties. He went on to marry his personal secretary there, Sabine Eychenne. Garat gave every evidence of conscientiousness in the memoranda he left behind from those years: 'It is to be deplored that the German authorities will not appear in these operations, which could cause unfortunate reactions in the populace,' he wrote, in a note signed and stamped by Papon, before the July 1942 roundup. Dead these last twenty years, Garat was a fugitive figure throughout the trial's six months, crucial but absent, here romancing his secretary, there appearing at Bordeaux police headquarters to give orders. He was there, for example, at 9 P.M. on October 19, 1942, for the purpose of sending officers out into the tenements of Méria-deck and the dank courtyards of old Bordeaux to hunt for Jews under the watchful eyes of the Germans. 'Tact' and 'firmness' were the watchwords, Garat told the police officers that night. Before the war he had joined the fascistic Parti Populaire Française, but some maintained that his subsequent experiences changed him. In any case, they didn't much hurt his career, since he was made a subprefect of the Gironde after the Liberation.

The defendant's relationship to the young man, only twenty-five when Papon arrived in Bordeaux, was one of the trial's mysteries. Now gingerly solicitous ('loyal, a little fragile', Papon said, 'maybe a little too young for such heavy tasks'), now standing back ('M. Garat was going beyond what he should have and could have said,' and later, 'a bit closed off, quiet, withdrawn'), it was understandable that he should try to maintain this distance, since Garat's own involvement with the trains was anything but abstract. '*Maître* Lévy lacks imagination!' Papon shouted at one of the lawyers once. 'We're coming back yet again to "Papon equals Garat, Garat equals Papon".' In fact, it was Papon's position that, within the Gironde prefecture's complicated skein of relationships, he was left out more often than not: 'The dossier shows with abundant clarity that I was largely short-circuited,' he said.

Actually the 'dossier' showed no such thing. The reports that Garat wrote were destined for Papon. The secretary-general had the authority. 'If one says "authority", one means "responsibility", no?' the judge had observed to Papon. Besides, the accused's entire subsequent career, a model of success, and his authoritative demeanour in the Bordeaux court made it difficult to believe that he was ever 'short-circuited' at any point.

Yet because of the trial's weaknesses and Papon's evident strength, it took patience to maintain the connection between the defendant and the victims. And it wasn't easy to keep up with the intensity. In the press, many were losing their stomach for it. You would see projected in court, at regular intervals, documents like the scrawled note of October 23, 1942: 'Received this day at 19:20 at the camp of Mérignac the 14 Jews hereinafter designated.' The normal context for such documents today is a book or a museum exhibit – a place where one can react in private. The neutral courtroom imposed a collective restraint, and thus a tension, and it restored – perhaps – bequeathed for the first time – a poisonous mortal tinge to the old papers. You were forced to focus on them as working instruments leading to the programmed death of the 'Jews hereinafter designated', their fate now becoming an issue in the trial.

For those living with the documents day after day, the world turned sour. Fellow passengers on the bus home, the smiling greengrocer – anybody apparently indifferent to what was going on in the courtroom – seemed hateful.

One late winter afternoon, after hours of listening to ambiguous witnesses of dubious veracity who may have been incriminating for Papon or may not have been, a well-known radio reporter muttered in the reporters' shed, 'And this is what they call their historic trial!' Sniffing the drift in public opinion, a sizeable slice of the media began to insinuate that the whole affair had been a gigantic mistake. One of the leading news-magazines demanded on its cover, 'The Papon Trial – Let's Get It Over With!' Another asked, 'Should Papon Be Acquitted?' In the press gallery, some of the reporters took to pulling out the sports pages as soon as the day's testimony started. The reporter for *L'Express*, Eric Conan, celebrated in Paris for the derision he aimed at the proceedings, was overcome by creeping lassitude, sinking further and further into his habitual seat as the weeks dragged on. Across the street, in the light of the gleaming mirrored café adjacent to the Palais de Justice, the lawyers looked edgy.

Papon on Memory

PAPON'S STRATEGY BECAME clear through the trial's long months. It consisted of thoroughly removing himself from the court's logic by calling into question the notion of memory itself, at least as it was applied to the distant period of the Occupation.

But it wasn't simply a case of the defendant dumbly reiterating the classic exculpation 'I don't remember.' This quasi-mutism wasn't possible for Papon, who was determined to be master of his own trial. Indeed, within a week of its opening, he had placed himself at the affair's centre with a long and cogent autobiography that astonished the reporters. 'The clarity, the careful phraseology, bear witness to an astonishing agility of spirit,' the *Le Monde* reporter, Jean-Michel Dumay, accurately wrote that day.

Papon needed to talk. But he didn't, for his own purposes, need to remember. He had his own relationship to the past, but it could not be comprehensive. So there could be no concrete reconstruction of those long-ago times. At first, this position was depicted as a matter of personal psychology, a function of his own rarely admitted deficiencies. He couldn't, for instance, say precisely how he had sabotaged German orders (one of his chief defences), remember the names of the Jews he had saved, or recall why eighty-one Jewish children wound up on the train from Bordeaux in August 1942. The projection, in court, of bills addressed to the prefecture for the children's transportation did not jog his memory. 'You're asking for concrete examples fifty-five years later! I'm not a genius!' he exclaimed one day. 'It's a terribly hard task to work up memories that are a half-century old,' he said a few days later. 'When you're eighty-seven years old, give me a call!' he shouted once to the government prosecutor.

But at the trial's midpoint he asserted this difficulty as a matter of general philosophy. Late in the afternoon of January

15, 1998, he rose to deliver one of the set speeches with which he liked to close the day's session:

> Memory makes its choices as a function of its own psychology, its own feelings, or quite simply of its own interests. There are inner workings that make the resurrection of lived facts impossible. Memories cluster around an idea, or a principal feeling, or they disappear ...
>
> [As for the] reconstruction of the past to utilitarian ends: it is done, in all good conscience, based on testimony and documents. In this work of research, it is the spirit of logic that prevails. One isolates events, one from another. But one can't restore to them the light of their context. It escapes us, because it has gone out. So one gives oneself over to hypotheses, with concern for the rational. But this is false, because life isn't rational. It is the spirit of man, who wants to govern events, which dominates and manipulates, according to his will, those events that are retained.[1]

So what was remembered was dictated by self-interest. It wasn't possible simply to call up, on demand, those memories one now wanted, or that the court wanted. The choice had been made long before, according to the 'interests' of the person concerned. It was a kind of confession, though one in which he had been careful not to name himself. He was suggesting that long ago it had been in his own interest not to remember. Therefore, like anybody else subject to the principles of the human intellect, he had forgotten many things. Others, like the vast majority of his questioners, had even less capability than he to reconstruct the past, because its 'light' had gone out. In a 'rational' world, events that 'in the spirit of logic' – for the sake, say, of accurate history – should be remembered, would be. But life, instead of being rational, was governed by 'will' or self-interest. So some of these 'events' were deliberately forgotten.

Papon was confronting the court with the logical impossibility of its own task. He was the only real witness to the history it was interested in. No one disputed that knotty fact. So the court needed him to remember. But by the principles he had enumerated, he was incapable of remembering, because for years it had been against his self-interest to do so. So perhaps he *was* guilty of having occupied the role the prosecution had assigned to him (and his speech didn't rule out this possibility). Yet it was impossible for him to confirm this, even if he wanted to, because as a matter of self-preservation, he would have, decades before, forgotten the details of his involvement. It had been necessary for him, in order to vault through the ranks of the administrative hierarchy, to shove into the farthest corners of memory the unpleasant wartime duties that in no way would be helpful to his ascent.

That day he revealed more of himself than at any other time in the trial. He had shown that his was a cold world, permeated by regret that the imperfect 'spirit of man' had the upper hand on the 'rational', which appeared to be lost. It was a world unabashedly dominated by self-interest, which he identified with the will. His speech was a monument to the egotism Maurice Papon said was all-powerful, since it posed as a general principle an argument that was exculpatory for himself. And yet, given the relative proportions of human sympathy and ego that he manifested, it was possible that his speech was sincere. He had demonstrated again that, of all the trial's participants, few could match him in acuity.

The Defendant's Mistake: Memory's Trump

NEVERTHELESS HE HAD made a miscalculation. Memory wasn't governed solely by self-interest. The proof of it was in some of those mansions on the Jardin Public, and it was sitting barely twenty feet from him, a mute chorus that occasionally broke silence to disapprove his words. The lives of the civil plaintiffs had been split, though not necessarily by what they had suffered directly. They had been teenagers or younger during the war, and their own moments of fear were mitigated by youthfulness. These people, in late middle age or older, were not like the rare deportees who had survived, for the most part irrevocably shattered. Nor were they like Bordeaux's bourgeois Jews, many of whom had found safe hiding places (unlike the Naquets), and who emerged frightened but relatively unscathed. An ancient lady from this class, one who had had to flee the large family apartment on the main thoroughfare of old Bordeaux fifty-five years ago, blandly told me she had never met any of Papon's working-class adversaries. One of the latter, in turn, spoke bitterly of the Jewish bourgeoisie's years of quiet 'manoeuverings' against their crusade.

The civil plaintiffs occupied a distinctive category. They were acting to redress what had been done to others, relatives who were missed. They didn't necessarily have a personal need for revenge. Elsewhere, some in their situation had chosen to move forward, to bury the past, to get on with their lives. And indeed for these inheritors of the victims, wholeness would have meant doing just that. But they had been unable to. True, some had built successful lives – one was a well-known psychoanalyst, another a chemical engineer, a third had made women's clothing. And yet they had suffered for years because they had allowed memory to fester. They had lingered over their own experience and the reconstructed last days of the people who had been close to them. Several talked of having spent years reading everything they could find about the camps.

When they spoke of Papon in court, they vilified him, as their lawyers did. 'A man devoid of value,' said Maurice-David Matisson, who hid in an attic but lost parents and siblings; Thérèse Stopnicki, whose two little sisters, five and two years old, were deported, said, 'I've got a big, big problem – breathing the same air as him.' During the crowded breaks, standing at the metal police barriers, some became adept at soundbites for the TV cameras: 'He's on the defensive today,' Michel Slitinsky commented once, 'a bit weakened. He's clinging to the idea that he waged passive resistance.' When they testified, the recollections they delivered in the narrow stuffy courtroom were specific, and almost invariably irrelevant. Not a single one credibly connected Papon to the fate of his or her relatives.

Yet they proved to be far stronger than he. They commanded attention, because they themselves were connected to the crime. They spoke with authority about the enormity of the mysterious occurrence that haunted the entire court – spectators, lawyers and Papon. They made real the truth that the ablest of the lawyers, Michel Zaoui, who represented the Fédération des Sociétés Juives de France, demonstrated with precision later, in the final closing argument: the bureaucratic crime required unusual and difficult means of contemplation, since there was no physical link between victim and perpetrator. The civil plaintiffs had the special ability to show that, even in the absence of such a link, and across the stretch of years, the effects of the crime were manifest.

There was a moment in the second week of December 1997 when the courtroom was frozen with an early realisation of this. A small quiet man of seventy-three told the story of how as a teenager he had dodged the roundups while losing a father, brother and cousin to them. In fact, the case of Hersz Librach's cousin Léon appeared to be one of the most damaging to Papon, because it was the only one in which an arrest order signed by the defendant had been found.

Hersz Librach, a retired tailor in an elegant grey suit, spoke precisely and deliberately, as if he were crafting a fine blouse. It was not an easy story to tell. When he was finished, one of the jurors, an earnest bespectacled man, asked him: 'What notion do you have of these fifty-five years that have passed?' And

Hersz Librach simply began the retelling of his story. Unsatisfied by this response, the juror asked again: 'These events seem so far away to us. What about for you?' The witness seemed to be in a kind of trance, eyes half closed, not hearing his questioner. 'I wouldn't say that this is an easy grief,' he said carefully. 'I would even say it is a perpetual grief.' He paused, and the courtroom waited. 'Perpetual,' he said again.

Musing and dream-like, he had created his own strange echo, a kind of unconscious onomatopoeia. He seemed to be speaking to himself. But the juror persisted, unsatisfied.

Hersz Librach appeared to wake up. 'Look,' he said, 'these events have lasted for fifty years. I've never been able to forget. I live with them. It's a wound that doesn't heal, that can't heal. There is something irreparable, something that doesn't move. It is the inhuman conditions that were the fact of the Shoah.'

He was speaking of events that never actually end, a new notion in the trial. Papon's theory of time's passage was evaporated by it. It seemed that Hersz Librach had undergone a more radical version of the transformation of memory experienced by Hugues Lawton. The pain left by what he called 'these events' had become gradually sharper, not weaker, with the years. The defendant, by contrast, had not allowed this festering process. He had cut off memory. The retired tailor said 'it was necessary to close the books' after 1947, when posters announcing returns from the camps had ceased to go up. But of course he had been unable to do so. Papon by contrast had had no difficulty in closing books, and writing wholly new ones (himself as *résistant*, for example).

'I'm going to speak without fear or hatred, but with rage in my heart, suppressed for fifty-five years,' said the psychoanalyst Maurice-David Matisson, immediately contradicting himself. 'The defence hasn't stopped bemoaning the absence of contemporaries. And we, then – are we not contemporaries?' In the most inclusive sense, they were contemporaries – the events in question and of all those present in the courtroom.

They wiped out the gap. 'All my life, I haven't stopped making this journey to Auschwitz,' said a tiny sparrow-like woman, Esther Fogiel, whose parents, grandmother and younger brother were deported. She transfixed the court with her terrifying story – that of a small child entrusted to a smuggler after the roundup of her parents, raped and abused by him, then, as the only Jew in a Catholic school, branded a 'little fiend' by the nuns.

The precise degree of Papon's connection to the trains going east, his knowledge of what awaited the passengers – the trial's two central questions of fact – became nothing but nuances in the face of this testimony. The inheritors had shown that the crime was not actually old but sharply contemporary. A few of them even seemed able to provide an exact measure of its increasing weight over the years. So Papon's mere presence in the prefecture back then was enough. It was particularly damning that life had simply gone on for him during those years, in the high bureaucrat's unvarying routine: the chauffeur picking up the young man at his apartment on the rue David-Johnston, taking him downtown, and dropping him off again in the evenings. In his diary for 1942, Papon noted some events that had preoccupied him: a country festival, a hunting party, an Allied bombing in the Bordeaux suburb of Lormont that killed 245. There was no mention of the Jews.

For six months, he was in a state of continual indignation. Indisputably, his longevity had put him in a spot dozens of other French functionaries could have occupied. 'This wasn't just about Bordeaux, but Rouen, Le Havre, Abbeville . . . Why is it that Bordeaux alone is answering for this national circumstance, one with consequences in all of France?' he asked, and his hands waved about to indicate the infinite possibilities. The guilt of secretaries-general in these other cities, at this remove, would have been equal to his.

The lawyer Michel Zaoui brilliantly demonstrated, in the

last closing argument, how the culpability of such functionaries should be measured. A locus of overall responsibility
didn't exist. A series of minute decisions, at myriad levels, led
to the departure of each train. In Bordeaux every one, over
nearly two years, had left the St Jean station on time. Thus the
machine had worked properly. It almost had the quality of a
mathematical equation. Papon was in authority in the prefecture; the Jews had been deported partly by virtue of the
prefecture's exertions; therefore he bore responsibility.

Only in the light of the present, at the end of the century,
would this equation have added up. It had taken more than a
half-century to measure the crime, and its estimation was
unfinished. Only now could the question of Papon's guilt or
innocence have been raised. So the frequent complaint that one
heard – that it was all coming too late – made no sense. It was
only at this remove that the trial could have taken place at all.
By the standards of the aftermath, he had not been guilty.
Measuring the crime now meant standing back far enough to
see its intricate pattern – and to see, disquietingly, the teeming
ranks of its perpetrators. The trial had confirmed what could
only have been dumbly sensed before: the suffering inflicted on
the plaintiffs – the suffering that doesn't go away and is caused
by memory – was the result of Papon's crime, the bureaucratic
crime of the nearly unquantifiable act. The suffering had been
intensified by the anonymity of these acts, represented by the
formal documents shown in court. The defendant (like his
academic champion Bergès) was lost in this welter of paper
and decisions. Papon justified himself in its complexity. And
for decades this would have been enough to exculpate him.
Now, however, it was more than enough to condemn him.

His own protestations of sorrow for the victims, inserted
with scrupulous regularity into the trial's ebb and flow, were
the best expressions of this. They showed that at the end of the
twentieth century, horror and wonder at the crime were so
intrinsic that expressing these sentiments was a reflex. More

than once the defendant used words like 'atrocious' and 'tragic' to describe it. He talked of the 'sacrifice of the Jews' and of their 'bereavement' in his last bitter words to the jury, the final words of the trial. 'What man, in truth, could resist without tears the pity and commiseration inspired, dictated by the premeditated, massive murder of an innocent people, awakened too late to its historic tragedy?' Papon asked amid a more general lament for his own fate.

He was, in the end, baffled. He didn't understand why he was back in Bordeaux after five decades. It was all the more bewildering to him because, as a man of orthodoxies, he partook of the late-twentieth-century outlook on the Holocaust. The idea that his actions might have contributed to it was hallucinatory. 'For him, I think, these acts have become totally inconceivable, absolutely unreal,' Michel Zaoui said. He had opened up a kind of abyss, demonstrating that a criminal enterprise could easily be populated by legions of people who were manifestly uncriminal. In his last statement to the jury, Papon compared himself to Joseph K. in Kafka's *Trial*. Kafka's heroes were victims of the arbitrary, the unknowable, and the disconnected. The defendant could see no possible connection between the *chevalier de la Légion d'honneur* he had become and the young man the court had revealed, the one who oversaw the roundups. At most he could depict himself, as he did early in the trial, as a youthful bureaucrat diligently sorting through the mail, dealing with the day's problems, tactfully waiting to see his boss. This was a thoroughly clean picture, one with no moral implications for the present.

It was true that Papon was not, in the plainest sense, a murderer. He remained what he had been once, an efficient administrator with limitless faith in his abilities. 'Thus their opinion of me,' he said once, speaking of the Germans, 'that I was a good professional.' He had tried to cut off the past. But unwittingly, with his long self-exposition over six months, he helped the court understand the young functionary he had been. Far from disavowing his earlier self, he was proud of the work that had been done. What was the meaning of that work? 'From an administrative point of view, I was indifferent, but not from a human point of view,' Papon had said in court. Having made this separation, he could have seen without difficulty to the roundups.

On the bleary-eyed April morning that followed a long night of deliberations, he strode into the glass box holding his briefcase, straightened his tie and sat up straight to receive the verdict. It was nuanced and subtle: the former secretary-general was convicted of illegal arrests and detention, but not of murder. The nine jurors had seen clearly the connection between the young man of many years ago and the personage in front of them. They had defied Papon and those who wanted to go along with him. The jurors had endorsed the idea of the underlying continuity of past and present. Afterward, the great hall of the Palais de Justice was packed with lawyers, spectators and reporters from around the world. But there was a strange calm, as if the appropriateness of the verdict had been recognized. A palpable sense of relief was in the air. The civil plaintiffs accepted this outcome, for the most part, but they looked uneasy. For them, the past was not over.

At the bus stop outside the Palais de Justice, I saw Esther Fogiel. She looked impossibly frail, so shrunken I had to bend forward to address her. Reluctantly, I asked for her reaction. 'I'm so tired, monsieur. So tired. Excuse me, I must go.'

II

• • • •

VICHY AND THE
PLEASURES OF FORGETTING

Bordeaux–Vichy

WHAT HAPPENED at Bordeaux would not be repeated. It was an extraordinary event, the hostility it provoked from France's best-known intellectuals proof of how unsettling it had been. Not all of those irritated by the trial were on the political right, but all of them had a stake in the country's self-image. On the national radio one Sunday a few months later, the former spokesman of the Socialist president François Mitterrand, the bestselling writer Max Gallo, declared, 'A whole career trajectory was put on trial in an emblematic, political, and ideological fashion.' He continued, 'And the entire attitude of France during that period.' The philosopher Alain Finkielkraut had been contemptuous of those seeking to draw lessons from the trial: 'For many of those born after the war, this judicial ceremony furnishes the opportunity to deny that the past is really past, and to inhabit that time of heroism and horror.' Oddly, he had substituted one of the trial's possible minor side effects for its essence. Henry Rousso, the historian who invented the notion of the 'Vichy syndrome' to describe France's waves of obsession with the period, was asked in *Le Monde* whether the trial had had any pedagogic merit. 'I think, very frankly, none,' he replied. He doubted Papon's 'exemplarity' in the historical sense, seeing him instead as a 'complex individual'.[1]

But it was Papon's very complexity that made him exemplary – the very fact that Papon was no mediocre ideologue like Eichmann, but someone who commanded admiration and horror at the same time, that made his trial so significant. He had spoken at length, sometimes plausibly, making it almost possible to identify with him. Papon's contemporaries in the prefectoral corps, some of them comparably gifted, and comparably culpable, but none of them prosecuted, were all dead. So the trial was exceptional not because the defendant was unimaginable, but because simple chronology made it the first and last of its kind.

The trial had brought to light hints of suggestive relations with the past in Bordeaux, though it was easy to imagine the city returning to its pleased self after the trial's end. Its mere presence there – an event the inhabitants instinctively recognised as historic – risked distorting the picture, exaggerating temperaments that might otherwise be complacent. A friend who had lived in Bordeaux for years, and was received everywhere in the town – she bore a famous name in the country's politics – told my wife she now felt an impulse to leave, for good.

I needed to examine a more omnipresent proximity to the past, one not dependent on the transitory. I needed to be in a place where the citizens had a permanent connection with what had happened before.

'Vichy' was born in Bordeaux, the lawyer Gérard Boulanger had said in his closing argument at the trial: from Bordeaux in June 1940 the harried French government, fleeing the Germans, had first asked for an armistice, setting in motion the compromises of the next four years. At Marshal Pétain's trial in 1945, the city's symbolic role in those last days of the French Republic was clear: 'M. Marquet made common cause with M. Laval, who installed his headquarters at the city hall of Bordeaux, which had become the fortress of defeatism in France.'[2] It was in Bordeaux that what became the Vichy government under the Marshal began to coalesce. I went to Vichy.

5

The Past Effaced

Unrecoverable Past

AT THE END of a long corridor in the attic of a former hotel, I saw a dim glow from an ephemeral civilisation. It was some lines of graffiti, written in blue pencil on the white plaster wall. I tried to read the words; the lights kept going out, leaving me and my companions in darkness. 'Quarter-master Ti-Tin', someone had written, and under this, 'Seaman Momo'. There was a series of numbers, all ending in '41' and '42'. Under a third name, 'Seaman Geo', you could make out a clumsy bit of doggerel. An elderly lady, who had known the building when sailors stood smartly at attention in the entrance and the fleet admiral's pennant fluttered outside, haltingly read the inscription before the light went out again: 'Not until crows fly white, and snow falls black, will the recollection of my squadron be wiped from my memory.'

People in Vichy would say, with an air of finality, 'You know, everything's been wiped away. There's nothing left.' The barely legible graffiti, had they been aware of it, would have been the rare exception that proved their point. If the longtime concierge of the Helder hadn't recently learned, to her amazement, that the building once housed the French Naval Ministry, and if she hadn't been wandering that corridor in the warren-like structure, the scrawl would have remained in obscurity. Its survival was an accident, its discovery pure chance, its continued existence a matter of indifference, or worse. 'What an idea!' the old lady who had been my guide scoffed when I suggested it should be preserved. So only a suspect nostalgic or a well-informed tourist would have any reason to connect the landscape of half-shuttered stucco hotels, including the Helder, with a particular situation that prevailed in and among them between the years 1940 and 1944. There had been so little reason to feel hangover that not even the names of these establishments had been changed. The Plaza was still the Plaza, just as it was when the Education Ministry moved in after the hectic summer of 1940, and the Moderne was the Moderne, as it had been for the Gestapo's French auxiliary, the Milice. The Helder was still the Helder. The Hôtel du Portugal, sinister to the Vichyssois because it had been a Gestapo headquarters in 1943 and 1944, had not changed its name. Even the Hôtel du Parc, the seat of national government for four years, long since converted to modest apartments, was forthrightly Le Parc. That continuity was all the more striking in that the mere name Hôtel du Parc, for all its blandness, years ago took on echoing resonance in the nation's collective consciousness as the place where Marshal Pétain and President Laval (third and second floors, respectively) carried out the policy that still haunted the country.

On a still autumn day, after the summer pensioners had departed and the little city took on the aspect of an undervisited museum, I went by the Hôtel Moderne. The stylised façade of superposed concrete pilasters and jagged projecting spits evokes an aggressive 1930s vision of modernity; the armed enforcers of Pétain's 'New France' had chosen well.

The hotel was deserted. I explained my purpose and asked to look around.

'The problem is, the hotel is completely closed,' the young man at the front desk said.

Just to look at the first floor, then?

'There's nothing left at all from that period. *Nothing*.'

From what I understand, this was the headquarters of the Milice for a certain time?

'That's right,' the young man said. 'Honestly, I know very little about that period.' He smiled a brisk, thin smile. 'So, that's it.' He looked suggestively at the front door.

'All gone!' the old lady at the Helder had said dreamily. She had her own reasons for a somewhat embittered nostalgia. Her father, a prominent local veteran, had been imprisoned at the Liberation for being a bit too devoted to the Marshal. In the coy domed villa that had been the embassy of the Republic of Argentina, and was now the home of the president of the local historical society, the president's wife said, 'There was a will to efface. It was because of a past that was more or less shameful.' She pointed out a fugitive trace in that very house: the lonely Argentine diplomats, shivering through frigid Vichy winters, had overused the mostly ornamental fireplace, leaving still visible cracks in the marble. When I arrived, her husband, the president, had said, 'It is a monumental error to look at the events of 1940 through the eyes of today.' Yet even the president, M. Tixier, found the contemporary viewpoint – the one that suggested averting one's eyes – unavoidable: the subject of that year, and the four that followed, rarely came up at his society's meetings. 'Too soon, too soon,' M. Tixier, himself the son of a deported Resistance man, mumbled. Topics like 'Dovecotes of the Auvergne and Bourbonnais' were to be preferred. At the city hall one day, a younger member of the historical society said, smiling, 'It's something that's just not talked about very much. It remains too' – he searched for a word – 'emotive.' In his years at the society only one paper touching on the town's moment of international stature had been given. It had been on Vichy's 'Liberation' – itself a questionable notion, since Vichy had been the nominally free capital of a nominally independent state. 'Look, the Vichyssois laid a wreath at the World War I memorial, and that was it,' an old Pétainist I knew said, scoffing. 'There were no Germans. There was no "Liberation of Vichy".'

From the perspective of the physical setting alone, a certain reticence was understandable. The décor was recognisably the same as it had been during the days of the État Français, Marshal Pétain's French State. In fact, it was nearly identical, if a good deal shabbier. There was thus an ongoing psychological risk, if only because the regime had come to be so closely identified with the hotels it occupied; its derisory nature was underscored by the fact that the functionaries had operated from hotel rooms, storing their files in bathtubs, bidets and armoires, next to the cured ham and whatever bread they could lay hands on. They sat on the edge of double beds to type out memos and cooked miserable meals on illicit hot plates. The best time to see these buildings was at dusk, when the already empty streets became deserted and the dim light covered up the cracks and peeling paint. Then, the entire town, and especially the one-time centre of government, the pastel-colored neo-Baroque palaces lining the Parc des Sources, seemed to have been frozen these past fifty-seven years – at the moment, say, in August 1944 when Vichy suddenly ceased to be the national capital and what remained of the panicked bureaucracy quickly packed up and left.

Evidence of the town's dilapidation reinforced this feeling. Inside the abandoned Hôtel des Ambassadeurs (with unconscious self-parody it had housed foreign diplomats during the war), the safe door gaped open, piles of unexplained rubble littered the floor and the wires had been pulled out of the old telephone switchboard. The formerly grandiose hotel, still faintly radiating the stupefying luxury it had once boasted, looked as though it had been deserted in a hurry. Of course, the Ambassadeurs had continued to operate for nearly forty years after the war, each year seedier than the last. But it required little imagination to picture the long-interrupted role of this nineteenth-century brick and masonry pile occupying half a city block. A long colonnade of creamy veined marble, overlooked by elaborately carved masks, sweeps past immense salons on the ground floor. At intervals there are huge panes of delicately frosted glass, incised with stylised art deco sunbursts, to radiant effect in this decay. I told the friendly estate agent who took me through that diplomats from thirty-six countries, including the United States, had once lived here. 'Ah, I had no idea,' he said.

'The people with direct memories of that period are extremely rare,' a thoughtful member of the city council said to me once. But the opposite seemed more likely. At promenade time, in the late afternoon, under the art nouveau ironwork galleries lining the Parc des Sources, shaded in summer by the dense foliage of the park's great plane trees, knots of slightly bent figures moved slowly back and forth. It was the gentle rhythm of old age, and of an earlier era as well. 'This is a city of old people,' a middle-aged doctor said bitterly. With resignation, a young man whose grandfather had been one of President Laval's chauffeurs summed up the main element of Vichy's populace as 'many who lived through that period, and have kept all their memories', adding a more plausible explanation than the city councillor's for the silence that enveloped the town: 'But they keep them inside.'

At the city hall, I asked to see the municipality's files from the war years. 'Oh, I'm afraid those records are not available to the general public,' the archivist said, smiling. 'They haven't been sorted yet.'

A man with a stall at the covered market, an echoing, windowless hangar built in the 1930s whose empty immensity testified to the town's lost importance, said to me: 'Besides, there aren't that many real Vichyssois left. Most of the people here are from somewhere else.' So Vichy wasn't really even Vichy. It might as well be called something else – a solution for which the local newspaper solicited ideas, in a kind of contest, just after the war.

These affirmations of an unrecoverable past were not state-ments of fact so much as a longing, an obscure but fervent wish for freedom, sometimes tinged with paradoxical nostalgia. It was a guileless hope, translated, for instance, by the continuity of the hotel names. The unexpressed thinking seemed to be: maybe no one will notice. Maybe Vichy will wake up one morning to its identity of the sixty glorious years before the war, miraculously recovered: one of Europe's most fashionable resorts, a super-luxury Hot Springs, Arkansas, a place where the rich and famous came to take the waters and attend the opera. And the little spa town would help, as it had over this past half-century, by not marking out a single one of the old ministry buildings with so much as a plaque.

No museum would commemorate the Pétain years. At the Parc, five initials on one of the mailboxes could be meaningful, but more likely would not. A.D.M.M.P.: Association pour la défense de la mémoire du maréchal Pétain, the organisation of Pétainist faithful that bought the Marshal's old rooms in 1960 and has maintained them, empty and locked, ever since. In the locked courtyard, a solemnly worded plaque affixed by the Nazi hunter Serge Klarsfeld (over protests from the apartment owners) reminds visitors that the August 1942 roundup of Jews in unoccupied France was planned here. The plaque is hidden, unreadable even if you penetrate the building. Behind a (locked) glass door on the right, up marble stairs that are the last vestiges of former splendour down the hall to the left, there is a rectangular patch lighter than the rest of the wall: a plaque, long gone, once signalled the adjacent rooms as Pétain's.

Across town, the little municipal museum, in an art deco building that furnished the Milice with torture chambers, has in its collection a few dusty glass cases with objects from what some people in town call 'the period'. The cases are inconspicuous, almost self-effacing. One of them contains yellowing telegrams from the Marshal thanking world leaders for their congratulations on Bastille Day 1941; another, coins engraved with Pétain's head. There is also a battered leather briefcase, said to have carried mail from the unoccupied zone of France to the occupied zone. This is the sum of the town's permanent, official recognition of the years when it was the seat of the national government. I never saw anybody visiting this forlorn collection. You can see more memorabilia at Sunday morning flea markets in the mountain villages around Vichy.

Since the late 1980s, on two summer afternoons a week, the municipal tourist office conducts an unobtrusive guided visit around some of the old hotels, identifying their functions during the war. If you happen not to arrive in town on one of the appointed days, or during one of the appointed months, the buildings maintain their innocence. In fact, if you happened to arrive looking for some tangible echo of that particular past, you might be well advised to move on.

Unease

I HAD COME to Vichy expecting certain cards to be frankly on the table. Bordeaux, like other towns in France, had an age-old identity in which to take refuge. But here people would have no choice, or so I thought. An identity conferred from the outside, possibly disagreeable, would have to be accepted. It was composed of a few widely known facts, some of which seemed more important now than they did at the time: Marshal Pétain and the rest of the French government, casting about for a place to settle after the armistice in June 1940, had established themselves in the town, attracted by its hotels and unrestive population; the government stayed for the next four years, becoming ever more repressive even as its authority disintegrated; under President Laval, it distinguished itself in making France the only country besides Bulgaria to hand Jews over from its own territory – that is, territory unoccupied by Germans.[1]

The French government was still hanging on in Bordeaux when the armistice with the Germans was signed on June 22, 1940. This short document was a blueprint for what happened next, at Vichy. It was an agreement, a coming to terms, nearly unique in the history of the European war. In exchange for vast tribute (disguised as 'maintenance costs' for German troops), the conqueror had apparently been magnanimous: the French state could continue – the French Ministry of Foreign Affairs, of Colonies, of Education, of the Interior, even of the Navy, all would go on just as before. There was no need for the government to go into exile, as had occurred in the other countries of Europe. Thus the rebellious General de Gaulle and his tiny band of followers in London represented only themselves. 'The government remains free, France will only be administered by Frenchmen,' Marshal Pétain reported to his countrymen, explaining the armistice on June 25. He allowed himself an expression of satisfaction: 'At least our honour is saved.' (Hitler's perspective was different: a new province had been added to his empire, and he would not have the bother of administering it.) What sort of French government would now exist that had as its founding act a deal with the Nazis? There were clues in the agreement itself. Those same French administrators were to 'collaborate' – the word appears in the armistice document – with the Germans who now occupied three-fifths of the nation, 'in a correct fashion'. Another clue, this one vague but nonetheless potentially menacing, came in Pétain's speech from Bordeaux: 'A new order is beginning.'[2]

For the creation of the new order, there had to be a new place. The birth of 'Vichy' was haphazard, the impulsive choice of a government suddenly almost a guest in its own country. Paris and Bordeaux were out – the first was already occupied by Germans, and the second was about to be. The major cities in the unoccupied zone presented problems: Toulouse and Lyon were bastions of the centre-left in prewar French politics, and Marseille was too wide open, too cosmopolitan. From Bordeaux, the French government made its way across the centre of France like some bedraggled oriental caravan, through Périgueux and Brive-la-Gaillarde to

Clermont-Ferrand in the mountainous Auvergne. But there were too many workers at Clermont's Michelin tyre factory, the city was drab, and the hotels were dingy. Dining with Pétain at the Grand Hôtel in Clermont on June 29, the exasperated foreign minister, Paul Baudouin, had an inspiration: 'I suggest Vichy, where the spacious hotels will allow us a suitable installation.' It was a nearly casual thought, flung out between courses at the hotel restaurant. 'The Marshal agrees to this idea,' Baudouin noted in his diary. US Ambassador William Bullitt wrote to President Roosevelt on June 30: 'As you know the French Government arrived in Clermont-Ferrand yesterday. Displeased by living arrangements it left today for Vichy.'[3]

From the perspective of Clermont, it was a logical choice. Barely thirty miles away, Vichy had more than three hundred hotels – plenty of room to stow the ministries – and its small population was well-to-do and conservative. The leafy town would be soothing after the trauma of defeat. 'Ah, Vichy, this is the kind of town I like!' Pétain is said to have exclaimed, on being driven past the tree-shaded stucco hotel façades for the first time. There were other advantages: a direct train connection to Paris and a telephone exchange that was among the most modern in France. Laval was enthusiastic, as his miniature château in the village of Châteldon was close by. And the mentally unstable, anti-Semitic justice minister, Raphäel Alibert, had had his liver problems treated there.[4]

So the paying guests were kicked out, the hotels requisitioned ('I was furious,' the manager of the Ambassadeurs wrote, 'and I refused categorically'; seeing it wasn't a matter of choice, he astutely landed the high-toned diplomatic corps), and the parliamentary deputies summoned, for the last time, to vote on a constitution for the 'new order'. In the first days of July, Léon Blum, the former prime minister, saw the ominous line of loaded delivery trucks in front of the hotels on the park. 'The Pétain government was moving in,' he wrote shortly after.

Blum, the Jewish Socialist, was perhaps the most hated man in Vichy. 'When that Jew is in the morgue, he will be in the one place suitable for him,' a Socialist deputy said to a colleague, strolling in the Parc des Sources. Blum was soon to be jailed by the new regime.[5]

Vichy was to be the seat of government. But the town would also become the centre of the octogenarian Marshal's personality cult, with all the familiar trappings – mass rallies, giant portraits, speeches from balconies and commemorative china (plates and dishes with Pétain's marmoreal image, hawked from shop windows).

A quantity of this debris had survived in the town's attics and back closets, last refuges of the long-defunct ideology. Generous inhabitants made me the recipient of several mouldering copies of the small book that contained Pétain's speech of June 25, 1940, describing the armistice. It would have been in many French homes six decades ago: the 1941 edition of the Marshal's most recent dicta, *La France nouvelle*, handsomely printed in the national colours.

I could see how the modest volume might have slipped into respectable households. There are anodyne pronouncements ('mistress of the hearth, the mother, through her affection, her tact, her patience, bestows on the life of every day its tranquillity and sweetness') shading into slightly more coercive ones ('in the country's misfortune, each of us will have realized that there are no such things as individual destinies, that Frenchmen exist only through France'). And then there are grim warnings: 'We will tell them that it is all very well to be free, but that real "freedom" can only be enjoyed under the protection of a tutelary authority: that must be respected, which they must obey.' Scattered here and there are approving nods to the conqueror and promises of racial renewal.[6]

Maybe the little books had been more ornamental than practical. The copies I was given contained uncut pages. Even so, you could be surprised that tranquil living rooms had harboured, for all these years, such an incendiary document. It was a complete statement of authoritarian racial nationalism – an outline, in fact, of the Vichy government's developing *révolution nationale*. 'What I really wanted was, at the end of the war, for Pétain and de Gaulle to shake hands,' a real estate agent in Vichy said to me once, echoing the common idea in town that the two had been equivalent patriots, politically neutral. But there was nothing neutral about the little book's pronouncements. Much of what is suggested in them had already been accomplished by the time it was published: anti-Semitism was state policy (the civil service, the press, academia, film and theatre companies were legally purged of Jews by the regime's third month), individual liberties – freedom of the press, the right to vote – had been suppressed, and an omnipresent police force, as a matter of official doctrine, was on its way. 'When he arrived in front of the Hôtel du Parc, he didn't dare enter,' says the narrator of *Le Piège* (*The Trap*), a political novel written during the war, published just after, and set in Vichy. 'It was crazy, but he was afraid that all these policemen – military, personal, civil, municipal – standing guard at the entrance, coming and going in the lobby, constantly whispering to each other, instead of directing him simply to the office of Laveyssère, would instead submit him to an interrogation which he wasn't at all sure he would pull himself out of.'[7]

Vice Premier Laval had warned the parliamentary deputies assembled at Vichy in the early July days: 'Either you accept what we are demanding, and you align yourselves on the German and Italian constitutions, or Hitler will go right ahead and impose it on you.'[8] But the Germans turned out to be not much interested in the internal doings of the Vichy regime, at least not until the very end. What happened at Vichy was a peculiar hybrid. It wasn't Italian fascism, nor was it German national socialism, nor was it Francoism. The earliest commentators struggled to define it adequately. 'The regime that has installed itself in France since the armistice is thus an authoritarian one. But that term doesn't suffice to define the current status of France,' the political philosopher Raymond Aron wrote from London in March 1941, before going on to avoid doing precisely that. Four months earlier he had opted for a simple label that was already sticking like tar to the new regime: 'Vichy', or 'the men of Vichy'.[9] Barely a week after the French parliament had voted to commit suicide, handing over power to Marshal Pétain in the sweaty Grand Casino at Vichy, on July 10, 1940, the Free French broadcasters in London were referring contemptuously to 'the government of Vichy', which 'proposes state absolutism' in order to 'bring us humiliation and suffering'.[10]

Sixty years later, through all the periodic upsurges of national memory (of which the Papon trial was the latest expression), the joining of 'Vichy' with Vichy had by no means disappeared. And it had left the present-day inhabitants of the town facing, more concretely than anybody else, a knotty problem. How does one integrate that four-year adventure in clerical authoritarianism into the context of the modern secular democracy? How was the late quasi-fascist regime to be lived with today? The rest of France could go for long periods without having to think about the various compromises of that history, but the people of Vichy could not afford this.

On the one hand, it was a wan-looking provincial town on the banks of a lazy river, a place the mention of which brought expressions of distaste to the faces of Parisians I knew; on the other hand, it was 'the only town in France you could stretch out on the psychiatrist's divan', as a well-known lawyer who spent summers in the gentle countryside near Vichy put it to me.

Was there some particular relationship to the past beckoning to the inhabitants? Of necessity, in Vichy the boundary between past and present was a porous one. As weeks there turned into months, I sensed successive layers of reimagining at work. What was buried beneath them? My stay there – for the length, say, of an extended cure – became an attempt to peel away these layers, an effort to identify the strategies in play. I wanted to determine the present-day juxtaposition of the town and the episode it had lived through. History couldn't be escaped here. How had it been integrated into Vichy's consciousness?

I had the luxury of free circulation in the neglected town. True, some were uneasy about my presence, but they were also curious about me. It was thought, hopefully, that I was 'working on a book about the Resistance', as someone said to me. Still, few outsiders, French or foreign, had until my arrival devoted so much time to the people in Vichy. The occasional journalist would stop in for a few days, deliver a usually sarcastic article, then gratefully leave. It was clear that the cards were definitely not on the table, yet the people had no choice. They would have to leave clues. The configuration of memory, shame and isolation that seemed to exist here was rare.

It was all very well not to have put a plaque on any of the old ministry buildings. These people were reminded of the past every time they so much as said the town's name, at risk whenever they opened up one of the national newspapers. They were 'ceaselessly confronted', an ironic local history teacher who had recently retired said to me, smiling maliciously. His father had been part of the regime's bureaucracy, regularly travelling to Vichy for Finance Ministry meetings in the art deco surroundings of the once elegant Hôtel Carlton. A woman in Paris told me of a colleague who, learning that she had been born in Vichy, blurted out an improbable explanation for his own birth there: his parents had made an unexpected stopover in the then national capital. Later she learned the truth, which she found amusing: the man's father had been one of the regime's functionaries, comfortably installed in Vichy. He had been too ashamed to admit it.

In France, the shame of the war years has had this singular characteristic: it can be delimited not just in time but in space. For years after the war, writers and politicians took convenient advantage of the regime's identification with the town. France itself wasn't compromised, only what emanated from that trumped-up little spa for the digestively troubled. 'The regime of Vichy', or 'the men of Vichy' – just repeating the name of the place, as the Free French broadcasters had done so often from London, had an incantatory, minimising effect. And after the Liberation, how useful and soothing it was to continue reducing the malign import of what had occurred by permanently affixing the now cursed town to it. 'Vichy still hasn't been liberated,' a local writer complained in 1946. For the rest of France it was a way of containing the damage. Of course, it was somehow unacceptable to call Pétain's regime what it really was, the government of France, legally constituted. (Hugues Lawton had declared exasperatedly that France was at *Vichy*, not London, during the war.) Yet the government had to be *called* something.[11]

Over the years, the unconscious tendency to designate it as merely the government of a small town, practically a city council, only became stronger. It was adopted even by those who, like Robert Paxton, showed that understanding the regime was essential to comprehending the whole of the modern French polity. The first words in the title of his book were, simply, *Vichy France*. Among its more powerful demonstrations was that much in contemporary France, administratively speaking, was born at Vichy. At Vichy, for instance, experts – professionals, technicians – became ministers, setting the pattern for the postwar years. Regional administrations were created, forerunners of today's *régions*. A national police force was established for the first time. In addition, the elite corps of civil servants who carried out government policy survived largely intact from the wartime regime to the one succeeding it. Paxton found that among auditors of public accounts, to take one example, 98 per cent of the personnel working in 1942 were still on the job in 1946. And the first government campaign against American cultural influences – jazz and films – was undertaken, a policy with a large future in French politics. The impact of 'Vichy' was durable, and it was national.[12]

By 1972, however, when Paxton's book was published, it was far too late to change the shorthand. The identification of the most reactionary regime since the post-Napoleon Restoration with the provincial town was stronger than ever.

And then there was a parallel phenomenon. As the years went on, as the men who had been at Vichy died out (the last of its ministers, the dapper and ingratiating former secretary of state for industrial production, François Lehideux, died in June 1998, barely two months after Papon's conviction), finally whatever direct link was left had been sucked back up into the unfortunate place. It had become a sort of national dumping ground of bad memory. Vichy was the last spot in the country where people would still be forced to think, on a regular basis, about France's long-extinct 'new order'.

Yet it seemed to me on my first morning in Vichy, staring up at the innocent façade of the Parc, that remembering, in this context, would not have the sense I had previously given it. A frozen fog hung about the bare trees, blending with the Parc's bland pastel. The town was opaque. Later, I asked the middle-aged doctor what position Vichy-as-national-capital had occupied in family dinner-table discussions in the 1950s and 1960s. 'Wall of silence,' he said. By the time she arrived in the town in the early 1970s, 'We talked about the water-skiing championship,' a woman said, 'never about Pétain.' Today the Vichy regime is a far more overt presence at a conclave of Paris intellectuals than it ever is in Vichy itself. Attending one such gathering after months in the town, I was nearly shocked by the freedom with which the word 'Vichy' was bandied about.

I began hearing a certain phrase, usually tossed off rather testily. It was a kind of polite exhortation for me to leave: 'Look, the people of Vichy had nothing to do with all that.' There was some truth in this, inasmuch as it described, in part, the relationship of a half-century ago. They had been extras, more or less enthusiastic until the war's great turning points in late 1942 and 1943 – the Allied landing in North Africa, the German defeat at Stalingrad, the capitulation of Italy. They were faces in the Sunday crowd, secretaries, telephone operators, billing clerks for the new regime. Still, this challenge to my continued presence was not the end of the story. Early on, I was aware that instead of unambiguous memory there was a sort of submerged tension. Signs of it kept cropping up, upsurges of the buried half-life of 'Vichy'.

One day I drove up to the Parc with one of the town's ex-colonials, a friendly retired shipping agent in his early seventies, M. Chervet. He was going to show me where he had stood every Sunday, in a crowd of hundreds of schoolchildren, singing the famous greeting to Pétain, '*Maréchal, nous voilà!*' An old magazine, its cover depicting the Marshal's emblematic cap, walking stick, and cloak, was lying in the back seat of my guide's car. He walked a few steps toward the Parc, stopped and went back. Carefully, M. Chervet turned the magazine over. 'Here, we don't want people to . . . ' he said, not finishing the sentence. One quiet Sunday, I walked by the Parc myself. I let my eyes wander up to the balcony on the third floor, where Marshal Pétain had stood to receive the crowd's acclamations; the balcony appears in dozens of official photographs of the era. A middle-aged man in a windbreaker emerged from the Parc just then. He saw me looking up at the third floor. For a long moment, he stared at me. Then he walked on down the empty pavement.

I was once in Calondre, one of the genteel pastry shops along the Parc des Sources, with Maurice Benhamou, who was then 105 years old. Tiny, wrinkled and pugnacious, he had miraculously lived out the war in an apartment across from the Hôtel du Parc, despite being both Jewish and a successful pharmacist. M. Benhamou, retired since the early 1960s, had decided to give me a demonstration of things seen and heard in those years, right in Calondre. Quietly but audibly, he began singing 'Maréchal, nous voilà!' Two stout ladies sitting opposite us, bundled up in furs, froze in mid-pastry. A look of mild panic came over their faces. My ancient companion, oblivious, continued singing the upbeat tune.

Outside the flower stand in the covered market one day, I heard a well-dressed lady say heatedly to her companion: 'Ah, Vichy, Vichy. Why always Vichy? The French are so stupid. And why not Paris? Three months before the Liberation the Marshal was in Paris. And the crowds he had!' The ladies bought their flowers and left.

The florist shook her head. 'They can talk, fine,' she said in a low voice. 'But let them do it discreetly.'

An essential, if inarticulate, clue was apparently provided by these furtive expressions. What did they mean? At the very least, that the town did not quite believe in its own protestations of innocence. It had not resolved the question facing it. How could it have, when, for instance, the rough draft of its own story, the one that translated into the ever-so-courteous invitation that I go elsewhere, was palpably incomplete? 'Let's just say the Vichyssois accommodated himself perfectly well to the Marshal!' a local Socialist, imprisoned by the Pétain regime, said with an indulgent laugh. M. Rougeron was perched at the edge of his bed in the hospice of Commentry, a nearby mining town whose mayor he had been for more than forty years. His wife had recently died, and his bare room, empty except for an old newspaper, was testimony to a certain resignation about the time remaining to him. He was nearly ninety, and he said, without complaining, that those days of struggle had been forgotten. At the Liberation, he had been secretary of the Comité Départementale de Libération – in other words, the top civilian authority in the local Resistance. His vision was irreplaceable: outsider, participant and historian, he was the author of a massive chronicle of the region in those years.

Later I looked through press photographs of Vichy taken on leafy summer Sundays during the war; they had been left behind by the decamping news agencies in 1944 and discovered in the basement of city hall. In these pictures the crowds wait five-deep for Marshal Pétain outside the Hôtel du Parc, faces beatifically smiling. 'To get the best spots, the most ardent have already taken position under the gallery,' a caption reads. People in Vichy often say the men and women in these crowds had come from somewhere else. Yet the daughter of the town's leading surgeon, then in her twenties, said to me, 'Every Sunday we were in front of the Hôtel du Parc, those of us who were patriots.' Smiling gently, she recalled, 'We sang that song.'

The wistful old lady was straightforward enough. Hers was definitely not a vision of Vichy as victim of 'Vichy'. Still, this was at least one accepted discourse here. (The people were 'increasingly exasperated' by government-imposed 'privations', the summer tour guide says.) And yet to say that 'the people of Vichy had nothing to do with all that' was like saying that New York had had nothing to do with the 1955 World Series. In one sense this was true. But it was also true that thousands of New Yorkers had flocked to Yankee Stadium.

The townsfolk had probably been no more explicitly complicitous than people in other places would have been, though some seven hundred people were locked up at the Liberation. Vichy's purge was big, six times bigger per capita than that of Paris, maybe the biggest anywhere. But the town's implication in those events had obviously been magnified by its small size, barely twenty-five thousand when war broke out, and the unlimited opportunities offered by the regime's presence.[13] The real degree of its complicity was not necessarily important, even if the denial of it was. The town was struggling to come up with a usable relation to the past, and it was conscious of some urgency in the task. The world had put Vichy in history's ditch. It was up to Vichy to dig itself out.

The Memory Hole

THE AVERAGE Vichyssois would indignantly deny 'having a complex' about the past, as he or she might put it. Everybody from the taxi driver to the greengrocer had ideas about how to handle the national ghosts inherited by the town, however chary they initially were in expressions of them. Resentment predominated over guilt. It seemed more likely, as I began to live inside some of the strategies for dealing with 'Vichy', that at its heart this was a problem of choice. Which strategy would be the best? Which would be the most plausible to the outside world? Which one would satisfy the Vichyssois themselves? The range of possibilities lent a kind of edge to the otherwise muffled life in the town.

First there were the memory holes, chunks of experience about to be forgotten. At the beginning, I stumbled on them frequently. I thought that perhaps the town had disposed of its past in this simple way. It was like what had happened to the placards. In photographs of Vichy during the war, white placards with bold lettering are clearly visible on the hotels, announcing, for instance, that a tall, narrow building with art deco floral panels, today a high school, is the 'Ministry of the Interior' (Papon had worked there before his promotion to the Bordeaux prefecture), or that the Hôtel de la Paix, now tightly shuttered, was the 'Ministry of Information' (the American correspondents had worked in offices to the right of the entrance).

These placards had largely disappeared from the memories of the people I spoke with. ('A sign out front? Ah, I don't think so,' said a woman who had been a clerk in the Education Ministry.) But they were perfectly evident to contemporaries, who took them as evidence of the performance of the enterprise. 'They are installing themselves for a good long while,' the central character in *Le Piège* tells himself, uneasy after seeing one such sign, this one posted inside a building.[14]

'No no no no no! No,' a woman shouted at me over the phone, the simple mention of my purpose having been enough. Her father, M. Ricou, had run a favourite restaurant of collaborationists and near collaborationists, a charming spot by the peaceful Allier River. She had moved from Vichy some years ago. 'Sure, we had President Laval,' Mme Dupays said, warming slightly. 'But you know, he went elsewhere too. Look, there was a little bit of everybody, journalists, Germans, Americans. M. Krug von Nidda,' she said, spontaneously mentioning the name of Hitler's consul general in Vichy. 'It was very ... what's the word I'm looking for?' I heard her shout to her daughter. 'Yes, cosmopolitan, that's it. No politics. It wasn't political,' she said. 'Sorry, I've got to go now,' Mme Dupays said. 'My daughter is waiting for me for lunch.'

M. Edier was a friendly short man, jolly and distracted, who had been in the Légion Française des Combattants, the veterans' organisation established by Marshal Pétain. This was a kind of militant adult scout troop, spreading the good word of the *révolution nationale* and reporting on those disinclined to follow it, like Jews and suspected Communists. 'A suspicious Jew named Gossel, living at the Hôtel du Lion d'Or, seems to be the rallying point for Jews of the town and surrounding area,' M. Edier's colleague in the Légion, named Andraud, had reported from the Hôtel Carlton, across the Parc des Sources, to police intelligence at the Hôtel des Princes in March 1942.[15]

The old *légionnaire* lived in a concrete apartment building by the river with a tiny yapping dog and his ailing wife. He often repeated certain words and phrases, not out of forgetfulness but as if struck by the judiciousness of his observation. The ministers at Vichy had had 'meetings with the Marshal, meetings with the Marshal,' M. Edier said. He was vague about his postwar transition. 'I took up my profession of hotelkeeper. With difficulty. With difficulty.' He frowned.

Later, in the archives of the Allier *département*, I found his name on one of the lists of people locked up at the Liberation. 'Names of Persons Taken to the Internment Centre at the Vichy Show-Jumping Stadium, from 26 August to 15 September' was the heading. In the hours I spent in his company, M. Edier never mentioned his stay at the Concours Hippique, the old-fashioned stadium with the jolly brass horses' heads out front. We covered much ground together, but not that patch. Yet passage through the primitive wooden barracks there was a defining Vichy experience. 'One found there a great number of shining lights of the deposed État Français,' a historian sympathetic to Vichy wrote after the war.[16] Stupefied former ministers and prominent local folk found themselves locked up in the barracks, cheek by jowl with, say, the cook at the Ambassadeurs, 'dancers', housekeepers to ex-luminaries, journalists, *miliciens* or a bicycle mechanic.[17] Jacques Chevalier, a philosopher who had been one of Pétain's education ministers, treated his fellow inmates to lectures on Descartes.[18] 'Oh, he didn't stay there long,' several people said to me, talking about acquaintances who had been kept at the Concours Hippique. Shuddering, a woman said, 'Frightful.' Her father had spent eight months in the barracks, forced to traverse the town in handcuffs on his way to woodcutting details.

A smartly dressed couple came to my door in Vichy one spring day. The man was smiling uneasily. M. Arnaud was solidly built, with a big square face, and his features were quite different from the local type. He hesitated. The archivist at the city hall had sent him to me.

'I'm looking for my father. I was born at Vichy,' M. Arnaud said slowly, smiling and showing white teeth. 'My mother never talked about . . . ah, no.' He paused again. 'Here, look at this.' He pulled out an old black-and-white photo. Two tall, confident-looking young men stand in a train corridor. Beneath the breast pocket of one, dressed in a fine tweed suit and showing a toothy smile, a slight bulge is apparent. Over his head, someone has pencilled in 'xxx' followed by three dots.

'Don't you think he looks like me?' M. Arnaud asked. 'My father was in the German police. He was with the Germans at Vichy.'

'In the Gestapo, then?' I asked.

'Yes, probably.' He smiled. 'You see, my mother worked at the Hôtel du Parc. For the *maréchal*.'

He worked in a bank in the port city of Toulon, and he was looking for the man in the picture, which he had found in a stack of old photos after his mother's death. A police expert had decided that the bulge under the smiling man's breast pocket indicated a gun, and that the newspaper carried by the other man was in German. The expert told him the men seemed to be German police.

Apologetically, M. Arnaud said, 'There were a lot like me, who were born at Vichy. They don't talk about it.' His mother had talked about it, but only once. 'She said, "It was an accident." And that was it.'

Three pasts had been dropped. In each case, it seemed an instinctive reaction. You could sympathise with the motivations. But if Vichy's problem could be dealt with so summarily, the ambient tension I was aware of from the beginning would not have been present at all. The memory holes turned out to be implausible to the majority, though they helped me understand, later, the better developed strategies in play. These disappearances would not present a good enough alibi to the outside world. The town's ambiguous collective destiny and its past weren't made for such brutal treatment. Vichy had a vocation to reimagine.

6

Reimagining the Past

IT HAS ALWAYS lived on an identity of make-believe. Vichy exists in a land apart. Even today, so many years after its period of prewar glory, some vestigial whiff remains, at least for the people of the surrounding countryside. 'Oh, it's like a little Paris,' a country woman from one of the neighbouring villages said to me, her eyes sparkling. A mix of awe and resentment colours these attitudes. 'The problem with the bourgeoisie of Vichy is,' the mayor of a dull suburb began provocatively, 'it is so . . . Vichyist!' He had used the adjective that was anathema in the town. The owner of one of the fancier pastry shops, raised modestly in a village in the nearby farmland, was forever gleefully passing me tips about the 'truth' of what had happened in Vichy during the war.

The town's apartness was amplified by its distinctive physical characteristics, commented on acidly by wartime memorialists. There was Vichy's peculiar topographical situation at the bottom of a bowl, surrounded by hills usually invisible from the town. The bowl trapped condensation. A 'colonial mugginess' prevailed, as one of the memorialists remembered – even the climate seemed to confirm the town's vocation as rest stop for people from the French dominions in Africa and the Far East. The light in Vichy was diffused. As soon as you reached the plains to the south or the gentle hills to the north, the weather seemed to clear.

Coming up from the sombre little Auvergnat towns to the south, with their narrow streets of dark volcanic stone, or down from the warm, cream-coloured ones to the north in the

Bourbonnais hills, places that haven't budged for centuries, you are catapulted surprisingly forward. The scale suddenly changes. This is a vision of modernity, firmly stopped in about 1938 and extending back from there perhaps a half-century. In the centre, art deco public buildings and villas rise, a few slim and elegant, like the rose-coloured structure that had housed the American embassy during the war, a beguiling series of bands and curves topped by a strange concrete arbour. Other 1930s buildings are heavy and menacing, like the Mussolinian post office, a mass of brutal grey concrete on a giant paved plaza that seems designed for fascist rallies. There are palatial stucco-faced hotels built around 1906, their huge size betokening long-gone splendour, their light colours falsely promising the south and the sea. Facing each other across the Parc des Sources are two sprawling temples to sensuality and pleasure: the riotous, bastard Second Empire cum Belle Époque cum art nouveau Grand Casino, and the Moorish-style Central Thermal Baths with its enormous yellow-tiled dome, an improbable vision of the Orient marooned deep in the French provinces.

In the surrounding streets that are the town's hinterland, there is a landscape of kitsch: a fantastic confusion of late-nineteenth- and early-twentieth-century architectural pastiches conjuring up Belle Époque dreams of luxury and escape. There are oriental minarets and cupolas against Flemish Renaissance palaces, twisting art nouveau gates setting off faux Gothic arches, faux medieval crenellated turrets next to classical dormer windows, loggias, caryatids, outsize Swiss chalets, shrunken Italian palazzi and miniature châteaux. There are villas that announce, in multicoloured tiles, that they are actually castles – 'Castel Gothique', 'Castel Français' (where the young future president of the republic François Mitterrand, Vichy bureaucrat on the rise, worked during the war), and 'Castel Alameda'. There are ochre villas with brown trim, pale yellow villas with green shutters, pink villas with light blue shutters and brick trim, bursts of yellow and blue ceramic cornflowers implanted on façades. The wavy rhythms of Vichy's undulating ironwork fences evoke the sea, or imaginary floral gardens, or lush billowing fields of grain.

The town was a self-conscious, elective fantasy. The cure-seekers could pretend they were not in a cold damp place in the middle of France, their stay not dictated by the medical necessity (or so it was presumed) of taking the sulphurous waters. Instead it was to be governed by pleasure, to be taken in a hundred different locales all over the world, but concentrated in one. The gaudy pavilions were about enticement, built by speculators competing for the liverish tourists.[1]

Today the inhabitants seem almost embarrassed by the remains of this showiness, in winter modestly scurrying about chilly streets where fur coats were once common. They rarely stop to contemplate their peculiar architectural heritage. The pale winter light on the pastel houses creates a wan tone throughout the town. The trees lining the streets are bare. Even when they haven't been abandoned, the dwellings look forlorn. The diminishing number of cure-seekers – from nearly 130,000 in 1936 to barely a tenth of that today – are resolutely frumpy. Jogging suits are the essential fashion. The town's motor, luxurious pleasure-seeking, has long since disappeared. But, mockingly, it is evoked on nearly every block. It is even in the street names, compliantly recalling, in the fancier neighbourhood, the home countries of the principal clientele: Serbia, Russia, the United States, England. It had been a town of accommodating virtue, a place alive under the sign of gratification and soothing. At the turn of the century there was a hotel for every fifty inhabitants, 573 hotels in all. The rates were so high at the Parc and the Ambassadeurs that a 1939 guidebook tells customers they are available only by request.

The precious Vichy poet Valéry Larbaud, translator and friend of James Joyce, wrote shortly after World War I of the town, which one couldn't name without smiling, as when one speaks, in the provinces, of a woman free with her charms . . . It is a town that deigns only to exist when existence itself is good; it wakes in the spring, and lives the whole of a summer in the shade of the plane trees.' It was a place that wasn't quite France, nor indeed anywhere specific. 'One would think oneself in foreign lands: in the streets, people are speaking in unknown tongues, and in the evening, in front of the illuminated terraces of the houses, Neapolitans sing "La Francesa".' Larbaud, eulogist of the exotic, is a fitting bard for his town, though he didn't spend much time there. 'And in heart of the season, there were the three daughters of the President of Bolivia, very young, more tender than anything one could see in a dream, beautiful, like holy images.'[2] There was also Grand Duke Alexis of Russia in 1892, the Shah of Persia in 1905, Sultan Moulay Abd al-Hafid of Morocco in 1912.[3] 'In the Parc des Sources, aptly called a "crossroads of races" one encounters a diverse crowd,' says the 1939 guide. The musical season was brilliant: the Grand Casino, containing the opera, a stone and brick temple of high culture, was said to be the one place outside Bayreuth where you could hear *Tannhäuser* with all sixteen English horns prescribed by Wagner.[4] For five months of the year, it was one of the most cosmopolitan towns in France.

To the disgust of M. Maes, manager of the Ambassadeurs, Vichy demonstrated its inclination to please when the Germans rolled through briefly at the end of June 1940. 'Some of them found, in the street, girls happy to accompany them. What shame for us!' he wrote in his journal. 'They took them for drinks in the bar, and we had to mount guard so they wouldn't bring them up to their rooms.' Three or four slipped by anyway. At his rival Aletti's Hôtel du Parc it was worse: there, M. Maes reported, 'about forty girls, running naked down the corridors, created a shameful scandal.'

The town's compact size was deceptive. With its thousands of (now empty) hotel rooms, Vichy was infinitely expandable.

Whole populations could suddenly appear and disappear into these rooms. The hotel names themselves promised the world. You could go from Seville to Russia to Algeria to Portugal and never leave town. The murderer in Simenon's mystery *Maigret à Vichy* 'deploys treasures of patience and cunning' calling hotel after hotel for days, trying to track down the sister of his victim. Inside the grandest of the hotels, the cramped perspectives of the little town become elongated. The dark corridors of what Vichyssois call the *palaces*, like the Hôtel des Ambassadeurs, seem to go on forever, with doors opening onto mysterious half-hidden staircases. In the late 1960s, the dying days of the Ambassadeurs, Simenon himself had haunted the lobby: standing in a corner, he observed that 'very far away, in another world, it seemed, four elderly persons, two men and two women, played bridge with slow movements. The distance gave an impression of unreality, like a scene shot in slow motion.'[5] During the war, the Resistance contacts of Suzy Borel, an official in the Foreign Ministry, flitted from hotel to hotel, quickly finding anonymous shelter or the menace of entrapment. When the local police were looking for Jews in 1943, the myriad hotels were a source of confusion, making the pin-pointing of prey difficult: 'Baruch Freilich, Polish, living at Vichy, Hôtel de Londres or Hôtel Bellevue, certainly warned,' a police inspector noted about one who got away. Then, in the late summer of 1944, the local purge committee filled pages with names of *miliciens* it was pursuing, noting their last known address – invariably a Vichy hotel.[6]

I lived in the bottom floors of a colonnaded, grey four-storey stone villa once owned by Florence Gould, the wife of the American railroad heir and banker Frank Jay Gould and one of the richest women in the world. In the 1930s the house had been her stopping-off point between Paris and the Riviera. The war kept Mrs Gould in what was then the former national capital, where German officers, including the cultivated young SS chief Helmut Knochen, were welcome at her weekly salon.

In those days, Knochen was meeting regularly with French counterparts to work out logistics of deporting Jews. Mrs Gould's guest was still alive in the spring of 2000, living anonymously somewhere in Germany, having served an abbreviated prison term in the 1950s. A friend of his I knew in Paris, declining to put me in touch with him, described him as 'weary' and 'bitter'.

At the Liberation, Mrs Gould had had passing 'difficulties', in the discreet common term, with both the French and American authorities. Her old Vichy residence, sold after the war has been drifting gently downward for years. It had been long since divided into apartments by a recently deceased doctor who had been a figure in the local Resistance. Plaster falls from the balconies, and the exterior looks badly in need of a bath. The city bus stops right in front of what had once been an exclusive Vichy address, 56 avenue Thermale, and a car dealership sits diagonally across from it. Inside, the fancy wallpaper, torn and stained, bore only traces of its original, subtly raised pattern. Still, in the neighbourhood, faint memories persisted of the two Rolls-Royces that once parked in the dilapidated garage, of the concierge and his wife who lived above them, and of Mrs Gould's flying visits between Paris and the coast.

The style of this pile (coyly named 'Les Adrets', or 'The Sunny Side'), with its frieze of foliage, scallop shells and dragons and its off-centre front portico, could be described as neo-Italian Renaissance. This vogue lasted four years among Vichy's architects, from 1910 to 1914, and succeeded a fashion for houses in neo-French Renaissance style, which in turn had succeeded other fashions.[7]

It was this promiscuity that so exasperated some of the more sensitive adepts of the Marshal's new order, including young Mitterrand. 'Vichy is ghastly (not disagreeable, not boring: ugly),' he wrote to a friend in 1942, 'nothing that catches the eye, hotels that are bulging or stupidly linear, pretentious villas planted here and there according to the dubious tastes of fat women.'[8] (Mitterrand is said to have avoided the town in later years, skipping it on visits to his close friend the budget minister, who lived only fifteen kilometres away.) Nobody captured the town's look more succinctly than these men who despised it. The place made a mockery of their would-be seriousness. The fascist writer Lucien Rebatet, turning his back on Vichy to return to the Germans' congenial embrace in Paris, wrote in 1942: 'Everyone knows that Vichy is a ridiculous hodgepodge of Turkish baths crowned by vaguely oriental domes, of kiosks, of casinos, of convolutions in tin, wrought iron, and rockwork, a place that displays more or less all the architectural incongruities of the last century, side by side with heavy samples of our contemporary style.' Pétain's aristocratic civilian chief of staff, Henry du Moulin de Labarthète, stuck in Vichy, was offended by this vulgarity: 'The eye is saddened to discover, jumbled together, these seaside cupolas, these Turkish-bath tiles, these promenades covered with doubtful sheet metal, these dreary streets, lit by dim lampposts.'[9]

The town was malleable. It was a kind of three-dimensional trompe l'œil, the literal representation of something it really wasn't. It could be adapted to a hundred identities. For a few years it was turned into the national capital.

The Pleasures of Forgetting

TRUE, I LEFT many of my interlocutors half convinced that this had not been the case – that somehow Vichy had been the victim of a giant conspiracy by historians. I would find myself wondering, with them, how anybody could be so ill mannered as to accuse the genteel resort of having harboured the État Français.

Obviously the idea was absurd. I warned myself that Vichy had a vocation as a trompe l'oeil, that things might not be quite as they appeared. But the town seemed so innocent you could, after a few months there, begin to sympathise with its sense of grievance. It was a habit of mind you could agreeably settle into.

'Vichy had nothing to do with it! Nothing! Damn, that makes me mad! Furious!' The elderly man with the bulldog face seemed to have good reason for this vehemence. As mayor of Vichy during the war, his father had accomplished a remarkable feat. I was reminded of it every morning: the street signs near the covered market, a half-mile from my house, bore the former mayor's name, a sure sign Pierre-Victor Léger had escaped the regime's taint. He was the only wartime Vichy politician so honoured. Even the old Socialist M. Rougeron had growled from his hospice bed, 'He conducted himself well.'

I was looking for unclouded memories, trying to see if any aspect of the town's wartime past could be recalled without difficulties. It would be a way of cutting through Vichy's perplexing fog. An autumn afternoon in the company of Pierre-Victor Léger's son and daughter-in-law held out promise. We sat at the dining room table for several hours in an empty art deco apartment building near the train station. It looked as though nothing in their lace-trimmed apartment had been moved for decades.

I asked the elderly couple, 'But what did he say when he found out he was now mayor of the national capital?'

'There was nothing to say,' Jacques-Pierre Léger replied. He added, 'Believe me, everyone in France was for Pétain in '40, '42.'

'So, the mayor changed his position,' I said. 'Why exactly?'

M. Léger said, 'Because of the turn taken by the Pétain government. Then, there was collaboration, but besides that . . . we hardly saw him.'

His wife cut in. 'Yeah, we were in Lyon in '42, we were not in Vichy. And in any case *Papy* would never have talked about it. It wasn't even worth the effort she said. He suffered enormously from that situation.'

'Did he talk to you about what he had suffered?'

'No, never,' Mme Léger said.

'Even after the war?'

'No, nothing at all.'

'After the war, he was very, very tired,' M. Léger said. 'Very tired.'

I asked, 'Well, was daily life different for him during those years?'

'Ah, daily life. That's something we had no knowledge of,' Mme Léger said.

'We weren't there,' the mayor's son said.

I went to see the mayor's granddaughter, a middle-aged lawyer in a glass and steel office building in Paris. The mayor was a mysterious figure to her. She showed me his pocket diaries, small leather-bound books full of crabbed notations; occasionally the name of a Vichy minister was decipherable. The diaries had been entrusted to her by her parents. But they weren't probative of anything.

The Légers had had no story to tell about the mayor's passage through the war, not even to their daughter. The war period, the most dramatic in Pierre-Victor Léger's long political career, might as well never have existed.

Yet alongside this silence, it turned out, there had been some details that had survived the passage of time. 'They wanted to name a street for Marshal Pétain, but there again he was firmly opposed,' the mayor's son had said. In the minutes of the city council meeting for January 15, 1941, one can read, 'The mayor presented to the council the interest there would be in revising certain street names.'[10] The rue du Parc had become the rue du Maréchal Pétain, and the street that had commemorated the great Socialist leader Jean Jaurès now was the rue Nationale. The État Français, having done away with elections, appointed the mayor to the post he had previously been voted into, in May 1941. He and his municipal council gratefully made it their first order of business to declare 'respect, attachment and devotion' to the Marshal.[11]

The mayor's son recounted how his father's wartime mandate came to an end. 'In '44 he was very tired, and Jean Barbier, a former schoolmaster, took his place,' he said.

A local Resistance captain, Étienne Asso, who had barrelled into town with his ragged colleagues, had more to say on the end of Mayor Léger's tenure. It came on August 30, 1944, four days after the 'liberation' of Vichy. 'Bordet and I entered Mayor Léger's office. We said to him, "You've got to get out. Your mandate is finished, along with Vichy's."'[12]

'One thing is certain,' the mayor's son said vehemently. 'As mayor, he never, ever, officially received Petain at city hall. Never.' Among the unpublished photographs in the city library, there is one of the mayor and M. Edier's boss in the Légion Française des Combattants greeting Pétain on the steps of the building. (A few days after I set the photo aside, the librarians were unable to find it.)

After I had left the Légers, I thought about a surprising remark Mme Léger had made. 'You know, happily for the individual, he suffers, but he also forgets quite easily,' she had said soon after I arrived in the darkened apartment.

A little taken aback, I asked, 'And you think this is beneficial?'

Oh yes, certainly. Because if one lived nonstop . . . Look, living with the past is fine when it's a good past. But you are not going to live with a past that was more or less deplorable. When all's said and done, you have got to forget it. You have got to go on living.'

Mme Léger's remark seemed to make more sense in the context of the other information that could be discovered about her father-in-law's career. Remembering had turned out to be a matter of choice. You could step in and exercise a will to efface. You could, in all gratitude, forget. This might be the mental equivalent of what had been done to the old hotels after the war, a general wiping away of all traces. The interior of the Parc, for example, with its linoleum floors and pink stucco walls, was irreproachably sterile and homely. In the town of trompe l'œil you could intervene and, for all that had happened, substitute – nothing.

Vichy in a Vacuum

IT SEEMED A strenuous way of living with the past. It required effort. The mayor's granddaughter, long since gone from Vichy, had been volubly frustrated over it when I met her. 'I grew up in an atmosphere of wondering,' she had said. 'Resistance, collaboration, compromise . . .' The sentence trailed off. Her meaning, in the hours I spent with her, was nonetheless unmistakeable: in the household of the son of Mayor Pierre-Victor Léger, 'Vichy' had not existed.

But clearly something had happened. To maintain otherwise was to invite ridicule. Besides, though this might have been an option forty years ago, it wasn't any longer. 'Vichy' was too much in the news, on television, and in the bookshops. So for many of the people I encountered, living with that past became an effort to separate the event from the place, to erase any connection between the sleepy little town and the État Français. These people were willing to acknowledge the reality of the regime, but for them it had unfolded in a vacuum.

'What I can tell you is that Vichy took absolutely no steps to entice the government here,' said Dr Lacarin, who had been mayor in the 1970s and 1980s. A music-loving doctor, M. Hilleret, who worshipped the glorious past of the Grand Casino, grumbled, 'It's as if, for some in the press anyway, we went out *looking* for the government.' What Dr Lacarin said to me at the beginning of our long conversation was repeated by almost everyone I met in town: 'Look, Vichy had fifteen thousand hotel rooms. This was the deciding factor for Pierre

Laval.' M. Hilleret said, 'We had an exceptional capacity to play the host.'

They considered this a certificate of the town's primal innocence, original proof that, as M. Léger's son and others put it, 'Vichy had nothing to do with it.' But to me it seemed just as much an unwitting admission that the Vichy government could not have existed anywhere else.

The immense opera hall, one of the biggest in Europe with fifteen hundred seats, was uniquely able to accommodate the old, fleeing government's parliament for the fateful vote of July 10, 1940, in which all power was handed over to Marshal Pétain. 'We had at Vichy our treasure, the opera, the only building large enough to house the two chambers of parliament at the moment of the vote handing over power to Pétain,' the former mayor said.

From the outset, it was the town's singular attributes, its jewel, that permitted the new order to come into being. There was thus a peculiar appropriateness to the designation 'Vichy'; a kind of symbiosis had existed between town and regime. As it took shape, as its distinctive mix of repression and sanctimony developed, it was subtly moulded by the hotels that sheltered it.

Wandering the dim corridors of the Parc, where I had an office, I had an instinct that the effort to divorce town from regime would fail. A half-century before, each door had represented a bureaucrat, or three; each corridor could be multiplied dozens of times over for the whole town. Tightly packed into the hotels, now unencumbered by meddling elected officials, the regime's functionaries – the number of government workers grew by 26 per cent between 1941 and 1946 – operated in what became a nearly pure bureaucratic state.'[13] In fact, a generation of efficient servants of the French nation, among them Papon, cut its teeth at Vichy. The legacy of the expansion survives through the death of his generation:

the country today has a higher percentage of its workforce on the public payroll than any of its industrialised peers.[14]

A man I met, living in a secluded brick villa at the edge of Paris, had wandered these same hotel corridors more than fifty years before, looking for a government job. His search had been fruitless, but he had understood the connection between the corridors and the bureaucrats. The man, M. Sjöberg, was a retired graphic artist. In 1945 this son of a Swedish émigré painter had published an eccentric book of satirical captioned drawings entitled *Hors-saison à Vichy* (*Vichy in the Off-Season*), these days found only by accident at speciality second-hand book dealers.

In these drawings, Vichy is the nightmare paradise of the bureaucrat, a place where the hermetically sealed functionary officiates unrestrained. In the corners of the sketchy drawings we see flights of stairs leading up into a void at the edge of the page. Meetings take place on the stairs, apparently significant – 'No time, dear fellow, I've got to prepare the incineration of the latest decrees' – and the stick figures clutching files are in a hurry, perched uncertainly in the middle of the image, floating just above the steps. These end at a vaguely titled ministry that no longer exists or that has been moved somewhere else. Shapeless drones with hairbrush moustaches exist to announce the hero's false step or to disappear down endless corridors; the hero exists to climb and descend the stairs, in hotels whose functions maddeningly shift, to the glee or indifference of the denizens.[15] 'I invented nothing,' M. Sjöberg explained. 'They said to me, "Go and see so-and-so, he'll give you a job."' But there was never a job, or it turned out to be temporary ('Your name is a problem,' the hero of *Hors-saison à Vichy* is told).

In Sjöberg's vision of Vichy, the ministries are as transient as hotel guests. Their plans are, in turn, as shifting and frivolous as those of tourists. They are hatched by agile youngsters crouched on the floor of tiny hotel rooms, the reduced space

nurturing a ludicrous febrility. At the Commission on Prolific-
ity, 'everything remains to be done ... and we're going to
make sparks fly!' The Commissioner in the Fight Against
Idleness says, 'Everything from scratch, now. What's needed is
audacity.'

M. Sjöberg was a quiet old man in a neat green wool jacket
and bow tie. My phone call had surprised him; his book has
been forgotten for years, though it bore the imprint of a major
French publisher, one he helped found in the 1930s. 'The
behaviour of those people had nothing to do with that of
people in a responsible, honest government,' he said. He spoke
in the spare, declarative style of his book of fifty-four years
before, and he shared the fastidiousness of its hero. His
darkened living room contained a number of featureless
wooden figurines carved by long-dead sculptor friends; M.
Sjöberg reminded me of these enigmatic carvings.

He had captured better than any memoirist or historian the
peculiar negative synergy of the hotel-state. He had recorded,
more precisely than anybody since, the essence of 'Vichy'. Yet
he was nearly indifferent to his achievement, handing me
copies of the rare book as though they were visiting cards.
What had stayed with him from his weeks in Vichy was a
strong sense of moral disapproval. As a young man he had
been disgusted by the spectacle in the spa town. He found
'motivations that were false, motivations that were ridiculous.
They were all delighted to have found a position.'

M. Sjöberg had affixed the obloquy of the regime to the
locale. He had brought a judgement against his contemporaries, and not just against those who were leaders. In Vichy I
had been specifically warned against doing this. 'Good gracious, what would you have expected, that we all up and went
to London? No! There were families to feed!' said a woman
who had worked in one of the ministries.

In the town there was a sense that too severe a judgement
could have the unwanted consequence of localising reproval,

of training it too sharply, just there. This helped explain otherwise surprising pockets of complaisance, in quarters where it might have seemed unwise. 'The Marshal had, in all probability, a grand conception of France,' said M. Bourdier, the deputy mayor. 'He was a great man,' he said, hastily adding that he was not a Pétainist. Others who proclaimed allegiance to the values of the Resistance easily referred to the Marshal as *'le père Pétain'*, slipping untroubled into the old soldier's favourite self-image as the country's father.

It seemed important, as part of the process of catapulting the Vichy regime into a void, to shy away from moral assessments of it. The current mayor, M. Malhuret, bristled when I suggested that there was necessarily such a component in contemporary judgements of the regime. 'It's a mistake to judge events of forty, fifty years ago from that standpoint,' said M. Malhuret, a former government minister for human rights. 'That's a very American point of view,' the middle-aged son of one of the period's important local functionaries said to me when I made a similar suggestion about the moral import of the past.

The mayor was keen on promoting the blandest possible relation between the town and its history. A voracious reader (several people in Vichy spoke resentfully of his intelligence), he nevertheless eschewed books on the subject. 'People in Vichy didn't live it any differently from people anywhere else.' M. Malhuret's features tightened. 'There is nothing unique about Vichy,' the mayor, a doctor like the rest of Vichy's governing class, insisted.

The idea that the town had trudged wearily along, really no different from any other place, seemed vital to its present-day functioning. I recognised it as part of cutting Vichy off from 'Vichy': Vichy was to be dissolved anonymously into the mass of the nation.

'We never thought of it as the capital. As for the Vichyssois, everything happened outside of us,' said a lady I met at the

Calondre pastry shop one day. She had been a nurse in a doctor's office on the park, and regularly saw the Marshal on his daily promenade.

When the presence of something unusual was acknowledged, it was in the guise of hidden knowledge, of information not widely known. 'All those little hotels around the Source de l'Hôpital' – one of Vichy's several hot springs – were occupied by ministries, you know,' an elderly woman said, confiding in me as if suddenly remembering a vital but forgotten fact.

The Town's Alternate Reality

I WAS BEGINNING TO WONDER. If Vichy had not been a capital crowded with bureaucrats, what on earth was it? Clearly, the memoirs and archives must be misleading, the ones that painted a picture of streets full of sour-faced functionaries uprooted from Paris. And yet in these documents, every aspect of life appears to be affected by the new presence a half-century before. You saw the regime's servants walking in the evenings, they kept you out of shops and restaurants, they flooded the train station. It had become a government town as surely as Washington has ever been. 'In spite of persistent and vain efforts by members of the staff, only one employee has been able to find an apartment, which is far from satisfactory (without central heating or bathroom) and may be requisitioned for the use of some French official at any time,' the American ambassador wrote home in September 1941.[16]

The population had suddenly doubled, and the newcomers hated their confinement. There wasn't much to do in the frigid little town. 'We would go out to dinner, three or four of us, and then we would come back to the hotel, and at that point the only thing on our minds was to pile on the jackets, because we were very, very cold,' said a lucid old man I met in Paris who had been at the Ministry of the Interior (Hôtel des Céléstins), as the top aide to the personnel director, until early

1944. Sometimes, as a special treat, he and others would descend to the hotel lobby and huddle around the static-filled radio.

As the months passed, the feelings of resentment became mutual. On October 29, 1941, city councillor Dulong declared sarcastically to his colleagues that the gastronomic challenge facing the ordinary Vichyssois was 'at least as worthy of interest as that of the functionaries taking their meals in the ministry canteens'.[17] Maurice Papon, an unpopular figure around the mess hall of the Céléstins, was envied his promotion to the Bordeaux prefecture, even as colleagues winked knowingly at the young man's cool careerism. Jammed into hotel rooms, sometimes doubling up, the younger bureaucrats tolerated this life better than the older ones. 'Come, stay in the room I'm sharing with a couple of friends, it's as simple as camping out,' Sjöberg's hero is told, but he flees on confronting a chaos of shoes, toothbrushes, clothing and sleeping bags scattered over the floor. 'The meals were not particularly tasty,' Sjöberg remembered.

What had been a modest-sized provincial resort soon took on the characteristics of an urban centre. 'In the streets of our city, the crowds of passersby, hands in their pockets and collars turned up, scatter in every direction like nervous ants,' a columnist for the local newspaper wrote in January 1942. Up above, the shivering bureaucrats had installed wood-burning stoves in their offices. 'Everywhere windows let pass the long black neck of a pipe, sweating drops of sooty liquid.'[18] Having perused the letters sent from Vichy in July 1943, the regime's postal censor wrote, 'They accuse these functionaries of invading *everything*.' The month before he had written, 'There is general uproar in the population, which is eager to see the departure of these undesirables in order to have better access to provisions.'[19] These people were tangible evidence that the town was, for a time, France's nerve centre, though as the Occupation lengthened, government agencies tended to drift back to Paris – even the proximity of Germans was considered preferable to remaining in the spa town.[20] 'Numerous Frenchmen burned to serve the new state,' the regime's finance minister, Yves Bouthillier, wrote maliciously in his self-justifying memoirs after the war.[21]

'We were in a sense occupied, but by Frenchmen,' Dr Lacarin, the former mayor, said, chuckling to himself. He was speaking from personal experience, the musty apartment we were sitting in having been bunked in by bureaucrats. The memory of them was thus in some instances unavoidable. The bureaucrats had once been in your house. They had been ubiquitous.

But in that case they were not serious. There was no heft to the structure they were supposedly upholding. They were not part of a real government. Vichy had not been a real capital. 'We couldn't stop ourselves from saying that it began to seem, very quickly, like the capital in an operetta,' said M. Frelastre, a city councillor, who was a young teenager in those years. 'An operetta capital!' a retired army officer said disdainfully.

Something besides the authoritarian administration of France by Frenchmen had occurred in Vichy. A coherent alternative reality could be substituted, one that clinched the town's innocence. This substitution makes use of two of the traditional elements in the national story of the war, the Germans and the Resistance. In Vichy, Resistance had battled Germans, just like anywhere else in France. But in this context, Resistance is aided by an unavoidable local figure, Marshal Pétain.

He is at the centre of the triptych, though morally rehabilitated. 'Look, I'm going to tell you something, and excuse me. You better not say anything nasty about Marshal Pétain in front of me, that's all!' said the retired shipping agent who had sung '*Maréchal, nous voilà!*' He described himself as a Gaullist, though he had kept his portrait of Pétain through the years, the standard-issue one that had been in every shop window in Vichy.

In the capital that wasn't, Marshal Pétain is not necessarily the head of state. He is a transcendent figure, outside politics. He does not sing in the 'operetta'. The Marshal exists in disembodied form, divested of the horde of functionaries who carried out his policies. He is seen from a distance, in the park or up on his balcony, a virtual statue whose height marks him out from everything around. 'My sisters would take me into town from up in the mountains. Sure, I saw Marshal Pétain, from across the park. Tall, with his kepi,' said the middle-aged *patronne* of a coffeehouse. She was then a small child. 'It impressed me,' she said.

'He would be strolling in the park,' said Dr Lacarin, the former mayor, 'the only contact one had with him. He was in civilian clothes. He was a great big tall old man. He carried himself extremely well. Cane, felt hat, he walked very slowly.' A man who had been a schoolboy said, 'Ah, he was so handsome, the Marshal, when he was in uniform.' Pétain in these recollections is often ten or twenty years younger than his age, and he is preternaturally robust. He seems approachable, because there are so few attendants around him, but he is actually quite distant. He is like the honoured guests of the prewar years, the people whose prestigious presence thrilled the town. As a middle-aged neighbour put it to me wistfully one day (though in her case she was referring to wartime Vichy), 'So many important personalities came through Vichy in those days!' Naturally, Pétain puts up at the fanciest hotel, the Parc. When he leaves, as one of his secretaries remembered with gratitude years later, he hands out envelopes stuffed with cash to his faithful attendants, like any self-respecting guest.[22]

I asked M. Frelastre, the city councillor, 'So, were people aware of the nature of the regime, that it was an authoritarian regime?' He replied, 'Oh, yes, yes. There were all those good folk from Cusset,' a suburb of Vichy. 'They were all employed in the hotels. They came in by bicycle. I can't tell you how many people said to me, "Oh, it's terrible, we passed in front of the Hôtel du Portugal at six o'clock this morning, we heard the cries, it was horrible, the bastards were torturing." We were all the more fearful in that the Gestapo wasn't in uniform ... So we knew that there was denunciation, torture, that it was a dictatorial regime. We knew this from the beginning.'

A dictatorial authority had installed itself in the town of Vichy, but it was not the one the historians or I had identified. 'Don't forget, there was the Gestapo at the Hôtel du Portugal,' a bourgeois woman warned me at the start of our chat. The moral profile of the Marshal is sharpened by his necessary evil counterpart. 'There was the Marshal, and there were the Germans,' the old nurse said. In Vichy's revised past, the Germans have the upper hand, sometimes in uniform, sometimes not. The Marshal is alone against them, just as in his own glory days, those of the Great War.

Germans and Marshal are juxtaposed. The Hôtel du Parc marks the culmination of the summer walking tour. Just before, the little group stops at the edge of a well-tended green lawn in Vichy's riverside park. 'There it is, the wall,' the guide says. Fifty yards away, at right angles to the Hôtel du Portugal, is a concrete wall, high and pockmarked, topped by a series of steel fence posts strung with wire. The Gestapo, in 1943, erected it to discourage prying eyes. Amid the verdure and just yards from Vichy's remaining luxury hotel, it is a startlingly grim intrusion. The ugly wall has a special status in the physiognomy of the town, though it serves no useful purpose. This is one of only two wartime structures that have been allowed to survive; the other is a disused pump house. For the citizens, the wall is a fixed reference point. 'Do you know about the wall?' people would ask me, trying to be helpful. The wall is the town's unofficial monument to the war years.

Because they are in the commanding position, the Germans look down from balconies or terraces. 'Up there is where we used to see the German officers at lunchtime,' a woman said, pointing to the terrace on the corner of the neoclassical mansion that had been the German embassy. 'They wanted us to see them up there, in uniform,' she said, looking up. 'He was on the balcony,' a man said, 'drinking something. He was in shirtsleeves, and he was watching the loading up. It intrigued me, and I was afraid.' Or their presence comes back through loud sinister noises, sometimes imagined from the tales of others: cars screeching to a halt, the cries of the tortured in the basement of the Hôtel du Portugal. 'When one heard a car stopping suddenly, and four doors slamming, one knew it was the Gestapo,' said the former mayor, Dr Lacarin, a young physician at the time. 'One could hear people crying out from the basement,' said a woman who, as a small child, was brought to Vichy from the countryside by her doctor father. It was not generally remembered that the Portugal was turned into a prison for collaborators at the Liberation. No one mentioned this to me, not even Dr Lacarin, who had been the consulting physician at this new prison (in January 1945, he recommended that sick prisoners be given a litre of wine a week).[23]

In the town's personal history, the Gestapo – the Germans – had been shifted front and centre. Their brutality crowds out all images except that of the Marshal himself. In the extended afterlife of the État Français, the Germans had come to dominate Vichy in a way they did not between 1940 and 1944.

It was true that the Gestapo had installed a regional headquarters in the town, in the last eighteen months of the war (and not 'from the beginning,' as the city councillor had said). But German uniforms were rare, even after the invasion of the unoccupied zone in November 1942, a deliberate policy on the part of the Nazis to preserve the French state's appearance of autonomy.[24] The Vichyssois acknowledge this. 'Ah, no. No no no no. No. Very little, I tell you. Sometimes at the train station,' one man said. 'Under the Marshal, there were no Germans at Vichy,' M. Edier said. 'The Germans were fairly discreet, fairly discreet.' At the very end, there were 182 people, including secretaries, in the Gestapo operation, and their compatriots numbered a dozen-odd diplomats, a few journalist-spies and assorted hangers-on.[25]

I asked the old man in Paris who had been at the Interior Ministry whether he was aware of the Gestapo in his Vichy days. 'Not so much,' he said. 'Not so much. Not so much.' The memoirs of the Marshal's men scarcely mention Germans in Vichy – apart from the importuning diplomat Cecil von Renthe-Fink, who installed himself in a room at the Parc during the regime's last months, irritating Pétain. Collaborators like Lucien Rebatet complained that the German influence was not evident *enough* in the capital of the French state.

The Portugal and the adjacent houses on the boulevard des États-Unis, also occupied by the Gestapo, maintain a hold on the town's imagination far surpassing any of the installations of the État Français. 'I would never live in one of those houses,' a fashionable restaurateur said. 'It took the longest time for that house to sell,' Mme London said, smiling confidentially, about a house on the block. The owner of one of them, a slim art deco mansion of the 1920s, took me on a tour of the basement one cold morning; he was having trouble renting it. Sure enough, there were sinister fugitive traces of the Nazi presence: thick metal bars over a high, narrow opening; a massive concrete wall doubling a thin brick one; a narrow cubicle of inhuman dimensions, awkwardly inserted into the existing floor plan, that could have had only one purpose.

At the Portugal and in neighbouring buildings, evil was done to Frenchmen. Besides the Germans, this block evokes the third element in the triptych of the substituted past, the Resistance.

Vichy had resisted. 'This was where the first resistance was,' a man said to me. He was indignant, provoked by my presence at the annual commemoration of Vichy's 'liberation' in the peaceful municipal cemetery at the edge of town. Vichy's one official plaque marking those years makes the same point: placed on a wall in the Grand Casino, it honours the *Quatre-vingts,* the eighty deputies who voted no to handing over power to Pétain in July 1940. It makes no mention of the 569 who voted yes. 'And you know, even during the war there were important acts of resistance,' Dr Lacarin said.

This was phrased tentatively, almost hopefully. Having been in town for some months, I understood why. It represented a desire more than a verifiable fact. Late in the spring I had gone to the local commemoration of National Resistance Day. On the little tree-shaded square that houses the town's hyper kinetic, neo-realist World War I monument, ten old men grasped faded flags while a dozen-odd elderly people, relatives, looked on. There was convivial chatting in the late afternoon sunlight. Pedestrians strolled by, barely looking over. It had the feel of a private ceremony. You couldn't say the event had drawn only a small crowd; there was no sort of crowd at all, big or small. 'Ah, Vichy,' a flag bearer in a brown corduroy cap said despairingly before getting back on the train to the nearby railroad junction of St-Germain-des-Fossés, a centre of Communist resistance during the war.

A local personage, wanting the memory of the Portugal to be represented in my work, directed me to a man who had been tortured there. The Germans had come for him on February 10, 1944, taken him to the basement of a pink villa across from the Portugal, and beaten him bloody. 'These were professionals. They knew what they were doing,' M. Saurou said. He was modest and soft-spoken, and I listened to his grim story – torture, deportation, concentration camp – over a long winter afternoon as his wife quietly urged him on. He turned out to be not from Vichy at all but St-Germain-des-Fossés.

All the ambiguity of Vichy's relationship to the Resistance is contained in the one street name that recalls the town's years as national capital. The rue Walter Stücki, a beguiling lane of parti-coloured villas leading to the river, is named for the Swiss ambassador to the État Français. Stücki is a hero in the memory of the town, credited with saving it from a column of bloodthirsty German soldiers during the götterdämmerung of August 1944, when the regime evaporated.

Yet this is a role Stücki doesn't attribute to himself in his memoirs. Instead, the upright and self-effacing Swiss tells of persuading the *résistants* (or *maquis*) waiting in the mountains not to exact reprisals on Vichy, which was terrified of these armed compatriots. 'Panic has set in at Vichy,' a diarist notes in his entry for August 11, 1944, two weeks before the end. 'The functionaries ask themselves whether they are going to be abandoned; the whole of the population fears above all the taking of Vichy by the *maquis*.'[26]

The nearby mountain villages had conscientiously named their streets for local Resistance heroes. It took Vichy fifty years to honour the man acknowledged as the leading Vichyssois *résistant,* Roger Kespy, a Jew who made radios and was horribly tortured for months before being shot in the forest of Marcenat. In 1994 Kespy was given the privilege of a tiny square's edge near his old house, a bit of turf that doesn't figure on city maps.

I asked the granddaughter of one of Kespy's Resistance colleagues, a frank, open-faced young woman, whether she had ever talked about this heritage with friends at school: 'No-o-o,' she said, looking down. 'What would have been the point? They wouldn't have been interested.'

Her peers were astonished when I told them about her grandfather, M. Gonnat. Her own father had been uninterested in M. Gonnat's Resistance exploits. But she had taken pleasure in accompanying old man Gonnat, before his recent death, to reunions.

In her wallet she carried blank identity cards René Gonnat had stolen during the war from the Vichy headquarters of the Pétainist Légion Française des Combattants.

'Why do you keep them?' I asked.

She looked down, embarrassed by the question. But she took care to explain that the cards were 'virgin', and therefore precious. The *résistant*'s granddaughter worked at the melancholy municipal museum, among the 'exhibits' from the État Français. What she had in her wallet was more interesting.

Another *résistant* left a message on my answering machine: he wanted to talk. 'For God's sake, if you call back, don't tell my wife I called you,' he said in his message. I phoned him. He answered with an elaborate charade: 'Ah, so somebody tipped you off about me then? Very good, very good.' Under his breath he explained, 'My wife doesn't like for me to talk about all this stuff.' I heard a woman's voice grumbling in the background. 'She hates what she calls "the rehashing",' the *résistant* said. The grumbling became louder, and I heard the word 'rehashing' being repeated angrily.

Later, at their house above Vichy, while her husband spread out an impressive array of postwar Resistance certificates – official-looking documents guaranteeing my host's membership in such-and-such a Resistance organization – she circled around the kitchen table like a restless fox terrier. He spoke at length about bits of trash he had fished out of wastebaskets and passed on to the Americans; she came up with a childhood Christmas card from Marshal Pétain, faux-naïf and sentimental.

I understood her point. The town's hold on resistance was tenuous, like its vocation as victim of the Germans. Given the severity of the purge and the threat from the *maquis,* the town might show more good faith in thinking of itself as a *victim* of the Resistance. It was a potentially tempting viewpoint, though of course unacceptable. By the same token, the mental monument to Pétain was a guilty pleasure, not to be avowed openly. This vision of the war years, encountered in various combinations throughout my stay in Vichy, had the structure of a dream; each part was dependent on the other, and all three parts worked handily together. Vichy's Pétain needed the

Germans to elevate his stature; the Germans needed the Resistance to accentuate their evil. There was a strange kind of harmony among the three parts. Like a dream, it seemed to make good sense when you were in the thick of it. But it could exist only within the mental confines of the town, in a sort of vacuum. Once the bridge over the Allier River was crossed, the dream tended to evaporate in the daylight of the outside world.

7

Interlude: Escape from Vichy

The Past's Density

'Is it possible to be a historian in Vichy?' the retired history teacher asked waspishly. After some months in the town, I knew what he meant. It was the worst possible place in which to achieve a level-headed view of past events. Vichy was like Baudelaire's forest of symbols, where every building and every corner had some associative value, some potential meaning for the passerby. The Carlton might just be the Carlton, an incongruous, superannuated art nouveau high-rise on the park where a respectable group gathered to play bridge every week. Or it might be the Ministry of Justice, where French officials had earnestly affirmed the legality of the new anti-Jewish laws. The teacher and his friends made a game out of all this, playfully telling each other to meet, say, 'outside the American embassy' or 'at the Ministry of Finance'.

Others I knew in the town were overwhelmed, the abundance of associations crowding in and confusing them. An ardent young man in his thirties who ran a subsidised theatre troupe had big plans to mount a 'Festival of Memory' in Vichy. 'We have to lance the abscess,' he said several times. 'There are too many silences around here.' He was going to invite Germans, Italians, historians, artists. They were going to talk, give speeches, act out scenes. But about what? He didn't know. 'We have to determine what questions need to be asked,' he said. His plan was inchoate. He could sense that some meaning could be extracted from the town, but he was unsure what it was. The rebellious scion of one of the town's great hotel families told me he steered clear of books and discussions on the subject. 'It's not so much that it doesn't interest me. It's that it makes me mad – makes me mad that people can't talk about the war of '40 with objectivity and lucidity.' Bitterly, he added, 'Look, for my mother it was a splendid time. She wore a different gown every night.' An enthusiastic local man phoned to tell me he was working on a massive project, the reconstruction of Marshal Pétain's daily agenda for every day of the four years of the État Français. He was going to put the results on a CD-Rom. He explained that he had no exact goal, but 'the historians are not precise enough, not *mathematical* enough.' Others would offer me old ration tickets, identity cards, portraits of the Marshal, coins minted under the État Français, letters opened by the German censor, a photograph of the dog of one of the American diplomats in Vichy during the war, certain that it all had some meaning, unsure what it was.

The retired history teacher led a small group of citizens that doggedly tried to penetrate the thicket. They called themselves the French Psychohistory Society, and they met every month in an insurance office across from the Concours Hippique, where collaborators had been imprisoned after the Liberation. The project of the psychohistorians was nothing less than the decoding of Vichy's still functioning debris. Patiently, they were assembling a critical dictionary of the key words and phrases of the État Français, explaining to themselves its symbolic language. The psychohistorians pored over the defunct regime's symbols, making notes of their own remarks, solely for their own consumption. The frigid night I went to the Psychohistory Society, its brightly lit meeting room was the only illumination on the dark street, the one renamed rue Nationale during the war. A cold fog had enveloped the town.

What could have induced the psychohistorians to come out on such a night? They were evidently not lunatics. 'We are the subversives,' the president – the retired history teacher – had said gleefully. It became clear that they were undertaking a sort of mental gymnastics, keeping themselves in shape. After months immured in Vichy's provincial silence, you could feel that this was both necessary and courageous.

The past was dense in Vichy. The citizens instinctively felt this. Their struggle to establish a connection to it was testimony to this density. The past hemmed them in. I couldn't help sensing it myself, journeying through the various phases of memory in the town – the memory holes, the will to forget, the separation of 'Vichy' from Vichy, the substitution of an alternate reality. You could experience this density as an enervating claustrophobia. Whatever essence there was in Vichy's relationship to its past might not necessarily be getting any closer. A friend in Vichy urged me, at the end of the long dead winter, to go south, because 'it can get so heavy around here.'

He spoke of leaving the town as nearly a necessity. I recognised this as an impulse that had moved back and forth across time, the density of the past's memory being, no doubt, a distant echo of what had been an oppressive present a half-century before. The will to escape was a kind of antithetical proof of the existence of something overbearing, an element nonetheless hidden.

In the memoirs of wartime functionaries, the word 'escape' recurs. Du Moulin de Labarthète, the head of Pétain's civilian staff, wrote after the war: 'Hatred of Vichy; that was the cry of all those who lived, struggled, suffered in that *bad* city, who felt themselves cloistered there for months on end, for whom the road to Gannat represented, for a long time, the only hope of escape.'[1] Gannat, a modest little town fifteen-odd miles from Vichy, was nonetheless out of the Vichyssois bowl. A Foreign Ministry official wrote: 'I took advantage of the slightest excuse to escape that rotten town (the minute one got out, the air seemed lighter and more pure).'[2] For Sjöberg's hero, Vichy is a 'jail', a 'trap with no bait', and on a rainy November Sunday he considers suicide in the Allier River as the best alternative.

Not being in Vichy, the ability to leave it on the special weekly train to Paris reserved for ministers, represented status a half-century ago. On the train from Paris one winter's day, I saw the mayor, M. Malhuret. Resentfully, people in the town said he spent much of his time in the capital. 'I'm very cosmopolitan,' he explained impatiently in his city hall office the only other time I saw him. He had helped found Médecins Sans Frontières and had spent his younger years in Afghanistan, Nicaragua and Lebanon before beginning a political career on the Gaullist right. 'Look, the history of Pétainist France, all that old France stuff, bores me to tears,' he said. He was a small balding man wearing a stiff dark suit on a Saturday, the type of brilliant, uncharismatic official who, in the United States, would never have been elected to anything.

What did he think about establishing some sort of museum of 'the period'?

With vehemence M. Malhuret replied: 'I absolutely don't want to get into it. To get involved with something around memory ... Look, I know what would happen, and I just don't want to get into it.' He talked as though 'memory' – the memory of the years in question – were a suffocating tar pit. 'There would be problems, problems I don't want.'

'Vichy' was a trap. It would drag him down.

The mayor had two computers and a cellular phone on his immaculate desk. He was starting up a medical software company, and he was soon off to Texas and California on business, a trip he relished. An American friend had once mocked him with the assertion that Frenchmen had largely collaborated during the war; M. Malhuret quoted this 'New York Jewish intellectual' with approval. At the end of our meeting, he treated me to a lecture on the virtues of global markets and free enterprise, castigating French preoccupations with republicanism', a concept he considered absurdly antique. 'You sound like an American,' I said, not usually a compliment for a French politician. He didn't flinch.

'How on earth did you wind up here?' a woman asked me, the only native-born American living in Vichy – the United States being sufficiently distant, from this perspective, for my presence to be surprising. Even when surprise turned to mild dismay, the reason for my presence becoming apparent, people would reassure themselves out loud that, being American, I would be open-minded and tolerant. The ancient, crotchety invalid who lived above us was provoked by my presence into remembering the bright white lights of New York in 1945; the France he left had been 'black', and he had returned to it only reluctantly. A woman who spent her adolescence in Manhattan during the war spoke longingly of returning. Passing a café in the central square, I heard a middle-aged woman say, to laughing approbation, 'I've always dreamed of marrying an American.' A man in Vichy said to me one day, 'You are over here, but we are trying to get over there.' M. Bardiaux, a television repairman who had been a teenager during the war, another scion of a local hotel family, grew misty-eyed when, taking his leave, he said, 'And thank heavens for the Americans.' Long after American tourists had removed the town from their itineraries, the local branch of the Franco-American Society, the Comité France-Amérique, still had a full roster of members, though few English speakers. The retired history teacher made regular trips to New York, proudly saying he could reach Manhattan faster than he could drive to his country house in southern France.

An unusual concentration of prominent streets in the town was named after American presidents – Woodrow Wilson, Franklin Roosevelt, Eisenhower and Kennedy were all within a half-mile of one another. Anglophone guidebooks sneered at this toponymic peculiarity: here Vichy was belatedly showing fidelity to the Allies. Yet America had a complicated and distinctive place in the local consciousness. America was the anti-'Vichy'. It might be a way out of the past's density. It offered possibilities of escape and redemption, perhaps even sympathetic deliverance from the morbid resentments of Vichy-despising compatriots.

The Americans at Vichy

THERE WAS A striking continuity in these sentiments. They too had survived across time. Many years before, during 'the period', the Americans had represented a promise of innocence and clarity. A mere encounter with them was like a vicarious escape. 'The Americans, the most privileged of the privileged, who brought us a whiff of the great open sea,' a retired journalist wrote in a sentimental memoir of Vichy's years as national capital. She had spent much of her time manoeuvering, unsuccessfully, for exit papers to the United States.[3] 'He's a man of tall stature, simple and direct, who gives a great impression of authority,' wrote the journalist Maurice Martin du Gard, observing the new American ambassador in 1941.[4] There is jealousy and condescension in these wartime reminiscences. They are evoked in banal contexts. A Foreign Ministry worker, recalling her meagre social life, wrote of a few 'dives into the pool of the Sporting Club, where Wallner, the secretary of the American embassy, gained my admiration because he did the complete roundtrip underwater without seeming in the least winded.'[5] The sentimental journalist Wanda Vulliez, encountering the ambassador and one of his aides at the Cintra, a fashionable bar across from the embassy, wrote admiringly, 'Here were two honest gentlemen, speaking without pomposity of the vagaries of their job in Vichy, that carnival of hangers-on.'[6] Thirty years after the war a prominent citizen of the town had written, 'The American diplomats left behind very good memories in Vichy ... Simple, direct, always a little puerile, but easy to chat with.'[7] I asked an elderly man in Paris who had spent time with American diplomats how they had been regarded in wartime Vichy. 'Oh, but they were everybody's darlings!' the man exclaimed, surprised at the question (he had used the French word '*chouchou*').

It was a forgotten corner of America's wartime history: American diplomats and journalists had witnessed the unfolding of the *révolution nationale*. The State Department had stuck by Pétain, to the consternation of those people at home the US ambassador in Vichy later derided as 'so-called liberals'.[8] Roosevelt mistakenly believed the Marshal to be 'the one powerful element in the French government who is standing firm against selling out to the Germans', as he put it to the man he had chosen as ambassador. Hoping to bolster Pétain, he went out of his way to flatter him, sending him William Leahy, an admiral who had been chief of naval operations.[9] Pétain had been delighted to get Leahy, staging a ceremonious reception between rows of marines presenting arms in the snow-covered Parc Sévigné in January 1941. But the policy infuriated a large swathe of American public opinion, which considered the Marshal a tool of the Nazis; the State Department felt obliged to engage a respected historian to defend itself immediately after the war. 'In the United States it generated no end of indignation and bitter feeling, and led to charges that frequently went beyond the limits of decency and reason,' the historian wrote.[10]

Yet across the ocean, in the town, the presence of the Americans had been experienced as a relief. Contact with them, however menial, conferred status. 'That really positioned you in those days. For a young man like me, it was really pretty great to work with the Americans,' said the last surviving Frenchman to have been employed at the American embassy. He was hunched over his dining room table in a gloomy mountain village above Vichy. In front of him was an official-looking document with a big red wax seal: 'United

States Embassy Vichy'. It certified Jean Corre as '*employé à l'ambassade des États-Unis*'. The thick, robust bond, with 'Foreign Service of the United States' printed on it in blue letters, contrasted with the flimsy stationery of the État Français I was used to seeing in the archives. The survivor had carefully preserved the document through the years, though he had been no more than a 'messenger boy', as he put it in English, a simple gofer.

This was a rare trace of the fugitive American presence in Vichy. Feeling the town's isolation one hot August day, I was determined to find another. I knew that the wife of the ambassador had died unexpectedly in Vichy in April 1942. I went to the municipal cemetery to see if there was any sign of Mrs Leahy. 'Name doesn't mean anything to me,' the caretaker said. He was sweating under his blue work shirt. Irritably, he looked through the register of notables. No Leahy.

As a consolation, he offered to show me the embalmed body of the mistress of the builder of the Suez Canal. She had been a dancer, he said; you could see her under a glass lid, still wearing her dancer's costume.

At city hall, the cemetery supervisor was sceptical. He couldn't find Mrs Leahy on his computer screen. I dictated the name, and he pulled down a leather-bound registry book from 1942. Still no Leahy. The supervisor didn't think this person had ever existed. 'You see, it could even be under her maiden name,' he said doubtfully.

'Here's an American name,' he said, idly flipping the pages of the old book. 'Harrington.' We looked at it more closely. 'The 21st of April, 1942, at 9:45, was deceased ... Louise Harrington, born at Colusa (California) (United States of America) the Fifteenth of February Eighteen Hundred and Seventy Six ... living at Vichy, 56, avenue Thermale ... wife of William Leahy ... '

This appeared to be the only trace left in Vichy of the American ambassador's wife, an abbreviated death certificate written in flowing script and signed by the mayor, P.-V. Léger. She had died of a blood clot after a routine hysterectomy in La Pergola, a private hospital that had boasted of its modern facilities. Later, going through the embassy's records at the National Archives outside Washington, I found that the French authorities were relieved that the admiral accompanied his wife's body home. They were afraid a funeral in Vichy would be the occasion for a pro-American demonstration.[11]

To my surprise, I discovered from the death certificate at city hall, months after moving to Vichy, that I had been living in what was once Mrs Leahy's home, the residence of the American ambassador, 56 avenue Thermale. Nobody had told us about this predecessor. The landlord had said, before we moved in, that he 'thought' American diplomats 'might' have lived in the house. The high-ceilinged rooms, with the curious swastika pattern in the tiled entrance and the toile de Jouy shepherds and shepherdesses on the walls, had once echoed with other American voices. They are evoked in William Leahy's postwar memoirs. There was a reception on July 4, 1941, for the reporters and American 'civilians' in Vichy (around seventy people present), a Christmas tea for the embassy staff (forty in attendance), late-night phone calls from Mr Atherton at the State Department in Washington, the Army–Navy game over shortwave radio in the upstairs study. 'We got a reasonably good play-by-play broadcast despite much static, and the Navy won, 14 to 6,' the admiral noted.[12] Eight servants had waited on the Leahys at 56 avenue Thermale: a cook, a kitchen boy, a butler, two chambermaids, a valet and two concierges.[13] In the winter, putting on a coat before descending to the basement, I thought of Mrs Leahy. She had 'finished' at Miss Cary's in Baltimore, was a pew holder at St Thomas Church in Washington, DC, and 'was rated a great asset to her husband wherever he was stationed, because of her poise,' the *New York Times* wrote. But she was unprepared for winter in the draughty summer villa on avenue

Thermale. Mrs Leahy struggled to keep the icy house warm, 'sealing the doors and windows with cloth and paper strips'.[14] Her death, on the eve of their planned departure, left the admiral 'in an abyss of emotional distress' in the lonely outpost, he wrote in his memoirs.

'Ah, how about that,' the elderly aristocrat who lived on the third floor said when I brought her the news about our predecessors. 'You see how ignorant I am,' she said with polite irony. She had lived in the building for nearly thirty years. A bland index to 'Requisitioned Vichy', available at the municipal museum (it generously gives equal space to the town's forgotten role during World War I), makes no mention of the Leahys.

Their presence was information that had disappeared. It wasn't that surprising. Perhaps it was risky to acknowledge the former ambassador too concretely; other potentially embarrassing acknowledgements might have to follow, like the fact that there had once been a government there. 'Oh, but that was something very ephemeral,' the president of the Comité France-Amérique said a little anxiously when I recalled the one-time existence of a real American embassy in the town.

Yet there was a memory of the American presence that had persisted. It was a hopeful memory, contiguous with the Americans' latter-day position in Vichy's consciousness as purveyors of escape, and with the vision of them as 'simple' and 'direct' discernible in the memoirs. It was a matter of universal certainty, for instance, that Leahy and Pétain enjoyed close relations. 'You know, Leahy and the Marshal, they were very close,' said another elderly aristocrat I knew, who remembered shaking the diplomat's hand at a reception. 'The rear of his yard bordered that of Dr Ménetrel, Pétain's personal physician. This was very useful for communicating.' Thus reads the text of a speech given to me by a city councillor – intriguing information, except that the city councillor misidentifies Leahy's house.

Leahy was blunt, plainspoken and ignorant of the country to which he had been assigned. He believed that Gaullists were not really followers of General de Gaulle but simply patriots identifying themselves with the ancient French nation, Gaul; months after the suppression of parliament, he was shocked by a Pétain speech in which 'the Marshal was going all out for authoritarian government'; and he considered that 'so far as I know, however, no Jewish houses were searched' under Vichy, apparently unaware that across the park from the embassy, the Commissariat Générale aux Questions Juives, the regime's 'Jewish affairs' agency, was busy registering and despoiling the country's Jews.[15]

He arrived with sympathy for Pétain as a fellow officer. He acknowledged in his memoirs that the Marshal 'asked for me often'. The old man, he said, 'seemed relieved to have somebody to whom he could unburden himself'.[16] But by November 1941, eleven months into his assignment, Leahy was contemptuously calling Pétain 'a jellyfish'.[17]

The idea that admiral and Marshal were actually close was a rose-coloured view of a more tenuous reality. Just as the Marshal apparently found Leahy's presence therapeutic, the town needed, in those years, to believe the two were complicitous, for its own psychological relief. Vichy continued to need this belief: Leahy as the boon companion of Pétain, who redeemed the old Marshal. Still, the former mayor Dr Lacarin acknowledged that he had doubts about this version of the story. 'It was said he had frequent meetings with the Marshal. It's a story that circulated in town. I think it's something we must have hung on to,' he said.

Looking back, these meetings are merely 'a story', though one that had clearly had importance. Dr Lacarin was keeping his distance from it. But there was no distance in the recollection of loss associated with the departure of the Americans in November 1942: the Allies had landed in North Africa, French troops were firing on Americans for the first time since 1799, and Pétain ordered the American diplomats to leave Vichy.

'You know, in '42, when we saw the villa of the embassy closing its shutters, we really had, at that point, the notion . . . we said to ourselves, "We're nothing anymore, the Americans aren't there anymore."' He drew out his words, speaking slowly and sadly. 'We felt as though we were orphans.' The Americans had promised protection, and their presence guaranteed a kind of legitimacy for the town, the regime and Pétain. Without them, the people of Vichy were 'nothing', as vulnerable as children without parents. Sympathy for Pétain certainly hadn't precluded attachment to the Americans; the 'story' of Leahy's frequent meetings with the Marshal was a demonstration. The Americans had been implanted in the middle of Vichy, one hundred yards from the Hôtel du Parc, yet they had not been harsh in their judgement of Pétain.

On occasion, they were obsequious. 'Allow me to express the hope that it will be given to you to watch for a long time still over the destiny of the French nation, in seeing through to the end the noble task you have undertaken,' an embassy official, H. Freeman Matthews, wrote in birthday greetings to Pétain in April 1941. 'Could you one day confide to me the secret of eternal youth? Please accept, *monsieur le maréchal*, the expression of my profound respect and my entire devotion.'[18] The Americans had offered the hope of escape, they had given a kind of benediction to Pétain, and they had gone on to win the war.

I wanted to test the present and past perceptions of the Americans. I wanted to see whether they had been capable of offering the psychological escape hatch from Vichy that was apparent in memoirs and recollections. And after some months in the town's fog, I was keen to see whether the American viewpoint might offer some clarity – might offer, in fact, a sort of escape. What could it have been like to have been one of the rare Americans in Vichy in those years? This viewpoint seemed beyond reach. There were the cables from the embassy, published by the State Department in the early 1960s, and there were Leahy's own memoirs. There were the sixty-two boxes of the embassy's records preserved in the National Archives outside Washington, DC. These are crammed with letters, memoranda, requests for passports, lists of personnel, replies to anxious American bank branch managers, analyses of coal and shipping resources, entreaties to Washington for more typing help, and a plea to the Vichy textile-rationing office that young Jean Corre, 'office boy and porter', who 'finds himself in a precarious position, clothing-wise', be given a voucher for a new suit. You could reconstruct the daily life of the embassy, but you couldn't gain a sense of the passage of time from these boxes. Voices from the early 1940s emerged from them, as faded and dated as an old movie – *Casablanca*, say, made in 1942 and set in Vichy French North Africa. It was difficult to discern what had survived as important through nearly sixty years of intervening life.

Leahy himself was long gone. When he died in July 1959, at eighty-four, having after Vichy served as chief of staff to Roosevelt and to Harry S. Truman, he was a 'virtual recluse' on the seventeenth floor of the Bethesda Naval Hospital.[19] Somerville Pinkney Tuck, the polo-playing bon vivant and first secretary at the embassy, who had given the barman at the Hôtel des Ambassadeurs a bottle of 1848 cognac on the Americans' expulsion in November 1942, had died in 1967 at the American Hospital in Paris, where he maintained one of his three homes, the others being in Geneva and Grosse Pointe, Michigan.[20] The State Department, searching its records, found obituaries for all but three members of the American diplomatic staff in Vichy. Two had been born before the turn of the century. They wouldn't still be around.

There was a third who might be. His name was not unknown to historians. He had been connected, on the periphery, to an initiative nearly unique in American diplomacy during the war, one managed by his former boss, the long-dead Pinkney Tuck. All through the autumn of 1942, Tuck, the chargé d'affaires since Leahy's grief-struck departure, had made desperate efforts to rescue thousands of Jewish children from the French and Germans through visas granted by the State Department.

Tuck was a descendant of Chief Justice John Marshall, and he had been in the foreign service since 1913. He was known for his coolness under pressure, and in communications with the State Department affected a kind of British style: 'I venture to say he is very much the right kind of timber for the service,' Tuck wrote, recommending a young man in August 1942. He wasn't immune to the embassy's latent Pétainism – 'the Marshal is an appealing figure,' he wrote in March of that year – and he was sympathetic to the US consul in Marseille, who complained that a Jew had been proposed for his staff: 'I share your views,' Tuck wrote, before thanking the consul for a shipment of tennis balls. After the war he quit the State Department; an Arabist, he was known to be angry over US recognition of the new state of Israel.[21]

But the cables from 1942 suggest that, late in the Americans' last summer in Vichy, Tuck had become increasingly agitated over a kind of anti-Semitism he had never seen before. His language to Washington was unusually sharp. 'Revolting . . . appalling situation,' he wrote in a telegram on August 26, 'bestial conditions'; on September 11, 'tragic situation', 'desperate'. After a conversation with indifferent officials at the Hôtel du Parc on October 3 about the children the Americans were proposing to save – the State Department was offering five thousand visas – he wrote, 'I had difficulty in restraining my anger.' He ended the meeting by telling President Laval's chief of staff, Jean Jardin, that 'he would do well to consider the effect which a rejection of my government's proposal would produce upon the civilized world.'[22]

The French officials stalled, the Americans were forced out in November, and the visas for the children were never used. Tuck, unlike some French contemporaries – Papon, for instance – had not insisted on his lack of certainty about the ultimate fate of their parents, or even of the children themselves: 'As it appears to be the intention of the Nazi authorities that their deported parents should not survive the treatment they are now undergoing, many of these children may now be considered orphans. To leave them in France is to expose them to constant danger, to the threat of possible Nazi aggression (even against Jewish children),' he had written on September 11.

Less than two months before, the Americans had begun to awaken to the fate of the French Jews. Late on the night of August 7, three weeks after the first large roundup, with Tuck on leave in Switzerland, a telegram had gone to Washington under the signature of a junior diplomat in the Vichy embassy: 'Laval made no mention of any German pressure, but flatly stated that these foreign Jews had always been a problem in France, and that the French government was glad that a change in the German attitude towards them gave France an opportunity to get rid of them.'[23] The cable summarised a conversation that relief workers unconnected with the embassy, American Quakers, had the day before with the head of the government. Along with a cable from Tuck ten days before, it was one of the State Department's earliest indications of the worsening situation of the French Jews.

Robert Paxton and his former student Michael Marrus quote the telegram of August 7, identifying it as coming from 'US diplomat Tyler Thompson'.[24] The name has left a faint trace in memoirs. It makes a fleeting appearance, misspelled, in the *Diaries of Pastor Boegner*. Boegner was a French Protestant leader who also annoyed Laval with his pleas for the Jews. 'Went to see the Thomsons today, of the American embassy,' he wrote on October 25, 1942. 'The departure of the Jewish

children was finally settled Friday in the Tuck–Laval meeting,'
he continued, mistakenly.[25] And it appears, again misspelled, in
the memoirs of the journalist Maurice Martin du Gard:
'Thomsom' intervenes for one of the American reporters in
Vichy. I saw the name on a sheet of onionskin paper given to
me by the grandson of the manager of the Hôtel des
Ambassadeurs. It was a list of all the diplomats staying at the
hotel in January 1942: 'Thompson, U.S., (2).' He had been
there with his wife. A faint outline emerges from these
mentions, that of a confident, socially adept young man.

Tyler Thompson was the third name on the State Department's list. The department's brief biography showed he had
spent all his adult life in the foreign service, starting as a clerk
under President Hoover in the consulate at Cherbourg in 1931,
moving on to Marseille and Paris, returning to Washington
after the war, and finishing in the 1960s as ambassador to two
minor capitals, Reykjavík and Helsinki. His solid career had
not come to the attention of the outside world, his late
postings barely rating a line in the newspapers. By the time of
the great renewal of interest in Vichy, in the mid-1970s, many
of the diplomats who had been there were dead. The historians
were not much interested in living voices anyway (in the 1960s
Paxton had been received in sumptuous Parisian salons by
surviving members of the regime, but there was hardly a trace
of them in his book), and the French journalists who were
writing about Vichy had plenty of elderly men at home to
occupy them.

In the summer of 1998 Tyler Thompson was nearly ninety-
two. One afternoon I phoned him at his home in Maine. The
voice of a very old man answered, lucid but quavering. It was
his first communication with anyone in Vichy in over half a
century. He protested that the span of years made his
testimony unreliable. But then he referred to Pinkney Tuck as
'Kippy'. I decided to go see him.

Last American at Vichy

'THEY'RE ALL dead now,' Tyler Thompson said, chuckling slightly over lunch in the family lodge in Hancock, Maine. There was amusement and perplexity in his voice. He had survived everyone with whom he sat around the bar of the Ambassadeurs: 'Woody' Wallner, 'Sabby' Sabalot, 'Kippy' Tuck, 'Wahwee' and her husband, 'Doug' MacArthur II, the general's nephew and, like himself, third secretary at the US embassy, Vichy. In the narrow confines of the Villa Ica, with its small rooms, he would have got to know them very well. Tyler Thompson's own wife of nearly sixty-seven years, Ruth, who had hated Vichy, had recently died.[26]

When, precisely? 'March,' Thompson said briskly. (Later, he derided President Kennedy's 'mushy sentimentality' for giving a plum ambassadorship to a bereaved diplomat.) It was now a late September Sunday, and there was a dazzling, preternaturally calm view out picture windows onto a small bay and a fir-tree-covered mountain in the distance. Nothing stirred on the water. The scene seemed almost frozen.

'We think it's the greatest view in the world,' Tyler Thompson said, moving determinedly through the light-filled living room. He had a shock of white hair combed straight back, like F. Scott Fitzgerald's in photographs, clear blue eyes, a small fine-featured face, and he used words like 'row' to mean 'fight', 'dandy' to express enthusiasm and 'goon' to designate somebody reprehensible. French words he pronounced with an old-time American-French accent – vowels drawn out, hard consonants and the first syllables emphasized: 'PAY-tan', 'VEE-shee'. He was dressed in a navy blue sweater and khakis, the retirement uniform of the local gentry.

His late-middle-aged son was about to take his yacht on an extended cruise. From another part of the silent house I heard him call out, 'Well, I'm off, Dad. I'll see you in January.' Tyler Thompson said nothing. The front door closed. A dour-

Maurice Papon, a young civil servant, looks at the camera and at Charles de Gaulle as the general addresses newly liberated Bordeaux, September 1, 1944. Fifty-three years later Papon returned to Bordeaux to stand trial for his role in the deportation of the town's Jews. © *AFP / STF*

Maurice Papon, minister of the budget between 1978 and 1981, leaving the Élysée Palace, seat of the French presidency. © *J. Cuinières–Viollet*

Vichy, April 1941. Marshal Pétain takes his morning stroll with Dr Ménétrel, his personal physician and secretary. At the far left, a poster for the *révolution nationale* is visible. © *LAPI–Viollet*

Vichy. Marshal Pétain in front of the Hôtel du Parc, headquarters of the wartime French government, after greeting a contingent from the Légion Française des Combattants, a veterans' group. M. Edier, a member of the group the author met in Vichy, is in the foreground, wearing a beret and standing at attention at the pavement's edge. *Ville de Vichy, Médiathèque Municipale. Reproduction interdite.*

Vichy, spring 1944. The crowd welcomes Pétain, who is returning to the Hôtel du Parc after a tour in northern France. *Photo Raymond Brajou. Ville de Vichy, Médiathèque Municipale. Reproduction interdite.*

Balustrade at the former Hôtel du Parc, Vichy, 1999. *Sharon Stallworth Nossiter*

American Embassy, Vichy

Tom Cassady T.T. Ted Curtis Kay Tuck Woody Wallner

Vichy, September 1941–November 1942. From the photo album of Tyler Thompson, third secretary, US embassy, Vichy. Above and below, Thompson with embassy colleagues. *Courtesy Tyler Thompson*

Hotel des Ambassadeurs

Sabby Sablot T.T. Kippy Tuck

sur le banc du Marechal

velo-taxis

Henri Sjöberg's Vichy. An official makes nocturnal use of his office at the Hôtel du Parc. M. Sjöberg said his satiric drawings of Vichy bureaucrats in *Hors-Saison à Vichy* (Vichy in the Off-Season) were made from his observations of life there. *Courtesy Henri Sjöberg*

A postcard from the 1960s of the former Algeria Hotel in Vichy, which housed the Commissariat Générale aux Questions Juives, the government's agency for Jewish affairs. Afterward, the hotel's name was changed to the Carnot. *Courtesy Henri Maingonat*

Xavier Vallat, the first chief of the Commissariat Générale aux Questions Juives, after his release from prison in the early 1950s. Vallat worked at the Algeria Hotel during the war. *Courtesy Les Amis de Xavier Vallat, Association Loi de 1901*

Tulle, June 9, 2000. The fifty-sixth anniversary of the hangings carried out in Tulle by the Das Reich division of the SS. Charles Godillon and some of his colleagues were hanged from the balcony of this house; each garland represents a victim. *Adam Nossiter*

The priest Jean Espinasse after the war. He accompanied the victims of Tulle as they were led to the town's balconies and lampposts to be hanged, and received last notes to their families. *Courtesy M. and Mme Georges Espinasse*

Two of the ninety-nine men hanged in Tulle on June 9, 1944

Left: Raymond Lesouëf, age forty, married with two children. He ran a workshop that made wood-burning engines. The Germans knocked on his door at 9:30 A.M. *Courtesy* Peuple et Culture, *Tulle / Mme S. Sainmont*

Below: André-Fernand Gamblin, age twenty-two, married with one child. He was an accountant at a local factory. At 11 A.M., when the Germans rounded him up, he was searching for milk for his baby daughter. *Courtesy* Peuple et Culture, *Tulle / Mme M. Gamblin*

looking dark-haired young man poked his head in. 'He's the latest addition to the family,' the old diplomat said. 'He married one of the granddaughters. I can't remember which one.'

Up in his office, a wood-panelled room under the eaves of the clapboard house, I asked him if he had ever been back to Vichy. 'Noooo,' he said, chuckling. The idea struck him as silly. 'No interest in it. Ha.' I showed him a photograph I had recently taken of the rose-coloured stucco Villa Ica. 'It almost looks . . . except there's no flag on it . . . the embassy building, Chancery building. But that's not it, because . . . no, I don't recognise that.'

His wife had carried away a strong image, albeit negative ('As a watering place it was very grey and unattractive'). But to Tyler Thompson, Vichy was simply a place where he had once worked. It had not stayed in his memory, for instance, as a resort town in the middle of France where a government and embassies had once strangely planted themselves. 'There should be a flag on it. That's why I didn't recognise it,' he said. In a diplomatic career stretching over nearly forty years, it had been one episode, since piled under a thickening accretion of others. On the walls of his modest office were pictures of two presidents under whom he had served, Johnson and Nixon, and little pennants, gifts from the Finnish cities he had visited as ambassador.

Posted to Paris three years before the war, he and his wife had lived and played tennis among a wide circle of friends – smartly dressed, elegant people, judging by the photographs he had kept, some of them with titles. In 1940 he watched the Germans march in, seeing heavy artillery drawn by horses. 'I could not bee-leeve my *eyes*,' he said, drawing out the words to indicate his old astonishment, just as he had, perhaps, on first telling the story.

He stayed in occupied Paris until the Germans ordered the remaining American diplomats to leave in May 1941; his name appears at the end of a *New York Times* dispatch that month, on a back page of the Sunday paper. At the German embassy his contact had been the keen young political officer Ernst Achenbach. Tyler Thompson saw this 'German Nazi,' as he described him, socially; Achenbach's wife was American. 'At one dinner party Mrs Achenbach turned to me and said, "Do you know where I can get some Quaker Oats for my baby?" And I said maybe we had some left at the house.' And so at the next dinner he left some packages of Quaker Oats at Mrs Achenbach's place.

Her husband, Herr Achenbach, was tall and energetic, 'less German-looking than Scandinavian' Du Moulin de Labarthète remembered, 'fairly stylish, full of courtesy,' nearly to the point of 'obsequiousness', with 'a look that could be caressing, or cold'.[27] After the war, Achenbach recycled himself as a liberal deputy in the Bundestag, getting himself appointed the West German government's representative to the European Commission in Brussels, in 1970. But then the Nazi hunters Serge and Beate Klarsfeld pointed out that he had once unleashed the SS in roundups of French Jews, ending his career. 'As a preliminary reprisal measure, it is intended to arrest two thousand Jews and deport them to the east,' Achenbach had written Berlin from Paris in 1943, in one of the telegrams that were later to prove troublesome.[28]

I mentioned some of this history to Tyler Thompson. 'That's all news to me,' he said. In his own dealings with Achenbach, 'I have nothing but a feeling that he behaved perfectly correctly, and as a proper good German, too.' He chuckled.

At Vichy, after the Allied invasion of North Africa in November 1942, Tuck had left him behind, with a junior officer named Keeler Faus as an assistant, to close up the embassy. Thompson was in his office on the ground floor of the Villa Ica when German officers entered to ransack it. One 'goon had a machine gun pointed in my stomach, which is not the way diplomats are supposed to earn their living,' he remembered with good humour. 'Jean, call the Swiss embassy,' Thompson had said to the 'office boy', Jean Corre, who was at the switchboard that day.[29] But it was too late. The Germans had already snatched the phone from Corre's hand.

Tyler Thompson had been the last ranking American diplomat in Vichy. After the embassy was closed down, he and the others were taken into custody – the French government had refused the Americans permission to travel by train to the Spanish frontier – then handed over to the Germans at Lourdes, in the Pyrenees.[30] They were shut up in a hotel in yet another spa town, Baden-Baden. To the bemusement of the locals, they played softball to while away the time, right in the middle of Nazi Germany (eventually they got 'proper' balls and bats through the Red Cross). Thompson didn't return home until the spring of 1944, to meet a four-year-old daughter he had never seen. 'I didn't know what to do,' he said. 'We met on the station platform in Elmira, New York. And I didn't know what to do. But in France we always shook hands. So I shook hands with her!' He laughed uproariously.

After the war he returned to the Paris embassy. 'We tried to pick up the threads, but that wasn't possible.' One day he called up an old friend, a Frenchman, and suggested getting together. 'Oh, you don't want to see us,' the friend replied bitterly. 'We were "collaborators".' Recalling a ceremony at the Invalides for two friends killed in the Resistance, Thompson wept, fifty-three years later.

In the wartime capital, he had been a young man, mostly an administrator amid what Admiral Leahy called the 'period furniture' in the improvised embassy. Moving up and down the narrow iron staircase, with its finely worked art deco balustrade, he oversaw day-to-day operations and kept the Villa Ica stocked with supplies. The Americans, trying to stay warm, plugged in electric radiators, overloading the circuits, destroying the wiring. Every so often, Thompson met with the government's protocol people, talking to them in French, now fluent from the ten years he had spent in the country.

Like all the others, he 'went to every bar in Vichy', made the wearying round of receptions 'too many dinners, too many parties', and gathered horse chestnuts in the mountains with his wife. 'All these diplomats were bored to death,' wrote M. Maes, the general manager of the Ambassadeurs. 'So they organised parties in their rooms, where they danced and drank half the night, making a hell of a racket.' The Cuban ambassador, Señor Guerra, relieved his boredom by sleeping half the day; extraordinarily, when the Allies invaded North Africa, he was already out of his room by 8 A.M., prompting M. Maes to insert an exclamation mark into his narrative. 'Most of them are herded together in the dreary Hôtel des Ambassadeurs where their chief preoccupation consists in arrangements for a bigger and better "black market",' Pinkney Tuck wrote of the Latin Americans.[31]

For the bored local gentry, the presence of so many sophisticated foreigners was a boon. M. des Ligneries, an elderly aristocrat who regretted the treatment Marshal Pétain received after the war, would cycle twenty-five miles in from the family estate just to attend the diplomats' parties. 'They lived very luxuriously!' he protested, impeccable in his plaid jacket, vest and corduroys. A *Bottin mondain*, the French social register, lay on the table next to him. He was disturbed by the idea that men like Tyler Thompson had wearied of the social life. 'And one didn't eat so badly in those years, after all,' said M. des Ligneries, who was proud that the only person executed at St Pourçain during the Terror of 1793 was an ancestor of his.

M. Maes distinguishes between the 'jokesters' – mostly the Latin American diplomats – and those who were 'serious'. Photographs taken by Ruth Thompson from her Ambassadeurs days are unimpeachably domestic, suggesting the couple would have been in the second group. She snapped their cat,

Monkey, perched on a bookcase next to a flower pot. Her husband, in fact, had been 'delighted' at his Vichy posting, even if the earnest, dark-haired Doug MacArthur, his contemporary, was assigned the sensitive political questions at the embassy. Still, Tyler Thompson felt he was 'back in the middle of things' after a few months of rustication in Switzerland. In the boxes at the National Archives there are hints of how he spent his days: the many letters he wrote to Americans stranded in France inquiring about passports, and the occasional dry political report, in which the young diplomat is careful not to venture his own opinion – in contrast to the reports of MacArthur.

I tried to picture the young Princeton alumnus, serious and somewhat distant as he appears in photographs then, with close-cropped bushy hair, three-piece suit and wire-rimmed glasses, navigating through the heartland of the flowering Pétain personality cult. He was one of the few Americans ever to be in close proximity to it. Soon after his assignment to Vichy, and shortly before his arrival there, late in August 1941, twenty thousand members of the Marshal's militant veterans' group, the Légion Française des Combattants, had crowded into the municipal stadium for a thunderous torch-lighting ceremony and a speech by the chief of state, all of it under a giant arch proclaiming *'Travail, Famille, Patrie.'* Then, in late December 1941 a thousand students had flooded into Vichy to greet the Marshal; in February 1942 a 'massed crowd' waited for him in front of city hall; in April 250 students acclaimed him in front of the World War I monument, a few hundred yards from the US embassy, to be given the advice, 'Always and everywhere, think French!'; and in May, at a sports rally at the stadium, thousands filled the stands to cheer the old soldier.

I asked Thompson if a certain prominent member of the regime had maintained a Pétainist line in conversation with him.

He scoffed. 'There was no "Pétainist line",' he said. 'I don't think that existed.'

Puzzled, I asked him, 'So what about this famous *révolution nationale?*' He chuckled. 'That was . . . I don't really know how to answer that. Other than, that was a general political movement on the part of the whole French government in Vichy. This wasn't a Pétainist deal, this was basically a Laval-and-the-whole-government-backed deal, rather than Pétain.'

The first edition of Robert Paxton's book about the Vichy regime lay on his desk. I asked him what he thought of it. 'Too much detail,' he said. He saw 'Vichy' through State Department lenses, circa 1942, as 'a government that was hostile to everything we were trying to do' – an enemy of American policy, of course, but not one necessarily dominated by the fascistic, anti-Semitic elements that haunt the contemporary consciousness.

A snapshot in Tyler Thompson's photo album shows the young diplomat, in blazer and khakis, sprawled on a hillock in the countryside near Vichy. Underneath, the photo, someone has scrawled 'Near *"le banc du Maréchal"*.' On that sunny day, he had been at a high place of the Pétain cult. The granite bench, or *banc*, was crafted by villagers, incised with the seven-star symbol of the Marshal's baton, and placed in a spot with sweeping views over the mountains of the Forez, the leader's favourite place for a Sunday stroll. The Resistance blew up the bench in 1944. ('Stupid!' said the wife of Jean Corre, who lives barely a hundred yards away. One day half a century ago the Marshal had taken her tiny hand there.)

An elderly couple I went to see one afternoon in an immense apartment in Paris, M. and Mme de Boissieu, had known Tyler and Ruth Thompson well in those years in Vichy, had been perhaps their closest friends. They had lived opposite the American ambassador's residence on the avenue Thermale, in a seedy hotel long since demolished, and Mme de Boissieu had been invited to tea several times by Mrs Leahy. She was, in all likelihood, the 'girl spy' who came 'from a good family' mentioned by Admiral Leahy in his memoirs, in his only approving reference to the Resistance.[32]

'One day, I remember, there was, outside the windows, a ceremony with Pétain, a presenting of arms,' Mme de Boissieu began, recalling a morning nearly sixty years before that had been spent with the Thompsons, in their rooms overlooking Vichy's war memorial at the Ambassadeurs. 'They were at the window, and I was at the back of the room,' Mme de Boissieu said. 'And I remember Ruth said to me, "Aren't you going to come watch?" And I said, "Out of the question!"'

She and her husband, then a low-level employee in the regime's Food Supply Ministry, were already serving as couriers in the Resistance. This clandestine activity didn't necessarily recommend them to their American friends. 'From the beginning of our encounters, we were aware, Michel and myself, of their scepticism toward the Resistance,' Mme de Boissieu wrote in an unpublished memoir some years ago. 'Their sympathy was for the Vichy government, for the fresh-faced, made-up Marshal, whose car one often saw in the streets.' The de Boissieus tried to bring the Thompson couple into contact with as many Resistance leaders as possible, but it was an uphill struggle. 'For them, the Marshal represented France,' Mme de Boissieu wrote.[33]

Her husband, a gentle retired Finance Ministry official, recalled with affection the 'extreme simplicity' of Tyler and Ruth Thompson. 'You know, for them, Vichy was, finally, the establishment,' he said. 'It was the France that endured. And you know, behind all of our adventures, there might have been – communism.'

His wife was less indulgent. I mentioned that the American government's Vichy policy had been sharply questioned back in the United States. She quickly cut in: 'For us, very questionable. Very questionable!'

In one of the opening scenes of *Casablanca*, first shown two weeks after the Allied landings in North Africa, a would-be refugee is shot by the French police. He falls to the ground under a giant poster of Marshal Pétain, sinister and nearly sneering, and the camera lingers over this disturbing visage for a brief moment. For wartime American public opinion, Vichy was evil. In May 1941, the *New York Post* columnist Samuel Grafton had said the State Department seemed 'virginal, ignorant and naïve' in its embrace of Pétain. Freda Kirchwey, in *The Nation*, wrote of 'the dismal farce of America's relations with Vichy', adding for good measure that 'the whole relationship has been a fraud, somewhat perverse, totally impotent.'[34] In the same journal, Waverly Root, later my father's irascible colleague in the *Washington Post*'s Paris bureau, said that relations with Vichy were 'a State Department policy directly in the appeasement tradition of Neville Chamberlain'. Liberal groups – the Committee to Defend America, Fight for Freedom, Inc., the Union for Democratic Action – lobbied for a break in relations.[35]

So were the people back home right to complain that the embassy had given legitimacy to Pétain's government? 'To us, no,' Tyler Thompson said equably. 'From the point of view of legitimacy, all the parliamentary approvals and actions had set up that government in Vichy.' But, he conceded, 'that it acted under the pressures and influences of the Germans was clear.'

We talked about the reasons he and the others had been in Vichy. 'What the Germans were up to, was one; two, what Vichy was doing to help the Germans,' he said. 'And then, above all, to backstop Murphy in his preparations for the landings in North Africa,' he said, referring to the American diplomat Robert Murphy. In newly-liberated North Africa, Murphy went on to install men who had served Marshal Pétain, reproaching an Office of Strategic Services agent who was bothered by this policy: 'Art, old fellow, if you have nothing better to do in Africa than to worry about those Jews and Communists who helped us, why don't you just go home?'

The journalist I. F. Stone called Murphy 'among the principal architects of our pro-Vichy policy'.[36] Tyler Thompson said, 'I consider Bob Murphy one of the great American diplomats.' (With pleased regularity, French television repeats the surprising newsreel footage of Murphy, Eisenhower and General Mark Clark standing around in amicable company with top Vichy officials immediately after the North Africa landings.)

I showed Thompson the cable about the Jews he had signed. 'This telegram would have been drafted by the political section,' he said. He had no memory of it. Were you and the others in the embassy aware of what was happening to the Jews? 'Not really,' he said, a note of pain creeping into his voice. 'And I often asked myself that question.' He paused. 'It was only after internment that we started to become aware of German atrocities against the Jews.' He had worked alongside Pinkney Tuck in the tiny embassy, and gone bicycling with him and the others on Sundays. But the unusual initiative that had preoccupied Tuck through the fall of 1942 had left no trace.

The boxes of files at the National Archives shade this outline. Tyler Thompson saw the reports on roundups of Jews that flowed into the Vichy embassy that summer. His initials – 'TT', in bold red pencil – are clearly marked in the right-hand corners of the documents, including one vivid report describing the infamous Vélodrome d'Hiver roundup in Paris, in which nearly thirteen thousand men, women and children were taken. In his same red pencil he had underlined a vigorous letter from a French priest indignant over the 'scandalous facts' concerning the treatment of Jews in unoccupied France. 'There have been odious scenes, of which I spare you the details,' the priest wrote, and Thompson underlined those words. The young diplomat was even taken to task by the State Department for having sent out from the embassy a cable written by one of the American relief workers describing mass deportations from southern France. 'It is not apparent what clearly recognisable American interest . . . is involved in this message,' the department had sternly cabled back.[37]

And yet the work that had survived in his memory took place almost by accident, in frivolous settings. He recalled meeting M. de Boissieu at a cocktail party, and counted as his greatest contribution a flattering invitation to 'a delicious meal' at a black-market restaurant with du Moulin de Labarthète, Pétain's top civilian aide. The ironic aristocrat passed on a warning to be relayed to Robert Murphy, then reconnoitering the North Africa landings. 'He's a great guy,' Thompson said, as if du Moulin, who died at the age of forty-eight in 1948, were still alive.

He had made a big impression on Tyler Thompson. For decades du Moulin's sharp-tongued memoirs have been a principal conduit into the memory of the regime. He recorded strange details that escaped others: the huge pile of cold cuts on the day Pétain met Hitler, a hallucinatory game of billiards in a deserted prefecture that night. His retrospective portrait of his master Pétain is surprisingly dipped in acid – though du Moulin was himself an architect of the *révolution nationale*. Of all the regime's memoirists he was the only one to have sensed its rapid disassociation from the real – of Pétain, for instance, he says, 'physical ugliness exasperated him.' Still, he omits important details, like his participation in the violent anti-parliamentary riots of February 6, 1934, or his presidency of the fascistic Action Française in the Sixteenth Arrondissement of Paris before the war, or the sentiments of a letter turned up by Paxton and Marrus in which he congratulates a police official for his 'firm execution' in a roundup of Jews.[38]

A week after leaving Vichy for good, Tyler Thompson typed a report recounting the last days of the embassy. With precision and meticulous detachment he documented his attempts to counter the exactions of the Germans, including their seizure of his tennis balls and cigarettes. He carefully notes that 'six out of thirty cartons were missing' by the time they were finished, though the tennis balls were intact.

'At 9 P.M. I rang at the Embassy and knocked on the glass door but without result,' he wrote. 'After considerable more ringing and knocking finally I heard hobnailed boots on the hard surface of the second floor. Rounding the head of the stairs the person slipped and his progress downstairs was punctuated by dull thuds as he hit each step. A red-faced German soldier with food in his mouth who had obviously been drinking opened the door.' Here the diplomat was observing himself from a distance. Focusing on the disarray of his subject, he finds it droll in his Yankee way. Why else would he record for State Department officials the precise sound the German soldier made as he tumbled down the stairs, or the colour of the soldier's face as he greeted him?

Looking back, Tyler Thompson considered the young man he had been in those years with amused indulgence. He talked about having been 'busy', using the word several times. Like many American civilians who worked during that era, he saw his daily routine as part of 'the war effort', I asked him what he did for diversion. 'Tennis,' he said. 'And black-market restaurants.' ('Monday, March 30, 1942,' I read in the Vichy diary of his former colleague Keeler Faus. 'Played tennis with Thompson, beat him two out of three sets, 3–6, 7–5, 6–1.')[39] He laughed quietly. 'I don't really know why I was so busy. If I kept a list of my activities on any day it would be very long, but I don't know what would be on it.' He laughed harder. I asked him whether he had been in charge of ordering supplies. 'Oh yeah, and whiskey! I don't know how we did that, but the whiskey came.'

In his affable company that Sunday, I had had the privilege of a window on a discrete moment, frozen in time and unaffected by what came after in the town or the country. Or had I? Was this simply a charming old man's unsteady memory? I recalled his anxious warning before I arrived. 'I hope you won't be disappointed,' he had said. And yet he had remembered enough to suggest that the moment was partly recovered. I thought of du Moulin de Labarthète's single mention of Thompson: 'The Thompson and MacArthur households played host to perfection.'[40] So perhaps the Vichy of Tyler Thompson – black-market restaurants, tennis, whiskey – as he had conjured it up for me, reflected a certain reality after all. This Vichy had conceivably existed. It was easy to see why its reflection, bouncing off the genial and optimistic Americans, had offered a kind of salve across the decades. This was a 'Vichy' more or less oblivious to the *révolution nationale* and the Commissariat Générale aux Questions Juives. It was the Vichy of Admiral Leahy ('a very brilliant and distinguished American,' said Thompson). It was a Vichy that had escaped 'Vichy', and in that sense it had been one more gratefully accepted illusion – one that had been transmitted over time.

8

Vichy and the Jews

Why History is Blocked in Vichy

IN VICHY, everything had the potential to be banal. You could say this was the town's way of expressing itself. The low, light-coloured buildings, the slow rhythms of the inhabitants, the predominantly grey sky: it could all be considered either soothing – 'he wasn't the same as in Paris,' Simenon writes about his hero, Inspector Maigret, who had come to take the waters, 'his comportment had become gentler, the features of his face less sharp' – or exasperating. Ruth Thompson, a handsome, forthright woman, called it 'the dreariest place I have ever been, in every way'. The refugee rescuer Varian Fry, another American who had passed through during the war (to be rudely rebuffed by Tyler Thompson's colleagues), called it 'one of the dullest watering spots imaginable'.[1]

This capacity for the unemphatic could be considered a boon for the locals. It had the effect of mitigating some preoccupations – shrouding once notorious buildings, for example, veiling relations with the past. Lulled by Vichy's gentility, it took me some time to realize which elements were the most pressing to the people living there. The problem of living with the past was crystallised by this aspect of it, and understandably so. The 'Vichy' of the Americans, of Tyler Thompson, was of no help. It could offer only a false promise of escape. At century's end, with the focus on a question that had been of secondary importance to Ambassador William Leahy, there was no escaping this most unpleasant aspect of the past. Living with it would have to be resolved around this point.

I became aware of a low rumble of resentment. Vichy was expressing itself, quietly but vehemently, on the subject that preoccupied me: the precise location of the centre of pain in its relation with the past. These remarks were often couched in polite terms. They were presented as simple statements of fact by people of courtesy who were, or at least seemed to be, well disposed toward me. I wasn't always immediately aware of their possible significance.

At the country home of a man who had been an important figure in local politics after the war, I wondered about the forgotten years during it. 'But we're not allowed to talk about any of that,' the man said. 'It's the Israelites. They don't want any commemorations of the period.' He had forgotten that the one (hidden) plaque, at the Hôtel du Parc, had been placed there by Serge Klarsfeld. He quickly added, 'Don't get us wrong, we have plenty of Jews who are friends.' Dr Lacarin, the old former mayor, bemoaning the stigma attached to his town, said, 'In national, even international opinion, there has been a lumping together that I would say has been sharpened by the media. Particularly, of course, by way of the horrors of the concentration camps. And more particularly concerning the Israelites. And it's something we can understand. But we cannot accept it. You'll agree, I'm sure.' A museum in the town, unfortunately, wouldn't be possible. 'Notably in relation to the Israelites, it would be badly received, whatever *our* sentiment might be,' the polite old gentleman said.

'But there was a Jewish problem before the war!' the son of one of the Vichy cabinet ministers said to me. 'The Jews had gone too far.' We were speaking in the musty unlighted family lodge, a sort of elongated brick summer cottage in ancient forests north of Vichy. He venerated the memory of his father and the Marshal, and was quietly bitter about history's judgement on both. After Pétain's conviction in 1945, 'I went into a corner and cried,' he said. He had had a distinguished career, far from politics and Vichy, but his library was crammed with books sympathetic to the long-gone regime, many scribbled in with agitated commentaries. 'Of course I wouldn't dream of talking about the Marshal like this with certain people, who are nonetheless my friends,' he said shyly, demanding that his own name not be used. His father, a favourite of Pétain, had himself been convicted by the High Court of Justice in 1946. He was now totally forgotten. The minister's son showed me photographs of his father taken during the 1950s, after his release from prison: he looked pale and distant. The son, not distant at all, seemed boyish for all his eighty-odd years, a characteristic accentuated by his overwhelming filial devotion. He was anxious for me to understand the truth – and the truth, in his telling, had to begin with the Jews. He had brought it up at the start of our discussion, unprompted by me. 'The anti-Jewish laws? Why, why? Because there was something there . . .'

It was as if all the opprobrium that attached to the regime, and thus to the town, came from the Jews – what had happened to them and their complaints about it. If not for the Jews, it might be possible to reach a sort of understanding with the past, even celebrate it in some modest way. The Jews had blocked a healthy relationship with history. That the Vichy government was execrated by a good many Frenchmen who were indifferent to its anti-Semitism didn't seem to matter. In Vichy, as elsewhere, the Jews were simply a source of irritation.

There was no particular reserve about expressing it. M. des Ligneries threw up his manicured hands in frustration: 'The Jews! But there's too much talk of them! And they make such a fuss. Believe me, we didn't talk about Jews in those days,' he said. 'As for myself, I've got Jewish friends, good friends,' M.

Edier, the former *legionnaire*, said. 'People who are not all involved in politics, really good people. People who don't have the Jewish spirit, but who are like us, sporting, *bon vivants*.' A cultivated antiquarian of the war generation said angrily, 'They weren't as hunted down as people say. I never saw the yellow star in the southern zone.' In fact, the yellow star was never imposed on Jews in the southern, or unoccupied, zone.

These suggestions of annoyance were all the more striking in that the Jews were inconspicuous in the town. The modest art deco synagogue, tucked into an alleyway, was invisible from the street. The president of the small Jewish community, audibly uneasy when I called, put me off, then 'forgot' after we agreed on a meeting. After synagogue services one day, a man who works for a French computer maker said, 'Eighty per cent of the people in Vichy are anti-Semites.' The statement was impossible to verify, except perhaps through the calm, matter-of-fact tone in which it was delivered. It was the same tone adopted by several other Jews, solid members of the establishment, in speaking of their fellow citizens. 'You just have to make do with it,' said Max Seror, a successful businessman whose ascendancy to the local Rotary Club had created a stir. Bemused, he enumerated the slights he had endured over the years.

At a dinner in the country one night, the Papon trial came up. 'That was just something to please the Jews,' said the daughter of a local aristocrat, a count who was accorded great deference in the region. She raised horses; her family had produced France's kings (even the egalitarian Socialist former deputy from Vichy, M. Belorgey, paid them court). She went on to explain why, as she put it, 'all we ever hear about' is 'what happened to the Jews.' There had been 'lots of other massacres,' she said. 'It's because the media are all held on a leash by the Jews. The Jews control the newspapers.' The talk turned to my recent encounter with a notorious local anti-

Semite. 'My father is like that,' the count's daughter said with a certain fascinated delectation. 'He just can't stand Jews. It's almost something physical. He's just disgusted by them. I can't explain it.'

After she left, my host, a prominent medical man, described the count as a lovable and impecunious eccentric, on bad financial terms with his daughter. The old aristocrat had had to sell the ancestral château. My host treated the count and members of his dwindling staff for free. In Vichy, he was far from alone in doing this. 'We know he can't pay,' my host said. I asked why people were so accommodating to the count. Sheepishly, he said, 'It makes us feel we are part of history.'

In Vichy there were a number of separate and not necessarily overlapping histories. To my host that night, for instance, it was important that the count bore a resemblance to his ancestor Louis XVI. Some Jews in Vichy would have found it more meaningful to place him in the context of a certain complaisance toward anti-Semitism, stretching back well before the official variety established by the Marshal. The prewar Jewish population was small – perhaps no more than twenty-five families – and exposed.[2] M. Seror, for example, recalled a child's fear of the rowdies who had trolled down the rue Montaret in downtown Vichy before the war, yelling 'Death to the Jews!' and terrorising shopkeepers like his father. Had the people of Vichy been favourable to these hooligans? Carefully, he replied, 'In the majority, I would have to say they were favourable.'

This complaisance seemed to be simply a phase of the resentment toward Jews that was, after all, never far below the surface. In fact, the mere mention of Jews was often accompanied by some expression of dissatisfaction with them. I began to wonder what the practical consequences of this sentiment might be for Vichy's relationship with the past. If Jews were the essence of the problem, what might be the solution?

In this respect M. Seror proved to be a valuable guide, without exactly setting out to be one. An unsentimental retired businessman, he ruefully remembered himself as a schoolboy in short pants singing '*Maréchal, nous voilà!*' in front of the Parc, along with everyone else. And he realized that the outbursts recalled from his childhood before the war hardly distinguished Vichy from other 'bourgeois towns', as he put it.

On the other hand, he had a keen eye for Vichy's singularities. He was one of the few people to sense that its bland façades might reflect something other than innocence – one of the few to remember clearly, for instance, seeing a government sign on one of the hotels. It was a sign he couldn't fail to spot every day, since it was affixed to a hotel just up the street from his family's house. Even as a young teenager he had a feeling that this sign was a useful, if disquieting, reminder. Sooner or later, he and the remaining members of his family, Sephardic Jews from Salonika, had best heed its undeclared warning.

'I wouldn't say it frightened us,' M. Seror said, 'but it reinforced us, in a sense,' he said. 'It meant that we were living in an anti-Semitic state, and we had every chance – hah, every chance, quote-unquote – of winding up arrested, or in prison, or deported.'

The Seror family's neighbour was the Algeria Hotel. A sign by the big swinging wooden doors identified it as the headquarters of the Commissariat Générale aux Questions Juives, a grotesque unconscious symmetry arising from the name of the hotel, its new function, and the regime's designation of the Jew as other, oriental, foreign. The Anglicized spelling and word order (in French it would have been 'Hôtel d'Algérie') implied modernity, an up-to-dateness not belied by the block-like functionality of the building's appearance. Directly opposite the Algeria Hotel, on the Boulevard Carnot, is the Villa Tunisienne, the most Moorish of the town's private residences, a fantasy of pseudo-oriental arches and blue and yellow tiles, topped by a squat shingled dome.

The perfect anonymity of the Algeria, by contrast, was intriguing. What clues might it hold about the town's relationship to the Jews and, by extension, to its past? If the building had at one time reinforced the apprehensions of a Jewish schoolboy, what could its desuetude today say about these relationships? It was now part of the town's unremarkable fabric. This in itself seemed promising.

After the war, the hotel's name had been changed to the less evocative Carnot. Although somebody had made a crude attempt to fill the letters in, you can still make out, on the side, above the heavy concrete mullions dividing the windows of the former restaurant, the word 'Algeria' etched in 1920s-style lettering. In the unlit lobby of the four-storey hotel, abandoned for the past eight years, only piles of trash are visible through the plate-glass door. Squatters have made it their intermittent residence. Halfhearted straggly graffiti is scrawled on the façade; the blue paint on the iron shutters has faded to an indeterminate grey. The ex-hotel is one of the more neglected in Vichy: in the summer of 1998 the owner received notice that the cornice under the roof and the outside window mouldings were threatening to crumble and fall onto pedestrians below.[3]

M. Bardiaux, the television repairman, had grown up in his own family's hotel in Vichy (it also had housed government bureaucrats, but he couldn't remember the agency they worked for). He had an intimate knowledge of the town's hotel hierarchy in former days. I asked him where the Algeria had stood in this ranking.

'It was what you would call a one-star hotel,' M. Bardiaux said. 'It was a one-star.' Chuckling, he added, 'Like the *étoile juive*.' He pointed to a spot on his breast where Jews had been forced to wear the yellow star.

Actually, the Algeria was officially classified as a two-star hotel, but that would have spoiled M. Bardiaux's little joke.

The Algeria Hotel

THE JOLLY PASTRY shop owner accosted me one day on the pavement. He was excited; he had a tip. 'Monsieur Nossiter, Monsieur Nossiter, did you know that the old Algeria Hotel, boulevard Carnot, was once the Commissariat Générale aux Questions Juives? I heard it on TV, from a lawyer. He's trying to find out the truth.'

In a town of little-known facts, the identity of the Algeria Hotel was one of the lesser known. The building did not figure in the seasonal walks organised by the tourist bureau. In the office of Vichy's consulting architect one day, I mentioned that the Algeria Hotel had been the headquarters of the regime's anti-Jewish agency. 'Ah, I didn't know,' he said politely. For a really superior evocation of those years, he recommended that I visit the Hôtel du Portugal and its neighbours. 'Very few people in Vichy know about this,' said Mlle Gonnat, the grand-daughter of the *résistant* René Gonnat. The ignorance was pervasive, extending even to those who had once worked there. I wondered if it might have something to do with what had occurred in the building.

'Look, personally I didn't have the time to find out what they did,' said Mlle Debarnot, who had been an eighteen-year-old typist at the Commissariat. 'I didn't have any idea about what was going on there, absolutely not.' She sounded impatient. Like others looking for a job at the Commissariat, she would have filled out a detailed application, with questions like 'Is or was your grandmother of the Jewish race?'

Her address as it appears in the Commissariat's old records is the same as it is in the telephone book today, barely a half-mile from the Algeria Hotel. 'They gave us things to type, and that was it. Look, I don't have a single memory of it.' She had to get off the phone.

I telephoned Mme Massiani, whose family had owned the building and leased it to the hotelkeeper. She herself had spent the war years as a child in a small village near Vichy. Ownership of the building had long since passed to her.

'The Commissariat Générale aux Questions Juives? You're telling me something I didn't know,' she said coolly. The conversation shifted. She said, 'There's a very powerful Jewish lobby in France, you know.'

Despite her ignorance of the property's wartime function, Mme Massiani had other memories of that period, when the Jews were not quite so 'powerful'. She remembered, for instance, that 'the days when the Jews were arrested, we said, "*Ouf!*"' ('Whew!') She explained, 'The black car – we knew right away whether it was for neighbourhood folk or for the Jews.'

What exactly had occurred at the Algeria? The black car that came for the Jews would not have been dispatched from Mme Massiani's family property. Potentially messy police functions were performed in other offices; the Algeria had been a world of intense paperwork and bureaucratic routine. On September 25, 1941, the head of the Service de l'Aryanisation Économique, the 'economic Aryanisation' division of the Commissariat, sent a note to his boss, the agency's head, like him lodged at the hotel: 'From certain reports that are reaching us from the regional directors, it seems that, in spite of the statutes now in force, numerous Jews continue to work in professions forbidden to them – notably in banking, and with the connivance of benevolent Aryans. It is apparent that, in this context, the goal foreseen by the legislation cannot be achieved unless Jews are deliberately excluded from any and every financial enterprise.'[4]

The bureaucrats in the new agency at the Algeria were meticulous. In business for only six months when this note was written, they had already purged Jews from the legal and medical professions, and from the ranks of architects and university students. They had undertaken a detailed census of all Jews in the part of France not occupied by the Germans (later put to effective use by the police). And they had begun the time-consuming, patience-wearing process of divesting all the Jews in France of their property, under the 'Aryanisation' law of July 22, 1941. That also was drafted in the modest four-storey hotel with the faux mansard roof. Of course, months before the Commissariat's sign appeared on the Algeria Hotel, the French government had begun imposing restrictions on the Jews. It began, in fact, some weeks before the German occupiers started their own efforts.

The new agency served to concentrate these efforts. It was established at the insistence of the Germans, but its work was nonetheless French – French-inspired and French-run. The very presence of the Commissariat Générale aux Questions Juives in Vichy, away from the Germans and not in Paris (though eventually most of its functions were transferred to the former capital), was testimony to the government's commitment.

The neat identity cards of the employees, portrait-studio photographs attached, still encumber the agency's personnel files at the Archives Nationales a half-century later. Many of them are smiling young men and women, a few quite stylish in high collars and checked dresses. (In a letter, the director of the archives told me it is forbidden to reproduce any part of these personnel files in any way.) More than a few emerge as small-time crooks, dismissed for passing bad cheques or petty racketeering – the Commissariat always had trouble attracting quality help. Box after box was brought out to me one afternoon, filled with appeals for jobs ('I respectfully request employment as a stenographer-typist in your Vichy offices; I was eighteen in January'), encomiums to promising recruits ('M. Guy de Durand is perfectly honourable, a very cultivated young man of vibrant enthusiasm tempered nonetheless by reason'), even successful requests in the 1960s for government old-age pensions, based on long-ago service at the Commissariat. A circular of July 1941 announced prestigious new hires at the Commissariat: senior staff members from the Council of State and the Chamber of Deputies were coming on board.[5]

Downstairs at the archives building that day, in the men's room, I read the graffiti on a metal divider: 'Arrogant Jews we are going to put you in your place! To the oven! Death to the Jews!'

The Commissariat's employees, in their circulars and memos, never employed such emotive language. To varying degrees, they worked toward achieving the government's goal: the elimination of 'all Jewish influence from the national economy'.[6] Of course they accomplished much more in the hotel on the boulevard Carnot. By first enumerating the Jews, then despoiling them, the bureaucrats smoothed the transition from economic to physical elimination. The Jews made destitute were plucked off all the more easily. In that sense the unremarkable building, its only possibly noteworthy feature the V shape it appears to fill, angling off into two streets, could be considered an essential landmark on the European map of the Jews' destruction (though there is no plaque).

It was a big job, and the enthusiasm of the first chief of the Commissariat Générale aux Questions Juives, the one-eyed, one-legged World War I hero from the mountainous Ardèche region, Xavier Vallat – to him, Jews were a 'parasitical element' – was not enough. Resources and manpower were needed. The agency nearly doubled in size by the end of its first year, its budget growing sixfold in three.[7] Within the modestly proportioned hotel, the submerged bureaucrat clamoured for space and amenities. Vallat was personally shepherding the great project to push French Jews out of civil society. At his trial in December 1947 he was to say that the Jew, imbued with a 'sense of superiority', was 'unassimilable'.

He continued, verbosely explaining his earlier reasoning to Pétain and François Darlan, the ambitious naval officer who succeeded Laval as head of the government and who was even more anxious than his predecessors to close a deal with the

Germans: 'That's why I told the Marshal and Admiral Darlan: "Under these circumstances, it is necessary to take protective measures against a preponderant Jewish influence in certain sectors, where the Jews can, by virtue of this indelible ethnic exclusivity, wind up by taking the most important levers of power, and commanding – notwithstanding that they are, and remain, a foreign element – the very people that gave them asylum."'[8]

His preferred portrait shows a balding, full-faced man with a black monocle, pipe in mouth, wearing a dark suit, features creased, earnestly looking into the camera. Vallat was a serious man, and a pious one. In Vichy, his day began with Mass at 6:30 A.M., to which he would hobble on his wooden leg, large black beret on his head. From church he would hobble to the office. 'His work habits? Nothing systematic, but order, constantly order,' his old secretary remembered, in a vibrant festschrift published for her former boss in the late 1970s. 'Order on his desk, in his papers, in his files.' He kept only a few books on the desk, and one of them was always the Bible.[9]

The microfilmed files tell the story of Vallat's painful adaptation to the constraints of a small hotel in a spa town. In April 1941 he demanded new carpet, in May he pleaded for the allocation of all the rooms in the hotel and a new telephone line (ministries with urgent business having complained about the difficulty of reaching him), in October he wrote that work on the third floor had created twelve new offices (though forty more were needed) and in November he noted gratefully that the hotelkeeper had 'put at my disposition four new rooms, and a bathroom'.[10]

It was intriguing, this intersection of the regime's Jew-hunting agency with quotidian detail. It proved that the Commissariat Générale aux Questions Juives had existed in a specific physical space, in spite of the near-perfect anonymity that space now enjoyed. The agency was not simply a letterhead on microfilm.

I wondered what other such proofs there might be. The archives hint at a mutual regard that might have existed between the hotelkeeper, never named, and Vallat, the royalist anti-Semite and former firebrand parliamentary deputy. In June 1941 he withdrew his request to take over the entire hotel, for the simple reason that since 'the proprietor continues to live in the building, several rooms have been left to his disposition, for his own lodging and that of his family.' This deference on the part of an important bureaucrat to a mere Vichy hotelier was unusual. After the autumn of 1941 the Algeria hardly appears in the files: Xavier Vallat lost his job the following spring, and the Commissariat began its move to Paris, where it was more or less fully reconstituted by the end of 1943. (A plaque was placed on the agency's former headquarters, near the Paris stock exchange, in 1996 at the instigation of a young historian, a specialist of the period, who happened to be working in the building; it is now occupied by the Ministry of Culture.)

At the end, as the Allies were grinding through Normandy, Xavier Vallat was back in Vichy to broadcast the Marshal's word on state radio – and to blame the war on the Jews. The Resistance men found him in his rooms at the Hôtel Majestic on August 27, 1944. They took him to the Hôtel du Portugal and from there to a barracks at the Concours Hippique, 'a sort of wooden box three metres high and two and a half metres long', as he recalled in his diary.[11] He was condemned to ten years' imprisonment by the High Court in Paris in December 1947, but was freed exactly two years later. His cellmate was the Interior Ministry official André Parmentier, who had been the last titular head of the Vichy regime after Pétain left. He was the designated successor, though his reign lasted less than a week. Parmentier remembered later that in prison Vallat was of good cheer, frequently recited the rosary and cooked for the other imprisoned officials, an activity to which he 'brought much care'.[12]

Life at the Algeria went on. In the Vichy city directory for the year of Vallat's conviction, a half-page ad. for the hotel features an ornate crest and the words 'Comfort – Elevator – Exquisite Cuisine.' The telephone number, Vichy 36–98, was the same as it had been during the years of the Commissariat. A Monsieur H. Maingonat is identified as '*Propriétaire – Chef de Cuisine*'. Old Maingonat, as M. Bardiaux called him, was well remembered in town: he had been the youngest hotel-keeper in Vichy when he started in 1937, and the oldest when he left fifty years later. But all trace of him had been lost.

I found M. Maingonat in a small desolate village high in the mountains southwest of Vichy. A few days before, on the phone, he had warned me not to come: the Commissariat Générale aux Questions Juives had really not been at his hotel for very long, after all (actually, in one form or another it was there until the very end), and besides, he remembered little. 'The head is empty,' he said. When I arrived at his house, a strange oversized thatched cottage on a grassy plot on a road to the countryside, all the shutters were closed. M. Maingonat wasn't there.

But from a slight rise in the centre of the village, standing across from an abandoned store advertising 'TSF' – *télégraphic sans fil*, the wartime name for a wireless – I spotted an erect old man. He was more formally dressed than the other inhabitants, as if he had once known a life of some sophistication, and he was walking slowly up the road, out of town.

In his darkened dining room, the former hotelkeeper received me with a mix of unease and bafflement. 'So you're in Vichy?' he asked. I could just as well, he said, have installed myself fifty miles away in Châtelguyon – where a handful of satellite agencies had been located during the war.

He had spent 'forty years in front of the stove', had never touched wine or women, and at Vichy in the thirties had 'worked my head off'. He said, 'I ask you, do I look eighty-seven?'

The war, he said, had hardly changed things. 'People still had to eat, sleep and drink, you know. They managed as best they could. They came to the hotel, we fed them and we gave them a bed. We did our best in any case!'

Had he known Xavier Vallat? 'Xavier Vallat? You better believe it! We had him in the hotel, all right. He was really something special.' M. Maingonat called up Vallat's handicaps from memory – his missing leg and eye. Was he demanding? 'Ah, no!' M. Maingonat was offended. 'There was no reason for him to be, no reason at all.' He had cooked for Vallat and his subordinates, and their successors, every day. 'This thing really worked, let me tell you. If you do it right, there's never a problem. You shouldn't ever gyp people to save a buck,' M. Maingonat said. 'Look, I'm not someone who talks off the top of his head!'

What was Vallat like? 'He was an awfully nice guy. He was a veteran, severely disabled. Actually, we were pretty close,' M. Maingonat said. 'I've seen some clients come and go, let me tell you.' And Vallat? 'It's true that he stayed for a good little bit, after all. Oh yeah. If we needed anything at all, we went to see him about it. Because he had connections, let me tell you. It's always the same, you know – it's the connections that do it. Oh yeah. He really helped out. He didn't hesitate at all, whatever you needed. He did whatever it took.'

I asked M. Maingonat if he had a notion of what Xavier Vallat did with his time at the Algeria Hotel. 'He concerned himself with culture . . . With all that space he needed, he was kind of stuck, you know.'

The grandfather clock, a large imitation antique in the corner, struck four. 'Ah, wouldn't it be time for you to return to Vichy?' he asked politely.

As I was leaving, he showed me two large bronze medallions, first prizes he had won for his cooking from the Vichy chamber of commerce. 'I was pretty well known in Vichy, you know.'

At the door he proudly mentioned his son Guy, a computer systems specialist with Lufthansa in Frankfurt. Guy was born in 1940, had grown up at the Algeria Hotel and had lived in Germany for the last thirty years.

'Look, my parents knew Xavier Vallat very well,' Guy said on the phone. 'They had great admiration for him.' M. Vallat's piety had made a deep impression on them, he said. Guy remembered his father saying, 'Every time he makes a decision, he consults the Pope.'

Guy seemed eager to talk. After the war, as a boy growing up in Vichy, he had known former employees of the Commissariat Générale aux Questions Juives: his organ teacher, for instance, who played at the Église St Louis downtown, had worked there to support his passion, music. Guy's grandfather, a country wine merchant who followed his son Henri to Vichy, also wound up working for M. Vallat. 'Those who worked there never talked about it,' Guy Maingonat said. And at home, 'This was something we never talked about. I think, from this point of view, my father was thoroughly naïve.'

The warmth that had been engendered during the war years lingered. Mme Vallat continued to make the Algeria her stopping place when she came to Vichy for the cure in the fifties and sixties. 'She was charming, that lady,' Guy said. Her husband, the ex-commissioner, would fetch her at the hotel. He was a 'gentleman who was rather distant', Guy remembered, 'a gentleman who placed great stock in polite phrases.' Xavier Vallat took over the editorship of the royalist *Action Française* newspaper in 1962; throughout the sixties he ponderously mocked de Gaulle in its pages, eulogized Pétain, and sometimes returned to the subject of Jews: 'One is forced to the conclusion,' he wrote in the summer of 1966, 'that it is the Jew himself who secretes anti-Semitism, through his refusal to assimilate, linked to his taste for domination, two reflexes he derives from his feeling of belonging to the people whom Yahweh promised would dominate the nations.'[13]

At his funeral, in the Ardèche in January 1972, the hospital chapel in Annonay was too small for the crowd of notables – local, regional and national, senators and deputies – who came to pay homage. Serge and Beate Klarsfeld also attended and annoyed the mourners by brandishing aloft copies of a thick 1950s study of the Commissariat.

'He was joyous and optimistic, like all those who have the privilege of leading their lives bathed in sunlight,' the priest said of Xavier Vallat at a memorial service in Paris after the funeral. 'Beautiful soul, noble character – have I said enough? Of others he demanded his own moral rectitude,' his former secretary wrote.[14]

I asked Guy if he knew what had gone on at the Algeria Hotel during the war. 'That's the nub of the whole problem,' Guy Maingonat said, a little confounded. 'I've seen a few documentaries about that period . . .'

He had no idea. I suggested that he read Paxton's books.

A few weeks later Guy Maingonat shepherded his father to Vichy for lunch. Guy was a slight, bespectacled man who looked younger than his years and spoke French with a faint German accent. He had no plans to return to France; the Germans, he was convinced, had developed a more 'democratic spirit' in the workplace. Quietly, he said his reading of Paxton had surprised him.

In my office at the former Hôtel du Parc (old M. Maingonat had never been invited inside – *that* hotel was for 'high society', he said), Guy's father mentioned that Mme Vallat had not been the only faithful client after the war. The widows of Philippe Henriot and Fernand de Brinon, two notorious collaborators, both shot, had also favoured the Algeria when they stopped in town for cures in the 1950s. 'Names that are well known, even if not very respected,' M. Maingonat said, chuckling.

At the restaurant, he was greeted warmly by the owner,

whose hotelkeeping family had also housed a government agency, though he couldn't remember which one.

Guy was impatient with his father, cutting him off and hurrying him along. We walked over to the Algeria Hotel. Guy showed me where his bedroom had been, and that of his grandparents. He pointed to the empty window boxes and said, 'Only begonias could grow in them.' It was a tour without nostalgia; he seemed grateful to have left it far behind. Old M. Maingonat walked around the shabby building looking disgusted, muttering, 'It's disgusting.'

Earlier, at lunch, the old man had been mostly silent. When the talk turned to Xavier Vallat, he interjected happily, 'After all, he was very competent!' His son looked mortified.

The Saved Jew

THERE WAS NO more reason to notice the Algeria than any of the other crumbling former hotels in Vichy. Meals had been prepared, rooms cleaned, guests greeted and sent off. For a relatively brief period it was requisitioned. Afterward, it had declined, then closed. The former hotelkeeper was a mild old gentleman who was greeted warmly by colleagues on his rare visits back.

How many hotels in Vichy had not followed this trajectory? It didn't deserve any more or any less recognition than the others. When Guy called a few weeks later to say that, actually, his father was a bit of an anti-Semite, it seemed superfluous – unnecessary to the reconstruction of the hotel's history. The Algeria could have 'really worked', as Guy's father had put it, with or without anti-Semitism. And the afterlife of the hotel was a success in the sense that it had managed with no difficulty to integrate itself into the town's unthreatening profile. Objectively, the building might carry heavy symbolic freight. More than any other, it might represent the junction of local, national and global history. It might have been the clearinghouse for more ruined destinies than any other single building in Vichy – more, say, than the Hôtel du Portugal.

Yet its past had not been the object of any particular cover-up, though it was certainly less susceptible to identification than, say, the Parc. A cover-up would not have been necessary. Its mere place in Vichy's gently mouldering landscape was enough to guarantee it a beneficent concealment.

So nothing had happened there – an idea that might be as true as its opposite. This seemed like a useful way of understanding a narrative about the Jews that became familiar to me over the months in Vichy. I was irritated by these soothing stories; they seemed to be no more than impulsive obfuscations, wilful failures to engage with real history.

Still, another interpretation was possible. The Algeria and its place, or absence, in the town's consciousness suggested these tales might be part of a more comprehensive, even if inchoate, view of this most sensitive past. Thus the notion that nothing had happened at the Algeria could have a more general application.

A bourgeois woman I knew who lived in a little château near Vichy, a place of rich wood panelling and Renaissance tapestries, had said to me: 'There were Jews who were saved, after all. Are you going to talk about the ones who were saved?' Another woman, whose father had had 'difficulties' when Liberation came, told me of the prostrate Jew on their doorstep one day during the war. Turning him over, her father saw the yellow star and decided to give him shelter. At a party in Vichy one Sunday, a smiling lady came up to me and asked, 'And what point of view are you adopting?' She said, 'You know, at my school we had Jews, and believe me, nobody told the Germans about it.' At another party, a man told me of sheltering a Jew who came knocking one day, capping the anecdote with an amused memory of the Jew's meticulous refusal to eat pork. A woman who had worked under Jean

Bichelonne, Vichy's brilliant minister of industrial production, said, 'When they saw that, how the Israelites were being hunted, we found spots for them. We found a spot for him [*sic*] as a teacher in a small village in the Puy-de-Dôme.'

The story of the 'saved Jew' often came at the beginning of conversations. It was, understandably, the preferred touch-stone for remembering the Jews. It was also perhaps a way of placating the questioner – me – who was quite possibly a Jew. These stories seemed meant, consciously or otherwise, to cast whatever conversation might happen to follow in a positive light. On the surface, 'saved Jews' constituted whatever usable memory might exist of them.

The town's self-image was that, at least until the advent of the Gestapo, Vichy had been a protective place, thanks largely to the government. 'The Jews, like the Freemasons, until the end of 1942 did not have a difficult life, though it was not normal,' a retired journalist and politico in the region, the right-hand man of two of Vichy's postwar mayors, writes in his recent book about the town's days as national capital. It is a work with wide currency in the town, frequently recommen-ded and prominently displayed in all the local bookshops. Following the heightened consciousness of the times, it devotes a chapter to the Jews of Vichy. 'At the Ministry of Labour so many Jews were planted, with the consent of the government, that rolling shifts had to be established,' he writes, suggesting that the regime, far from rounding up the Jews, had actually given them jobs.

In fact, the new anti-Jewish laws had specifically excluded Jews from all government positions. About these laws the retired journalist writes, 'At Vichy, capital of defeated France, the government vacillated despite German pressure to enact the repressive laws' – an inversion of the government's real attitude.[15]

The consistency of this optimistic point of view – Vichy was a haven where Frenchmen saved Jews – suggested it was a

function of some inner logic in the town's psychology. Max
Seror, for instance, remembered being called 'dirty Jew' and
'yid' at school ('Wasn't much fun,' he said). And M. Benhamou recalled fellow pharmacists, hoping to take advantage of
prevailing circumstances, who publicly asked, 'What are they
waiting for to arrest him?' It was a matter of historical record
that Vichy and the surrounding *département* of the Allier were
in fact uniquely *in*hospitable as a matter of government policy.
As refugees trickled across the line from the occupied zone of
France, all Jews, except those few well established there, were
officially banned from the town as of June 6, 1941, a measure
without equivalent in all of unoccupied France (but not
mentioned by the retired journalist).[16] Xavier Vallat had asked
for the Jews' removal, since 'their very presence at the seat of
government was harmful.'[17]

The Jews expelled from Vichy moved on to other towns in
the Allier, like Néris-les-Bains. 'The local population received
them well, even if there were a few grouchy, envious
tattletales,' the journalist writes. A letter of October 1941 from
the subprefect to the prefect, preserved in the archives, makes
note of the strong complaints of the mayor of Néris about the
'Israelites' in his town.[18] In fact, the archives at Moulins, the
ancient capital of the Allier, are full of letters from the wartime
mayors of Vichy's neighbours, complaining about the presence
of Jews and demanding some action by the government. 'The
city council unanimously asks *monsieur le préfet:* 1) to ban all
Jews from the municipality; 2) to forbid them to live in the
neighbouring municipalities,' the mayor of Lapalisse wrote in
August 1941. In 1942 the mayors got their wish: Jews were
banned from the *département* altogether, and even forbidden
to swim in the Allier River.

I was sometimes told that the synagogue in Vichy had stayed
open throughout the war. This was advanced as proof of the
benign prevailing climate, though the entire leadership – the
rabbi, the secretary, the president of the community, the

administrator, the officiating minister, the sexton (M. Seror's uncle) – was deported. Their names are at the top of a long granite plaque on a wall of the diminutive structure. It lists 132 other local Jews who did not return from deportation or were otherwise killed. Perhaps it was true, though, as the retired local journalist writes, that 'they were all arrested by the Gestapo or the Milice,' entities long since consigned to general and uncomplicated obloquy, and ones connected to 'Vichy', but not Vichy.

Still, I wondered whether there might be some concrete trace of a counternarrative to the 'saved Jew' stories. At Vichy's outdoor market one day, a Jewish bedding merchant, who had annoyed the synagogue hierarchy with his obsessive, if disorganised, interest in the war years, said to me, 'I have the impression nobody gives a damn about all this.' He carried around thick stacks of spiral-bound photocopies of the 1941 register of the Allier's Jews, which he offered for sale, though there seemed to be few takers.

He had made the copies at the Moulins archives. I wanted to see for myself what light the old files might shed on the fate of Jews in Vichy. They contained: orders from the prefect of the *département* to intensify the search for Jews living in hotels, furnished rooms, on the road; pathetic appeals from Jews to visit Vichy for medical reasons, which were rejected; solicitations on behalf of already arrested Jews who had previously 'given complete satisfaction'; arrest reports on fleeing Jews in the *département*'s small towns, including one of a Paris man who told officers that his wife and daughter had already been rounded up, 'on July 16, 1942, and I don't know where they are.'

A letter dated February 27, 1943, addressed to the subprefect of the Allier, leapt out at me. It was on stationery bearing the familiar logo of TPN (Transports Paris–Nice), a bus company whose travel agency today occupies a prominent corner downtown, its large sign dominating the junction. TPN also has a billboard outside Vichy's tourist office, advising potential customers to inquire within, the only private company represented there. During the high season, its bright green and yellow buses are visible everywhere in town.

It is one of Vichy's oldest family-owned companies, and its logo had not changed over the half-century. The letter in the archives says, 'Please find enclosed our bill for the requisitions of 25th and 26th February. I should be grateful if you could provide us, as quickly as possible, fifteen litres of gasoline we were obliged to advance.' TPN was owed 4220 francs.

The company didn't note the reason why its buses were pressed into service, though the subprefect of Allier, at the top of his letter, does: 'Roundup of foreign Jews.'[19]

TPN's latter-day ad. boasts of 'fifty years of experience, the trip you've dreamed about, the smart trip, the business trip . . . ask us.' I wrote to TPN about the letter in the archives. After several weeks, the company had not answered my letter. I telephoned. 'If he hasn't responded, it's that he's not interested in doing so,' said the secretary of M. Baylaucq, the company president. The next day M. Baylaucq was 'in a meeting all day and couldn't possibly be disturbed'. I heard nothing further.

The roundup of the Jews took place on the morning of February 25, 1943. TPN's twenty-eight-seat buses made a circuit of perhaps twenty miles, starting in Vichy and proceeding to the villages in the gently rolling countryside. Of the thirty-one Jews looked for, only nine were found, including five in Vichy itself. 'The gathering of the arrested Jews was carried out by bus, with an escort of four gendarmes of the motor squad, under the command of an inspector from the police at Vichy,' the local police commissioner wrote to the subprefect. He uses '*ramassage*' to characterize the operation, a word often used in connection with the gathering of inanimate objects – leaves, debris – or children. The Jews spent the night at the Vichy police station before getting back on the buses at

7:30 the next morning for the one-hundred-mile trip to the train station, under local police escort.[20]

'All of these operations took place in absolute calm. No incident whatsoever to remark on,' the police commissioner reported. Three of the Jews mentioned in his report finished their journey as names on the plaque at the Vichy synagogue: Hermann, Kerner and Matarasso. This last, a shopkeeper and volunteer in World War 1, was the subject a week after the roundup of a pathetic letter from his wife to the prefect, also preserved in the files. Mme Matarasso begged him to help 'an unhappy spouse ... made desperate by this so unjust measure against my husband ... never involved in politics, with no care other than family and work'. But by this time it was too late, the train having left the Montluçon station at 10:45 P.M. on February 26.

The three men on the plaque had been arrested by the regular police of Vichy, operating from the same turreted police station in use today. They had not been arrested 'by the Gestapo or the Milice', as the retired local journalist had it. The connection between their fate and Vichy was closer than that.

In fact, the old police reports are surprisingly straightforward about the import of these 'operations'. The language is descriptive, even a touch anxious, and hints at something dark in the future. These are not 'saved Jew' narratives.

'The Jews arrested made no trouble at all and seemed to accept their destiny with a certain fatalism,' the police commissioner wrote on February 26, 1943. 'Certainly, the separation from their families was painful, but it never went beyond the point of silent tears.'

The 'destiny' of a person arrested is not usually the concern of a policeman. Nor is the emotional state of that person at the time of his arrest. Similar language is found in reports after the big earlier roundup, on August 26, 1942, which was carried out all across the unoccupied zone. In recent years this roundup has taken on great importance in condemnations of the Vichy regime, since it occurred months before the Germans occupied all of France.

That August morning, the police began knocking on doors at 5 A.M. Six men, eight women and girls, and three children were arrested in the Vichy police district, though only one man was taken in the town itself, Arthur Glück, described on the old lists as a thirty-eight-year-old father of three from Czechoslovakia. His name does not appear on the plaque at the synagogue.

'The separation was the occasion for a fairly painful scene, which we were at pains to shorten and attenuate,' the Vichy police commissioner wrote about the arrest of a seventeen-year-old girl, Marion Petruschka, in the nearby village of Mayet-de-Montagne. Her mother and bedridden father were left behind, though he was swept up later, in the February 1943 roundup. Inspector Labuche of the Vichy police wrote that 'the girl Marion . . . demonstrated great courage in leaving her parents . . . [but] before arriving at St Pourçain the young Petruschka, until then quite normal, had an attack of nerves . . . showed signs of mental imbalance.'[21]

By 2 P.M. on the 26th, sixty-eight Jews had been placed in a disused textile factory at the edge of Montluçon, the *département's* industrial capital, hastily converted into barracks. (The site is now occupied by a bowling alley on a featureless commercial strip.) Most of them were 'apathetic', the police inspector reported, 'apparently only interested in their immediate well-being'. The next day their money was taken from them, and the police squad was reinforced. More Jews were rounded up, and on September 3, 1942, at 3:55 P.M., 144 left the Montluçon station in five cars. 'The departure took place without incident,' the police inspector noted.

There are hints of apprehension in this language. Was the arrest of young Petruschka 'painful' for the officers as well as the family? And why would she have needed 'great courage' if she was simply going, as the official story held, to a labour camp? Why *wouldn't* the Jews have been 'only interested in their immediate well-being'? These policemen – or at least their superiors – seem concerned about the larger import of what they were doing. They report on the reaction among the citizenry. Why would this have been a preoccupation? 'Some criticise the early morning hour in which the roundup operation was carried out,' the Vichy inspector wrote on the day of the roundup. 'Conversations reveal a certain compassion in respect to the Jews. Anti-Semitism, in general, is not particularly sharp, even if, incontestably, it is present.'[22] At that moment the citizens of Vichy seemed touched by the fate of the Jews among them, even if in a mitigated way ('a certain compassion') and even if having been awakened early may have been a principal concern (the language of the report is ambiguous). The local police themselves appear to have been under no illusions about the 'destiny' of the Jews they were arresting.

Yet I found no memory of August 26, 1942, or February 25, 1943, in the town. Even some Jews were surprised when I mentioned that roundups had occurred in Vichy itself (and the retired journalist omits all details of them). I told a doctor I knew about these small-scale roundups. He immediately shot back, 'Jews were sheltered in Vichy, you know!'

There was no narrative to dispense about the roundups. It was more likely that I would be directed to see M. Benhamou, the ancient retired pharmacist. He was mentioned to me as an indispensable contact, an exception who somehow proved the rule. During the war, he hadn't bothered to go underground. His longevity and his extraordinary story – a Vichy Jew who had kept on surviving – made him the object of special attention. He was a 'saved Jew' who continued, improbably, to be saved. Having passed one hundred, his birthdays were celebrated at city hall and covered in the newspaper. Nevertheless, he was an ambiguous figure, disliked for his aggressiveness (he was in the habit of suing his enemies) but appreciated for his symbolic value. Other Jews in Vichy despised him, insinuating that he was an accommodationist. But for the population at large he was a kind of preferred living narrative.

M. Benhamou hadn't moved from the apartment above the Parc des Sources where the Milice had come looking for him during the war. The same brass nameplate in elegant 1930s lettering, 'Maurice Benhamou, Docteur en Pharmacie', was still on the outside of the downtown building he had once owned. I took the elevator up to the second floor, the one the *miliciens* had taken, and found him waiting for me in darkness, hunched over a cane, in a long oval room. The dusty art deco furniture with rounded edges, the giant radio with the old-fashioned tuning rod showing all the cities of Europe – everything spoke of fashions circa 1935. He had a keen, startled look, as if he were concentrating hard, so as not to miss anything. In a low, gravelly growl punctuated by odd grunts, he talked about having been mobilised when war broke out – but he did not mean World War II.

He was 106 years old. I had to shout my questions at him. Why hadn't you been deported? 'I escaped because I had a pharmacy, and at the pharmacy I worked hard.' Why did Xavier Vallat patronise your pharmacy when there were twenty-five others? 'Because of my character. He knew that the pharmacy was well run. I think it was that.' Were you afraid during those years? 'No, not at all. I was esteemed by many Frenchmen who were not of the Jewish faith. Everyone respected me.' What about the 'provisional administrator' placed over your business, like those of all other Jews? 'I protested. The pharmacy couldn't have borne an administrator. With a pharmacy, you've got to be there yourself.' It had taken one phone call, he said, to have the provisional administrator removed. Did you hear anti-Semitic talk during the war? 'Never would anybody have dared to say in front of me, "dirty Jew". I would have bashed them without thinking twice.'

He had 'held up', as he boasted, not just through the war but into a distant era. He had been arrested three times, but he had survived. He had dutifully registered as a Jew, and indeed I found his name in the prefecture's wartime registry of Jews in the Allier *département*. There was a strange obliviousness in his account, as if the menace hanging over the Jews had barely existed. 'The Germans,' he said, 'couldn't abide me, because I am of the religion they do not like' – an echo, perhaps, of the simple explanations M. Benhamou and others might have given themselves sixty years ago, before the word spread that something more deadly than 'liking' or 'not liking' was involved.

His pugnacity stood out in the muted atmosphere of Vichy. 'I'm really quite astonished, because I ask myself, at one hundred and six, soon one hundred and seven, if this can be true,' M. Benhamou said. 'I ask myself why?' He chuckled. 'I'm not in the least dissatisfied.'

It was an acknowledgement that he was improbably clinging to life with a kind of bullheaded tenacity. Had this contributed to his survival years before, as much as his Catholic wife and his well-placed protectors had? None of these were guarantees, to be sure. He may have been a 'saved Jew', but he was hardly a representative one.

His professional circle was of no help. Then, as now, pharmacists occupied one of the social summits in Vichy, below doctors but well above other tradesmen. They had not been well disposed toward him. 'They were jealous,' said M. Benhamou. His wrinkled bird-like features sharpened. 'There was one in particular, he's dead now.' He wheezed. A flicker of excitement ran through him. 'It's his son who's got it now. He was a bastard.' He brandished his cane at the window, toward the pharmacy on the corner, Then he invited me to have tea with him, to ward off the chill winter evening.

A Man of Ideas

THE TOWN WAS so benign, it was tempting not to come to any conclusions about the stories I had been hearing. Their exponents were manifestly civilised folk. At most they seemed guilty of a certain laziness. Some were practitioners of what people called '*antisémitisme de salon*'. ('*Ouf!* My parents are like that,' a scion of the family that owned the Ambassadeurs said wearily.) But they wouldn't necessarily let this get in the way of good manners. It was true that for a long time I had a disquieting sense that these people were purposefully leaving something out of the story of Vichy's relation with the past. Some townsfolk had undoubtedly taken chances for the Jews, and some hotelkeepers had doubtless helped conceal them, as several hotel families insisted to me. Yet Vichy had hardly been a haven. The story of the 'saved Jew' was particularly inapt. Could it be a courteous way of expressing some deeper instinct?

Nonetheless, I was tempted to agree with the sentiments of a longtime resident I met one pale winter's day. 'I like this little town, characterless and agreeable,' Robert Faurisson said distractedly, using a complicated literary construction. He was a retired literature teacher who had gained notoriety in other areas.

The toneless setting had been propitious for his major endeavours. He was the town's most famous inhabitant, though few Frenchmen knew he lived there. For the past decade, he had been shunned by the journalists who once quoted him. Under French law, it could be considered illegal simply to report his conversation. That very morning, he had had to explain himself in front of a local judge: a flyer containing some of his ideas had surfaced. In his basement library, surrounded by books he had inspired or was inspired by (among them *The Auschwitz Myth* and *The Hoax of the Twentieth Century*), he showed me a stack of photocopied cheques made out to the French treasury, mementos of recent

204 · *Vichy and the Pleasures of Forgetting*

fines. 'This is the life of a revisionist,' the contemporary avatar of what some call 'negationism' and others 'Holocaust denial' muttered.

He was a mild-mannered, greyish man of seventy, living in a plain, off-white concrete and stucco house with a gabled roof on a quiet street of pastel villas. Bland floral paintings, his wife's weekend diversion (he offered to sell me some), hung on the walls of the living room, a classical statuette sat on the walnut sideboard, and the heavy oak furniture was covered in red velvet. Listening to Robert Faurisson, it was easy to see how some of his former colleagues in the provincial lycée had been 'disconcerted', as the retired history teacher had put it.

The schoolteachers with leftist leanings had been most susceptible. It was the late 1970s, the Faurisson 'affair' had just started (with an article by him in the most respectable of forums, *Le Monde*), and a generation of '68ers moving into middle age still harboured resentments from their days on the barricades ten years back (Israel, agent of American imperialism and oppressor of Arabs, was a scandal, after all).[23] They would have had to overlook certain curious episodes that were widely known – he had once asked the history teacher, for instance, to prepare a slide show with photographs of Jews *leaving* Auschwitz. He had the sort of memory that could cause others in Vichy, where powers of recall and wide reading were not common, to waver, to wonder whether or not he was on to something.

He had once had a fine career, having moved from the lycée in Vichy to the university in Lyon. But for some years now, no one with any claim to respectability could associate with him. Yet he still imagined himself as someone connected to the larger world, mentioning, for example, his admiration for the British journalist Christopher Hitchens, whom he said he had met at a dinner. He also felt obliged to discuss his own biography with any and all comers. So with minute precision, in a soft voice, he recounted the incidents he said had led to his 'revisionism'. He described the dimensions of a flap of wood in 1942, the soup he had for dinner in 1947, the fact that he had arrived late at the family table that night. The episodes he related – a foolish teenage experiment in anti-Vichy graffiti, the unjust purge trial of a cultivated *milicien* – seemed secondary. It was a hyper-realist tableau, the details, many of them apparently irrelevant, all set in place under a harsh light.[24]

For an hour or more, as the afternoon faded, he proceeded with his monologue, employing the language of the disinterested scientist. 'One has to learn to be dry,' he said, hammering the last word. He abjured me to stick to 'the hard facts', which came spitting out in oddly inflected English as 'the herd fects'. He didn't mention Jews or the Holocaust, but there was a controlled tension in his voice, building slowly. Giving me 'advice', he said, enunciating each syllable, 'One should be able to finish M. Nossiter's book to-tal-ly mystified about his preferences.' He continued: 'Each of us can, by virtue of his origins, religious or otherwise, by virtue of his upbringing – and don't I know! – have preferences.'

He was quietly working himself up into a rage. He turned to the Jews of Vichy. Many of them had not survived. Some had. This was enough for Faurisson. 'Look, if you please, at the individual destinies. Look closely! Does this correspond to what one is always told about the Jew – constantly pursued, prevented from working, chased from here, chased from there, shot, deported, tortured? Not at all!' His face was red. He was quite excited. He looked at me accusingly. 'Excuse me, but you are definitely a Jew!' Calming down, he tried a compliment, lapsing into a queasy stereotype. 'I see that you are subtle but tortured.'

By now the room was almost dark. I had taken pains to avoid engaging him on his favourite subject, but it was impossible to stop him. He became animated again. 'You say you believe in gas chambers? Have you ever seen a gas chamber?' It was his clinching argument. Did I know, he asked, that the figure of six million was invented by a rabbi in 1944? 'And the Jew, we have the right to typecast him! How on earth do you imagine that one would not be irritated by them!' He saw me writing down his words. 'Hey there, what are you writing there?'

He had claimed he was treated with courtesy when he went to play tennis at the Sporting Club, still considered the summit of local society. It was a claim that was difficult to judge, though there had been expressions of sympathy after his beating by young Jewish militants in the parks along the river in 1989 – even visits to his hospital room. 'He's someone who loves history,' said an acquaintance who sympathised with him. 'He's very, very French,' she said. 'And, by the way, very Catholic.'

But it was also true that simply mentioning his name brought a look of anxiety to the faces of some Vichyssois. 'No one even knows he's there,' said a solid member of the medical establishment. 'His presence is completely unknown.' In one sense, he might just as well not have existed. His name never appeared in the local newspaper, and his writings could not be found in the town library. A local bookseller who had threatened to beat him up said, 'I have clients on the far right who think it was fine that the Jews were killed during the war, but they can't stand Faurisson.' Admittedly, among its more notable residents Vichy had sheltered one of the conspirators in the assassination attempt on de Gaulle in 1962, a courteous bibliophile with a taste for sixteenth-century poetry. But the collective obliviousness required for ignoring Faurisson demanded some effort. It reminded me of a scene I witnessed almost every afternoon from my window at the Parc: in the middle of the genteel Parc des Sources, a drunken band of youths congregated with their yapping dogs. They were a challenge to Vichy's respectability, undermining it insidiously. Yet in spite of the menace they posed – they combined their panhandling with intimidation – day after day the citizens crossing the park would resolutely turn their heads away or look down as they passed the rowdy youths.

Faurisson spoke of no deeper connection to the town than chance – he had accepted a teaching appointment there years before his public adventures in 'revisionism'. It was clear, however, that Vichy had become an important source of inspiration for him. It was a font of continuing outrage.

'I would say that "Vichy" has remained largely taboo,' he said acidly. 'Very scandalously, the name of Vichy is associated with that of Auschwitz,' he continued, recalling Serge Klarsfeld's book *Vichy-Auschwitz*. He castigated the town's failure to acknowledge its own history: the absent or misleading plaques, the peculiar little museum with the mail sack. 'The taboo against revisionism is the same as the taboo against Vichy,' he said. 'You've got Darlan-Pétain-Laval, with Auschwitz as the backdrop.' The idea that the regime's anti-Semitism loomed large in contemporary assessments infuriated him. 'The scandalous assassination of Bousquet,' he had spluttered, referring to the murder in 1993 of René Bousquet, the Vichy police chief belatedly indicted for rounding up the Jews. 'The shameful trial of Papon!' he said, his face reddening again.

Auschwitz had blotted out 'Vichy'. If not for the 'scandalous' association of the two – one of them, Auschwitz, a lie in his universe – 'Vichy' could exist, its past proudly acknowledged, the admirable men who peopled it honoured. The town with its effaced history served as proof of his system. 'I would remind you that "Vichy" doesn't exist. It's "Vichy-Auschwitz",' he said. Each time he drove past the Hôtel du Parc and saw no plaque indicating it had been the seat of French government for four years, he could blame it on the Jews. The town, with its ostentatiously hidden past a source of both rage and vindication, was the ideal place for him.

The thought was unnerving. Nonetheless, Faurisson had pinned the town's disjunction from its history on the Jews. So had others in Vichy. It was true that he had taken his resentment of their suffering off a lunatic precipice: he had eliminated that suffering from the picture. Others, it seemed, had only tiptoed around the abyss. They had worked various transformations on old and unpleasant realities, reimagining and displacing the past, and had wound up with the stories of saved Jews. There was scorn for Faurisson, but there was also a complicated fear, born of unease.

Faurisson was destabilising to Vichy not because he could be considered a madman. In that case he would simply have been dismissed as harmless. The sympathetic acquaintance had said of his work, 'I think it's the truth.' That frankness was rare. Nonetheless, there were disturbing elements of recognition in the relations the town had with him. Perhaps the same held true for fellow citizens outside it as well. (In a recent poll published in *Le Monde*, 31 per cent of those questioned considered that 'the Jews have too much power in France.')[25] Why else was it necessary to employ an elaborate judicial machinery to repress him, a national law specifically aimed at silencing him and his epigones? Horribly, Faurisson himself had recognised this link when he said, drawing the lesson from the trial of the cultivated *milicien*, 'Your enemy is a man.' It was an insinuating plea for recognition.

At the end of the afternoon his wife arrived home, a meek-looking woman with a briefcase, a teacher like her husband. She seemed embarrassed by my presence; visitors from outside her husband's circle were evidently uncommon.

I took my leave, disoriented – a feeling I recalled from encounters with Ku Klux Klansmen in vastly different contexts. On the pavement I watched Mme Faurisson close the heavy metal shutters, just like any Vichy housewife, settling in for the evening. She didn't look down at me. In the twilight, the town seemed even emptier than usual, as if Faurisson and his fulminations, at the moment of their eruption, could exist only in their own universe – as if there were nothing else in it but his own rage. I cycled home down the street and didn't spot a soul.

That night Faurisson phoned me. 'You weren't too shocked by my statements?' Then, with concern, he said, 'My wife found you very hostile.'

9

Vichy Lives

ONE DAY in the spring M. Benhamou died. At lunch several days later, among people he had known well, he was remembered for his annoying lawsuits; his funeral had been attended by hopeful relatives he hadn't seen in years. Obituaries in local publications omitted the most salient fact of his existence: he was a well-known Jew who had survived the war under the nose of Pétain.

At the Helder one day the concierge apologised for being late to an appointment. 'We had a death in the building today,' she said. A visit to the cemetery had been incorporated in her day's round.

One week the shutters above us had not been opened. 'And M. Giraud?' I asked. 'M. Giraud is dead,' said the old lady on the second floor. On a quiet summer morning a month before, slumped in an armchair, M. Giraud had spoken to me of Vichy's animated bustle nearly sixty summers ago. He came looking for work in the new État Français, though he had been an aide to Georges Mandel, the Jewish cabinet minister of the 1930s, murdered by the Milice in 1944. M. Giraud hadn't left his apartment in years, and there was nothing in the Vichy of today that would tempt him to, he had said contemptuously. After that morning I didn't see him again.

'Vichy is a town that is dying,' said M. Hilleret, nearly shouting. 'It may already be dead!'

Appearances were deceptive. I had come to realize a

paradox: Vichy was intensely alive. Once all the hesitations, the more or less voluntary lapses, and the complexes were removed, Vichy could allow itself a trembling guilty pleasure in communing unimpeded with its past. This was a Vichy that could be conjured up only gingerly, but its excitement, even at this remove, was palpable.

'It was absolutely swarming,' M. Hilleret said, his eyes sparkling. 'It was a town that was really moving, swarming with people,' he said again. 'A hundred thousand people. And in the ministries it was mostly young people, men and women. You went into a café, it was full. You went into a bar, it was full. There were people everywhere. Everywhere everywhere everywhere.' He leaned over confidentially. 'Here, just behind us, was the Cintra,' he said, referring to the bar that had been across from the American embassy. 'Just between us – and don't put this down – it was an absolute sexual hothouse.' He trembled slightly.

This could have been the essence of the 'living' Vichy. Buried deep in these memories was the echo of a kind of sexual charge that had existed many years before. Intuitively, it made sense given the limited diversions and the promiscuous packing together of so many young men and women. There was contemporary evidence for it: Sjöberg, the artist, had drawn a naked man and woman, passed out side by side amid disorder and champagne bottles, in room 243 of the Parc: 'Thus, a certain Director of Propaganda was refused entry to his ministry (which also happened to be the Hôtel du Parc) for having noisily used his office all night according to its original function.' M. Sjöberg assured me that the drawing was made from memory.[1] The sentimental journalist Wanda Vulliez, in those years a sought-after beauty, recalled frantic propositions from an American reporter, his passions stirred by the atmosphere of German menace and the absence of his wife: 'Coming close, he pressed himself against me, murmuring:

"Don't you want to become an American and live in New York?" '2

M. des Ligneries, the elderly aristocrat, remembered a local countess 'who had a certain weakness for young diplomats. We called her the "Corps Diplomatique",' he said in his fluty voice. 'And there was another one who was torn between a Romanian and a Hungarian. We called her "Transylvania".' It was awfully amusing! (In a luxurious apartment overlooking the parks on the river, a couple of antique dealers told me of seeing the now aged 'Corps Diplomatique' shuffling around a Paris apartment in slippers, clutching a piece of bread and compulsively watching the television for glimpses of Catherine Deneuve.)

Among younger generations, the passed-on memories of this sexual energy contributed to a kind of despair, even if it was, for some, the preferred way of thinking about the time of the État Français. 'I hope you will write about how gay it was in those years,' a melancholy doctor in his late forties said. 'I mean, life went on. People enjoyed themselves. There were all sorts of cabarets, nightclubs. And the whores – there were huge numbers of whores in Vichy then.' The thought seemed to cheer him momentarily. (I remembered that the Bordeaux lawyer Ducos-Ader's memory of wartime Vichy had been reduced to a single recollection: that of a 'sumptuous' brothel.)

No hint of this sexual plenty remained today, except among several doctors in Vichy who had abandoned their wives for younger nurses. What was currently referred to as the 'morality' of Vichy – or the absence of it – was frowned on by the respectable bourgeoisie in the countryside. 'When you get an invitation, you never know if it's going to be in the company of their wives or their mistresses,' a prosperous rural landowner said. His wife avoided going into town, full stop. Their library contained a surprising number of tracts by collaborationists like Philippe Henriot, inherited from parents and probably unread for years, if at all. Like many of their peers around Vichy, they had a weakness for Marshal Pétain. Speaking of de Gaulle and Pétain once, the husband said, 'Both had their uses.'

Vichy's one-time incarnation as a living, breathing organism, pulsing with energy, sexual and otherwise, was a feeling difficult to disassociate from its politics, even if the link was not explicitly made. (Pétain himself, characterized by Paxton as a 'discreet roue', was said to have had a passion for the Wagnerian soprano Germaine Lubin.)[3] 'What was absolutely breath-taking for me – and I was twenty in 1940 – was that you had the impression of being in *France*,' M. Hilleret said. 'There were French flags everywhere, because of the ministries. Every month a battalion paraded up the rue du Parc. It drew huge crowds,' he said, especially of local citizens. 'Every week you had music from the Garde Républicaine at Chamalières. You had an exceptional military band, the youth corps, bugles and drums. Forgive me for using an expression that may be a little vulgar – it really got the blood going. You could be proud, or satisfied, or both.'

I understood his apology for the indelicate language. He was a decorous old man in a blue blazer and polished loafers, at ease in his book-lined study, in a charming tiled villa behind the Hôtel du Parc. For him, as for others, only one man could be behind these long-ago impulsions of energy.

He took me over to a glass case containing miniature lead soldiers. Reaching behind the soldiers, he pulled out two large bronze medals, one with a likeness of Admiral Darlan, the other of Darlan's boss, Marshal Pétain. He had bought them in Vichy during the war. 'I'm not going to attack Pétain just because I can praise de Gaulle. That's certainly not the way I operate!' M. Hilleret said heatedly.

'Look, here's the Marshal,' M. Edier said, pointing to an old photo. 'And here I am,' he said, pointing to a somewhat melancholy-looking figure in a beret and white trousers standing near the aged soldier. Pulling out another picture, he said, 'Here's the Marshal, and here I am.' M. Edier reached into his box again. 'Here's the Marshal in the crowd at Vichy. Here's the Marshal. And I'm here. Here he is in front of the Hôtel du Parc.'

I said, 'He was pretty popular at that point, wasn't he?' M. Edier replied, 'Good God, all of France was with the Marshal. And you can see that I was right up close to him.' He pulled out a picture of a ceremony at Vichy's World War I memorial. 'There's the Marshal, and I'm right there, in front of the memorial.'

I looked at the picture. 'You seem a little uneasy there, no?' I said. M. Edier answered, with apparent inconsequence, 'No, we didn't worry about the Germans. The Germans didn't bother us at all.'

This was puzzling at first, but it made some sense: there was really no need to worry when one was in such close proximity to Marshal Pétain. How often? 'Me? Oh, twenty, thirty, forty times.'

M. Edier pulled out some more recent photographs of himself, taken in the 1960s when he had become a respected hotelkeeper and mayor of the First Arrondissement in Paris. 'Here's President Pompidou. Six months before dying. And I'm right there, see.' And he had other pictures: himself with President Chirac, himself with Gaullist dignitaries.

M. Edier had the hotelier's instinct to please. Politely he praised the Americans for having saved France. He mocked his countrymen, mildly, for being too attached to sensual pleasures, like those of the table. I was his guest that winter's afternoon, and as a hotelkeeper, he wanted all guests, transient or long-term, to be happy.

Like nearly all the people I interviewed at Vichy, he brought up the unwilling departure of a famous guest in the town. The guest had wanted to stay, and the feeling had been mutual. But this particular guest had been forced to leave. M. Edier was revolted by the idea that a guest would have to depart before he was ready.

'But the Marshal was taken prisoner by the Germans, to Germany!' he said. 'The Marshal was a prisoner,' he said. 'He was a prisoner, the Marshal, he did not leave on his own!'

'Look, these are things that aren't known even today,' said M. Chervet, the retired shipping agent. 'Look, he was kidnapped – kidnapped!'

M. Lacarin, the genteel ex-mayor, declared, 'The Marshal was kidnapped. He didn't want to leave. The Germans broke down the door of his apartment.'

The taking of Pétain by the Germans was planned the night before, as was much of his final morning in Vichy, August 20, 1944. The careful stage-managing no doubt helped ensure that the last hours could be quickly 'inserted' into the 'Pétainist legend', as the popular historian Henri Amouroux put it (though Amouroux, the most widely read of all French writers on the period, doesn't discuss this orchestration).[4]

The central image of that day – uniformed Germans breaking down doors to seize the octogenarian Marshal – has been irresistible to those faithful to his memory. It was true that the fleeing Germans, unwilling to give up this valuable hostage, ordered the Marshal to accompany them, and that he refused to leave Vichy. But nearly everything that followed was choreographed, including the hour at which Pétain was taken away – 7 A.M. – the smashing of the glass front doors of the Hôtel du Parc by the *Feldgendarmerie* (Field Police) and the Waffen SS, and the breaking down of the door to Pétain's own room. The Swiss ambassador Stücki, who had worked out the plan with the Marshal's aides, even reminded the German general Alexander von Neubronn to bring the necessary tools the following morning.[5]

M. Bardiaux, the television repairman, said, 'I've got documents that prove the Marshal didn't leave on his own.' He later brought over a faint photocopy of Pétain's famous declaration to his countrymen announcing his capture.

'Pétain was arrested. Very few people know this,' Faurisson had said between denunciations of Jews.

At the local historical society one autumn afternoon, the subject of Vichy's war was addressed for the first time in memory 'a historic occasion', said the ironic history teacher). The topic was Pétain's kidnapping. After the lecture, a man called out from the audience, full of righteous indignation, 'I can assure you, my cousin was there – von Neubronn said, "I didn't become an army officer for this."'

The town was innocent. Pétain was innocent. Even the Germans had managed to preserve some honour. Vichy's most famous guest had been on the right side after all. The proof had come late, but it was definitive.

'The Germans burst in at six in the morning. The Marshal wasn't even wearing a tie. In simple shirtsleeves. Not even a tie!' said M. Edier.

10

Postscript: Xavier Vallat at the Parc

AT NOON on Saturday, August 26, 1944, Xavier Vallat left his
office in the Hôtel du Parc to have lunch next door at the
Majestic. It was six days after Pétain's 'kidnapping', the last
Germans had left the night before, and the Forces Françaises de
l'Intérieur, or FFI – the Resistance men – were streaming into a
joyful Vichy, relieved that the end was to be peaceful. It was
the final day of 'Vichy'.

Vallat had agitatedly sought refuge with the diplomats at the
Ambassadeurs, but the stolid Stücki had kicked him out
(Vallat doesn't mention this in his diary). So he had had no
choice but to return to the Parc. Strolling by the pleasingly
rounded corner, past the luxury Barclays store (the sign is still
there), under the ironwork balcony Pétain had stood on so
often to greet the crowd, Vallat noticed that the front of the
Belle Époque Majestic was covered, for the first time in years,
in French flags. But at the same time, workmen were busy in
the windows, taking the flags down.

'What are you doing?' Vallat called out to the tall man
directing the operation. 'There's word of a German convoy on
the road from Gannat,' answered M. Aletti, the owner of the
Parc and the Majestic. 'It's more prudent, for the moment, to
take them down.' (M. Aletti's widow remembered, on a
summer day fifty-five years later, how her husband – Marshal
Pétain had awarded him the *francisque* for hosting the

government – later had to flee the FFI using secret underground passageways in downtown Vichy.)

'After lunch, I return to my office, on the fourth floor of the Hôtel du Parc, to await the visit of these gentlemen,' Vallat wrote in his diary entry for August 26, 1944. 'I am alone in the immense building,' he noted, 'with a detachment of the Guard that has remained on the ground floor.'

As the sultry afternoon wore on, he awaited the end in the empty building. At around four o'clock, he stepped out on his balcony. In the distance he heard shouts and the sound of the 'Marseillaise'. Coming down the long curving street that runs alongside the park, from the direction of the Hôtel Thermale, he saw a column of girl and boy scouts, six abreast, carrying the flags of the Allies. They were chanting something more ominous than the national anthem: 'Down with the traitors.'

The column reached the Parc. 'Long live Pétain! Long live de Gaulle!' the girls and boys shouted, word having not yet reached Vichy that this evenhandedness would not apply in the days and decades to come. Vallat, taking in the scene from his balcony, spotted another group on the pavement, far more partisan. It was softly singing, '*Maréchal, nous voilà*.' Of course, Pétain was no longer there to hear it. There was only the ex-commissioner general for Jewish affairs, the last official at the Hôtel du Parc.[1]

III

• • • •

TULLE: LIVING MEMORY

Vichy–Tulle

SOME MONTHS after leaving Vichy for good, I attended a conference at the Assemblée Nationale in Paris that brought together a few faces familiar from my days in the town. It had been organised by Vichy's representative in the Assemblée, a solid, plainspoken Socialist from one of the small working-class villages in the surrounding hills. Sensitive to the irritations of his constituents, M. Charasse had proposed a bill in the national legislature that would ban the mention of the word 'Vichy' from all official references to the wartime French government. 'It is time,' he said with solemnity, 'to put an end to a mix-up that is absolutely appalling.'

The participants, most of whom had come up to the capital on the train for the day, thought M. Charasse's bill was a good one. Several rose to express their indignation at the idea that Vichy could be considered anything other than a pleasant, leafy summer resort, a place where, as one man put it, 'it was good to be alive.'

The frustration was sincere. It made me think of the double life lived by many of Vichy's citizens. They could be content simply thinking about the abundance of trees in the parks, the huge beds of flowers and the insouciant architecture. They could ignore the past or at least pretend to.

Elsewhere, there would have to be a more brutally direct relationship with the past, one that could not be based on concealment or obfuscation. I went to a place where the citizens would not be able to avoid thinking about what had happened a half-century before.

11

Its Normal Life

As I WAS LEAVING her apartment, the elderly lady gestured
vaguely at the picture window, which looked out on a steep
hill, a little train station and a clump of modest two-storey
houses. One of the houses had a long, monotonous iron
balcony running along the front. She started to speak, in an
even tone: 'My husband was hanged over there. Near the post
office.'

Her calmness startled me. It seemed not in keeping with the
collective wisdom I was encountering in the town of Tulle. It
was an article of faith in the provincial capital that it had never
stopped suffering from a certain day in June 1944 when
German SS troops marched in, rounded up most of its male
citizens, hanged 99 of them from balconies, lampposts and
telephone poles on the bleak thoroughfare between the
armaments factory and the train station, and sent another 101
to die in concentration camps.

It was sometimes the first thing people would say to you –
that Tulle had not actually got over it. 'Monsieur, I would
like to tell you,' said Mme Roubinet, whom I met in the nearby
countryside. 'Even today, I don't know if you realise how
much people are still suffering from '44.' She was the
daughter-in-law of a well-known local Resistance man and
she had moved to Tulle in the 1950s. She had suddenly begun
speaking, after sitting silently through several hours of desul-
tory discussion with her husband about the Resistance. 'They

are really profoundly sick from it, in their sensibilities,' Mme Roubinet said.

A man who had by chance escaped hanging that day observed, 'Its normal life? It has never regained its normal life. Practically, you might say.' A lady said, 'No. We've never got over the Ninth of June. Because it was the entire flower of all the youth. They hanged them or deported them. They were just youngsters.' We were standing on the roof of her apartment building, in the Souilhac district. 'You see there,' she said, pointing down the street and reimagining a sight she could not forget. 'It went all the way down to there.' Another man began talking about the impact on the town. He made a statement that seemed obvious after I had spent some time there: 'It was rare to find families where there wasn't a relative, a cousin or a friend' who was killed. I telephoned the sister of a young man who had been hanged outside his parents' butcher shop. Could we meet? 'No. No. I can't.' Her voice was shaking. 'Look, it's been fifty-six years, but I'm not sure I would be able to control my emotions.'

Still, if Tulle continued to suffer, it didn't seem much more torpid than other working-class towns of fifteen thousand deep in the French provinces. At lunchtime the two restaurants on either side of the Corrèze River were packed with workers from the prefecture and the departmental council, but by 6:30 P.M. the streets were deserted. True, where you might have found, say, a respectable clothing shop in other prefectures, Tulle, the capital of the Corrèze *département*, had a butcher and a fishmonger near its main crossroads. There was no gleaming Belle Époque brasserie where the local elite might forget they were at the bottom of a valley 310 miles south of Paris. There were few signs pointing tourists toward the town's medieval streets. Until June 9, 1944, nothing significant had ever happened there; Tulle had not contributed any native son to France's roster of heroes.

You were conscious of modesty. On a wall in an alley in the

Souilhac district, a carefully lettered old inscription enjoins, 'No Pissing or Parking of Bikes.' There was a gentle resignation about the citizens. On hot days I glimpsed them at their windows, looking into the distance from the tops of buildings. It was the edge of southern France, and the people spoke with a hint of the singsong that becomes more pronounced the farther south you go.

The predominant colours of the façades are brown and grey. In the centre of town, flat space is at a premium, and even the ancient half-timbered houses are built tall. They hang over the narrow streets, blocking out the sun. The distinctive covered balconies, small galleries built one on top of another, create rectangles of deep darkness at the tops of the old houses. On the quays the sinister-looking Hôtel St Martin, a yellowish 1920s pile crowned by an odd truncated pavilion where the Germans tortured their prisoners in 1943 and 1944, has been abandoned for a year. The landscape of Tulle is dotted with dirty concrete rectangles, reminders of the country's housing crunch after the war. Except at rush hour, when the workers flee, it is a quiet town. At midday, you could stand on the bridge over the river in Souilhac and hear the water rushing underneath. It was the same peaceful sound you might have heard on the afternoon of June 9, 1944. Then, the near silence was disturbed only at long intervals: a few bursts of gunfire, a radio playing accordion music, guttural orders, a man's desperate cry.

Tulle didn't ask to be liked, nor did it particularly ask to be visited. To get to it from the north or east, you descend abruptly on steep winding roads as though you were 'falling into an abyss', a seventeenth-century divine, Mascaron, wrote.[1] At the bottom is the town, stretching out six-odd miles along the narrow river valley. 'Tulle is all twisted up,' a lady I met there said apologetically, somehow evoking its history without meaning to. As summer approaches, in the first weeks of June, the cherry trees are laden with bright red fruit, enlivening the colourless landscape. It is a country town, but from the centre you don't see the surrounding country, only modest suburban villas creeping up hillsides. The tall Gothic spire of the cathedral rises up in the middle of the valley, dominating the town but dwarfed by the surrounding hills. Evoking the distinct urban physiognomy, a man wrote of his childhood in Tulle in the 1920s: 'You had to climb up to the attic in order to get out into the yard.'[2] In Tulle, if you overshoot your destination, you can drive up steep inclines for a considerable way before an opportunity to turn presents itself. The few writers who bothered to visit dismissed it in a condescending sentence or two and moved on. 'Little town, squeezed into the depths of a narrow valley by steep mountains that seem to forbid it all expansion,' Prosper Mérimée wrote in the 1830s.[3]

A man at the city hall, a teenager fifty-five years before, blamed the empty shopfronts on layoffs at Tulle's ancient armaments factory and not on any sort of lingering trauma from the 'events of the Ninth of June'. Tulle had lost more than a third of its population in the past twenty years; the munitions plant, where more than half the victims of 1944 worked, had dropped from 1500 workers to 500 in the same period. None of this was because of the Germans. The man at the city hall was mildly exasperated. 'We do like to keep going back to those moments,' he said. There were those, he said with discreet impatience, who 'wallowed' in them.

This suggested that whatever contemporary preoccupation Tulle had with its terrible history might be a touch forced. So some people could attribute the town's shabbiness to the fact that Tulle has 'not forgotten, and will never forget,' as a woman said to me, but objectively this wasn't so and at this late date Tulle had best get over it. This seemed reasonable enough; the man at the city hall certainly wasn't callous. He had plenty of unforced sympathy for the grief of the town's families, and he himself had lost a close friend that day.

Nevertheless, I was intrigued by the conviction that the town was still suffering. I asked everybody I met what signs of it there might be. None could supply me with one, beyond the ritualised commemorative procession held every June 9 for the past half-century. This exercise, full of uniformed officials, doesn't even draw all the family members still living around Tulle. Grim faces line the hot mile-long route, but also smiling ones. Old friends and acquaintances are happy to be reunited. The balconies are festooned with garlands of flowers, one for each victim, creating an incongruous festive effect. 'Tulle hasn't forgotten,' a lady sitting at one of the cafés facing the train station said solemnly, not getting up from her drink as the procession started.

But after listening to the citizens for some weeks, you sensed that this lingering trace, if it existed at all, could exist somewhere else – somewhere besides whatever torpor there might be in the town's rhythms, the annual procession, and the reiteration that Tulle had not got over it. There were people who had last seen their fathers as very young children, and could call up, with subdued fervour, the distant memory of a 'silhouette' or a 'presence', as one woman put it to me. In the old town centre one night, a middle-aged restaurant owner lamented the emptiness of the street and the abandoned apartments all around. Tulle was dying, she said. Then she told me that her father had been deported when she was twelve years old. 'Oh yeah, there were a lot,' she said, turning her head away.

You could wonder at the paradox of the sudden equanimity displayed by Mme Godillon. She trembled when she pulled out her husband's pathetic legacy, a few fragmentary identity cards found when his remains were dug up, months later, from the public garbage dump where the Germans had forced a humiliating burial late on the night of June 9. The plastic in which these cards had been encased was strangely blistered by the extreme heat of the dump. Charles Godillon had been a lathe operator at the arms factory, thirty-six years old, a father of two and expecting another child. You could still make out, in faded pencil, the note he had scribbled to his wife on one of these cards before being led out to die – not knowing, as it turned out, how: 'Goodbye my dearest, my little ones, and all my family that I loved so much. Call the one who is coming: Charles, or Marie. I am leaving to be shot: goodbye, my love, my dear ones.'

She was visibly shaken by this forced dredging up of her most painful memory and I left her feeling ashamed of my inquisitiveness. Mme Godillon had talked, with emotion and sorrow, of others who had died that day, of her own grief, of her intense struggle to make ends meet afterward, and of her solitude. Yet when she made reference to the murder of her husband fifty-five years before, for the first time her tone had abruptly shifted. There was a kind of release. Her statement was like a window onto an intimate reality, one so essential its relationship to the normal pain of loss was not the expected one.

12

Unavoidable Past

WHY? Were there any general circumstances, beyond Mme Godillon's obviously private grief, that might help to explain this intimacy? And what was its connection, if any, to the broader conviction that Tulle was still suffering? Perhaps 'suffering', in this context, might mean something slightly different. In French, as in English, to 'suffer' something also means to endure it – to live with it. Surely, the same level-headed people who seriously invoked this word would have scoffed at the idea that the citizens went around in a kind of stupor of pain. Mme Godillon, for one, had raised three children by herself and operated a newsstand for fifty years. Yet there was no mistaking the sincerity of my interlocutors' belief: they and a substantial number of fellow residents still entertained a particular relationship with the past, one that involved some measure of pain. Pain was not the only element, however.

It was certainly true that if you had arrived in the town in the weeks and months following June 9, 1944, you might have been able to tell, simply by wandering the streets, that something had happened there. People continued to leave their houses to do the shopping or go to work, but they did so in a near daze. On June 17, 1944, a lady who lived near the train station wrote to her sister: 'Everywhere, in the street, you see faces that are thin, sad, filled with consternation, women in tears.'[1] A muffled half-life existed in the town for weeks. 'We lost, I don't know how much weight,' a woman I met remembered. 'We slept badly, badly, badly.' On October 13, 1944, with the rest of the country exuberant over Liberation, radio listeners in the regional capital of Limoges were warned: 'If by chance your travels should one day take you to TULLE, you will be struck by the heavy atmosphere weighing on the town, by the sadness of the faces ... In the expressionless gazes that meet your own, a glint of horror seems to pass.'[2] A woman from Marseille, the cousin of a victim, recalled her visit in the autumn of 1944: 'What I remember, my memory is, everybody was dressed in black.' In the early 1950s, the English travel writer Freda White noticed that 'there is something sad about Tulle,' speculating that it might be 'too shut in by the riverbanks'.[3] A woman who had seen three young men taken from her household that day said: 'My mother wouldn't allow me to go to the dances. So I went out very little. We couldn't. It caused too much pain.'

Few towns in France could have had an experience of war and memory like that of Tulle. Few could have inherited such an abundance of grief. Other places had suffered terribly at the hands of the Germans, notably the village of Oradour-sur-Glane, where a unit of the same SS division massacred 642 men, women and children the day after the hangings at Tulle. But Oradour was burned to the ground, and there were hardly any survivors who had witnessed the full unfolding of the event. At Tulle most of the town survived what it had just seen. After the war Oradour became the pre-eminent symbol of martyred France. A new village of Oradour was built; the adjoining ruins of the old village were designated a national monument and carefully preserved. More than four hundred women and children had died in Oradour's church alone, incinerated by the Nazis. Oradour, itself necessarily mute, was adopted by the French nation and made to speak by it. Today its haunting ruins are a place of pilgrimage and tourism.[4] Oradour, only seventy miles from the scene of the hangings, immediately overshadowed what had happened at Tulle. Tulle was muted because the world, outraged by the next day's killings, wanted to hear about Oradour. Within a month of the massacre, with Allied troops still fighting to liberate France, the New York Times carried a story on its front page about Oradour; it was mid-October before the paper reported on Tulle, in a four-paragraph snippet on an inside page. The number of victims was given as 120, and the anonymous writer contented himself with quoting an inaccurate description of the events given over Radio Brazzaville.[5] The state did not intervene to preserve the balconies and lampposts of Tulle. De Gaulle visited Oradour less than a year after the massacre; he didn't come to Tulle until 1962.

Outside Tulle – in Vichy, for instance – I rarely encountered people who could tell me exactly what had happened there, yet everyone knew about Oradour. Until a highway bypass was constructed in the 1980s, Tulle was best known to other Frenchmen as the grimy, narrow strip of a town where you got stuck in traffic between Bordeaux and Clermont-Ferrand. The poet Paul Claudel wrote, 'It's no more than two or three long winding streets descending to a large factory and a small train station.'[6] A few books, popular histories of France's war that can be found in the town's bookshops, devote a chapter to June 9 in Tulle. But unlike at Oradour, there is no stand selling postcards, videos and graphic accounts of what happened there.

'Will people talk about Tulle one day?' asked Antoine Soulier, whose son was hanged on June 9.[7] He was a school-teacher – Socialist, republican and anti-clerical – and his published account of that day has the authority of writ for the modest citizens. 'Look, Oradour put Tulle in the shadows, everyone knows that,' said Pierre Diederichs, a recently retired high school teacher whose father, rounded up that day, escaped hanging but didn't return from the concentration camps. When the SS of Oradour were tried at Bordeaux in

1953, 'it wasn't a little squib in the press, like the trial of the
Tulle hangmen, but a real event that aroused the greatest
interest throughout the country and even abroad,' M. Soulier
wrote.[8] Le Monde devoted one paragraph to the verdict in the
Tulle trial, buried on an inside page. Shut up in their deep
valley, the citizens of Tulle were left to talk among themselves.
As much as possible, they avoided doing so.

It wasn't because they had nothing to say. Many of them
had seen a great deal that day. The executions were deliberately conducted in public, and they were conducted slowly,
over the course of an afternoon. Not only the men taken
hostage and forced to watch from the little square outside the
arms factory, some five hundred of them, like Antoine Soulier,
witnessed the hangings. All the householders between the
factory and the train station could see what was happening,
through windows and half-open shutters.

If you happened to be at your window between four and
seven o'clock on the afternoon of June 9, 1944, in the Souilhac
district of Tulle, you would have seen men being hanged.
'Look, we watched through the shutters,' a woman I met said,
as if making a confession. 'I have the impression I am not
alone,' wrote a woman who had, in all innocence, penetrated
the hot, empty streets of Souilhac as the hangings were
starting.[9] Because the houses of Tulle spread up the sides of the
valley, people on the heights, some distance from the scene,
could also see what was going on. The hangings were
conducted in a vast outdoor amphitheatre. I asked a middle-
aged woman whether her mother had witnessed anything. She
looked at me with surprise: 'But, the events of Tulle, everybody
who was at Tulle was a witness,' she replied impatiently. Even
those who hadn't witnessed the killings were inevitably in close
contact with someone who had. The scene thus became part of
the firsthand experience of dozens of people. The terrible
image fixed itself in the consciousness of the town. On June 23,
1944, before the number of victims had been officially

established, the prefect of the Corrèze *département* wrote to President Laval in Vichy: 'The 120 corpses hanging from the balconies and lampposts on the Avenue de la Gare, on both sides of the street, for a distance of 500 metres, was a spectacle of unforgettable horror.'[10]

Mme Godillon, for one, could see the executions in the immediate vicinity of the train station. She had seen men hanging from balconies, though not her husband. The house where her husband had died, with the balcony on which an engineering battalion of the Waffen SS had attached fourteen evenly spaced ropes on the morning of the ninth, and returning that afternoon, after its lunch break, to kill her husband and some of his colleagues, was fifty yards from the newsstand where she had spent her working life. She would have seen that house every day for more than half a century.

I thought about how I had begun my afternoon with her, in the spartan concrete apartment block in the heights above the arms factory. 'The memory? Oh, it's always the same. You know, to me it seems like it all happened just yesterday. It's like what some people ask me: "How can you remember so long afterward?" But, you know, it's difficult not to remember. Oh yeah, it's difficult.'

It was almost an acknowledgement that she had no choice. So perhaps Mme Roubinet and the others, though unable to explain exactly how, were right: the town had not shaken June 9. What form could such a gaping public wound assume so many years later? I wanted to know in what ways it might have lingered, not just for those who had been witnesses, like Mme Godillon, but also for those who had lived with the tales of the witnessess – the sons and daughters of men who died or were deported. Was it possible to measure any connection between what they said today and what had happened fifty-five years before? Had any traces subsisted?

Over the years, most of the nearly tangible evidence had disappeared. Even in the departmental archives, a bunker-like building overlooking the town, there isn't much: long, yellowing cards listing what was found on the bodies ('COMMUNIER, Paul: one tube of aspirin, one metro ticket, 950 francs, a visiting card'); the small battered wallet of André-Fernand Gamblin, twenty-two, an accountant at a local factory, still holding coins and banknotes; Gamblin's family record book, on which he had scribbled, 'My dear Pierlotte. I am going to die. Take good care of the little one for me. I hug you tight in dying'; and various newspaper clippings.[11]

Across the street from the arms factory is a mansard-roofed house, tall, grey and concrete with brick trim, one of the last landmarks the men would have spotted that day. On one side of the house there are a half-dozen small round craters, hard to distinguish unless the sun is shining on them. They were made by artillery shells on June 8, 1944, during the Resistance attack that led to the hangings. This was one of the few places left with physical evidence from those days. Was there a more vivid persistence of them elsewhere?

13

Measuring Silence

I ASKED a municipal employee, a soft-spoken, reserved man,
whether he had ever read anything about that day. His father,
rounded up on June 9, had escaped hanging but had died at
Dachau nine months later. He replied quickly, 'I can't.' Pierre
Diederichs, the retired high school teacher, said, 'When I was a
student, I too, if you like, I wanted to *live* something else.' He
was a thoughtful man, a former member of the city council
with an interest in philosophy, and he expressed himself rather
formally. 'As for myself, I consider that faithfulness to the
memory of my father consisted more in the *engagements* that I
might have had,' M. Diederichs said, referring to his commitment to the Socialist Party. 'It was more in the engagements I
might have had than in reading about the past,' he said again.

'At home, we never talked about it,' said the municipal
employee. 'It was a taboo subject.' A woman who had been a
teenager in the Souilhac district fifty-five years ago said,
evoking the succeeding years, 'We *never* talked about it. Never,
never. Because we lived the same things. What on earth good
would it have done? I know that she knows, she knows that I
know.' Mme Raze talked with bitterness about her siblings'
lifelong silence on the subject of the absent parent: 'I would get
this incredible response: "Oh no, we didn't talk about it." This
is very hard to understand, and terrible to live with.' I
telephoned the son of a man who had been hanged that day.

'No. no. We're not interested,' his wife said on the phone. 'It just stirs things up to talk about it. What good does it do?'

I was sitting one evening with the municipal employee and Mme Raze's sister in her plain bare house on the heights above Souilhac. The discussion had begun, a discussion in which he played almost no part.

'So, the hangings took place at what time?' he asked hesitantly.

'Five o'clock,' she replied.

'You see, I don't know. I don't know.'

She said, 'It's because you didn't want to know.'

'Yes.'

'Look, I understand. I understand.'

The narrative of what had occurred at Tulle was readily available. But in its details – in the fraught background of the event and in the drawn-out account of the hangings themselves – it hardly existed. It was not a subject of discussion, exchange or reading. On the surface, nothing had happened.

'You might look for witnesses, and they were right close by, but you didn't know who they were,' said Mme Raze. The paradox was that if the town was haunted, it gave the outward appearance of being just the opposite – that is, unconcerned. The Souilhac district, where the hangings took place, has been transformed in the decades since the war: houses have been torn down, a brutal dark grey concrete housing tower was planted in its heart, and the little square from which the bulk of the assembled hostages were forced to watch has been partly changed into a traffic circle. The house where the first men were hanged was recently demolished. 'Everything has been rebuilt, everything has been effaced,' said Mme Raze. She was a child in her crib when the Germans came for her father, a tuner at the accordion factory. He was a champion player, affectionately known as 'Ricou'. The fact that 'this historic district', as Mme Raze put it, no longer resembled the Souilhac he had known seemed to weigh on her.

The Paris writer Denis Tillinac began his career in Tulle. He kept a morose diary of his time there ('what distinguishes Tulle from a real town: no whores'), a work that makes a single, erroneous reference to the events surrounding June 9 – demonstrating that it was possible to be a newspaper correspondent in the town in the mid-1970s, even if an unusually self-absorbed one, and not have those events impinge on one's consciousness.[1] It seemed reasonable to agree with one of Tulle's professionals who said, 'It's, it's every year, in the month of June, this fervour.' In other words, if you happened to absent yourself from the town during this month, you might not notice anything in particular weighing on Tulle.

Yet at certain points in the town's postwar history you could have sensed what amounted to the release of a collective inhibition – points when, as M. Diederichs put it, 'the steam burst out of the valve.' On November 29, 1970, a Sunday, people spilled out of the town's community centre onto the pavements to demand the extradition of the former SS general Heinz Bernhard Lammerding, commander of the Das Reich division. He had gone on to build a prosperous engineering business in Dusseldorf; for years, the impunity of the man responsible for Tulle and Oradour had rankled the region. In the late 1960s several frustrated citizens of Tulle had taken turns phoning his home late at night. More than five thousand people from all over France marched that Sunday in Tulle. Within its narrow confines, the crowd seemed like 'a vast human wave', and the event made headlines in the national press. The mayor of Tulle, Jean Montalat, 'was unable to respond to the questions of journalists, the emotion was too strong, the memories too cruelly present in the minds of all'.[2]

Then there were other moments, more specific to the town itself, when, unexpectedly and almost embarrassingly, the citizens revealed the depth of their preoccupation to themselves and to one another. In 1994 a local filmmaker, Jean Pradinas, wove together a number of interviews about June 9. It was the first time a large number of townspeople had spoken, more or less in public; several of those delivering important testimonies in the simple, moving film died shortly afterward. The first showing was that summer, in the art nouveau Théâtre Municipale on the river, to a packed house.

'You could have heard, for the entire length of the film, you could have heard a pin drop,' one woman said, still surprised six years later. When the film ended, 'what was very striking, when the people left the theatre, no one said a word,' the retired teacher remembered. 'There were people who still had tears in their eyes. Everyone's face was very serious. No one could speak.' Even this moment of communal revelation was silent. A lady whose father had been deported said: 'You know, monsieur, the day this film was shown in Tulle, at the theatre, lots of people were invited. And the people left in a silence of death. Nobody could speak. Nobody.' She nearly shouted the last words. Posters advertising the film consisted of family snapshots of the victims; they created a 'shock' in the town, said one of the producers, the director of a local arts centre. There was a 'mad rush' for copies of the poster, he remembered. A doctor who keeps it in his waiting room, hanging next to innocuous representations of local flora and fauna, said, 'Every day people plant themselves in front of this poster.' A whole generation of the town's young manhood stares out from it. The faces of the smiling men brought back what had been collectively forgotten: the victims' youth.

Sixteen years before the film was made, an event in the life of the sleepy town provoked such turmoil its memory still agitates the citizens. On September 22, 1978, a Friday, a white Mercedes pulled up to the pharmacy across from the train station, in the Souilhac district. Out of it stepped an elderly, bespectacled woman with a mane of grey hair. She walked into the pharmacy and, in a slightly guttural accent, asked the pharmacist for news about his predecessor, whom she had known well. Then she asked after one of the grocers in the district; he had sold her butter from his store on the ground floor of the former Nouvel Hôtel, across the street, where she used to live.

As she left to go to the clothing store next door, the woman told the pharmacist her name, Paulette Geissler. And she made a somewhat enigmatic remark: 'You know, some time ago I was in the headlines quite a bit.'[3]

La chienne, 'the bitch', had come back. For thirty-four years the fury of the town had been concentrated on this German woman whose nickname, bestowed immediately after the hangings, was ineradicable. She had been the secretary of the German-appointed director of the armaments factory – and, some said, his mistress. Her role, as described by M. Soulier, the schoolteacher whose book on June 9 remains authoritative for the citizens, wasn't in any doubt: she was the 'lewd female' who drank that afternoon away in the company of ogling SS officers at the Tivoli café, sniggering obscenely at the spectacle in front of her. She was the 'monster in the white blouse' who ran into the middle of the street to blow cigarette smoke in the faces of the hanging men, the lone female who that morning had circulated among the SS as the victims were chosen, the woman who 'gave advice, orders, called out'. With a familiarity that is not friendly, M. Soulier addresses her directly in his narrative: 'We see you often, Mademoiselle . . . coming out of the Nouvel Hôtel at the train station, where you lodged.' She is spotted one day, before the hangings, near the level crossing, a 'soft and terrible Amazon' who sits 'astride an enormous horse, your legs apart' (twice M. Soulier describes her with 'legs apart'). Then, one evening several weeks after June 9, she becomes a 'streetwalker all dressed in red, wandering with a huge black dog. A final vision that explains everything.'[4]

It explained the place she held in the minds of the townspeople. In September 1978 news of her return travelled fast. An emergency meeting of the city council was held: 'I have the obligation and the duty to transmit a piece of news the seriousness of which, I am quite certain, will not escape you,' said the deputy mayor, M. Montagnac, solemnly opening the session. A delegation of former *résistants* and family members gathered, then walked briskly along the quays and up the long rue du Trech in order to make a protest visit to the prefecture. 'Under no circumstances will we tolerate the presence of Frau Geissler at Tulle, and we will be ready, eventually, to organise a very vigorous protest,' the spokesman for the delegation announced. Everyone was in perfect agreement.[5]

'The people around here said, "This just isn't possible," and there was a whole bunch of people who wanted to demonstrate, who were just horrified,' M. Diederichs, the retired teacher, remembered. Emotions ran even higher than during the rally against General Lammerding – and Lammerding, in any case, was dead. Plans were hatched to launch an armed manhunt in the region.

By mid-afternoon Frau Geissler, a retired employee of the chamber of commerce of Ulm, near Frankfurt, had quietly resumed the expedition she had undertaken with several travelling companions. They were looking for *foie gras* in the adjoining Dordogne region. Later, back in Ulm, she told an interviewer of her disappointment at not finding in Tulle the charming 'Romanesque' town she remembered from her younger days.[6]

Mme Godillon's son Charles, the one born after his father's death, had alerted the authorities to the presence of Frau Geissler. I asked Charlie Godillon if he had seen her that day. 'It's better that I didn't,' he said. He chuckled grimly. 'It's probably better that I didn't. Right, look, I'm telling you, it's probably better that I didn't.' Into December of that year, rallies were held in the town to denounce *la chienne*. A photograph of one of these meetings hangs on the wall of Tulle's little Resistance museum, near a picture of General Lammerding's garage.

The clothing store owner complained that the people of

Souilhac had harassed him for weeks merely for having spoken with her. 'She sat right there,' he said to me in the dim store, pointing to a curved iron chair that had not been moved in twenty-two years. Nor had the one next to it, in which he himself had sat while trying to answer her questions. 'Look, she was very polite. Perfectly correct,' he said. 'Believe me, she was a lot more polite than some of my clients.' He grumbled, 'I've had it up to here with all that.'

The town is fixated on her. She presides over M. Soulier's account and Tulle's consciousness as a goddess of death, the evil tutelary deity of Souilhac, exuding a maleficent sexuality. A man who avoided speaking of the details of June 9 asked me, 'You know about *la chienne*, don't you?' A woman who had seen a great deal that day, but not *la chienne*, nonetheless insisted on bringing her up. At a café in Souilhac, nearly facing the long-defunct Nouvel Hôtel (you could still see the words incised in the plaster), a woman said vehemently, 'Look, there was this German woman, a young woman. She smoked, she mocked the victims.'

Her role in the collective mind recalls the *tondus*, 'the shaven-headed ones', women accused of sleeping with the conqueror, in history grimly assigned the name of their punishment. At the Liberation they were symbolic targets for years of pent-up rage over German power and French impotence, paraded through the town streets of France to increase their humiliation. June 9, 1944, at Tulle was a terrible moment in this four-year dialectic. 'A feeling of powerlessness that was absolutely insane,' said a woman I spoke with. 'Powerlessness, and fear too.' A man who saw his brother hang, interviewed in the film by Jean Pradinas (who has since died), said, 'We were absolutely powerless to do anything at all.'[7]

The mere presence of a woman smoking cigarettes amid such suffering was enough to trigger fury, regardless of her precise role. In 1951 the Bordeaux military tribunal sentenced *la chienne* in absentia to three years in prison for 'nonassistance to a person in danger'. The court found that in 1944 she had been called on by the SS to pick out those 'indispensable' to the operation of the arms factory. She had fatally snubbed an engineer, Cazin, though the court recognised that she had saved seventeen others.[8]

Given the likelihood that her role was actually quite limited, the vehemence of Tulle's preoccupation with Frau Geissler could be difficult to account for. The most authoritative witness, a priest named Espinasse, never mentions her in the account he wrote in the weeks following June 9. He told an interviewer in 1978: 'I saw her that day. She didn't insult the hostages, nor did she dance in front of the corpses. She *did* smoke. But she smoked all the time.'[9] Nevertheless, with her ample body, so full of insolent life, in the memory of the inhabitants ('she had the physique, a real Gretchen, everything one doesn't like,' a lady said) she has a function beyond that of mere historical actor.

'At Tulle, we don't speak of the Ninth of June '44. A collective sense of modesty suppresses the evocation of that day of horror,' a local memoirist, Alain Postel, wrote several years ago.[10] You would not want to talk about the Ninth of June, but you could always talk about *la chienne*. It was easy to be outraged by her disgraceful performance. Given the town's reticence, *la chienne* becomes the substitute of choice for a more detailed engagement with the narrative of what happened at Tulle between 5:45 A.M. on the morning of June 7 and 11 P.M. on the night of June 9.

14

A Difficult Story

HE HAD BEEN talking about his grandfather's latent guilt over having survived that day while seeing his own son disappear forever. 'So, um, another aspect of things that you should know about,' the retired high school teacher began, moving briskly from the particular to the general, 'but that's still difficult to bring up because, here again, even today, it, ah, it provokes arguments, even fights, is the background to the events of Tulle as far as the role of the *maquis* is concerned.'

In one sense, it was easy to understand the town's 'sense of modesty', as the memoirist Alain Postel put it. The story of what had happened was painful. Contemplating its details was not pleasant. There was often a deliberate spareness in the recounting of these memories that suggested efforts of self-control. A woman I met said, 'And then, in the afternoon, you could see that things were going on.' These words were conveyed slowly, quietly, with an air of wonder. The people of Tulle could hardly be blamed for keeping silent. Yet in other places – Oradour, most notably – the process of mourning involved a continual evocation of history. The people of the rebuilt Oradour lived, almost literally, within this history. At Tulle, the events were difficult to evoke openly for reasons, as the retired teacher had suggested, not necessarily related to the pain their memory caused.

In order to understand what happened on June 9, it was necessary to know what had occurred on June 7 and 8, 'the background to the events of Tulle'. You had to know that the *maquis* had attacked the German garrison on those two days, that German soldiers had been killed, and that the Das Reich division of the SS had entered the town on the third day and exacted reprisals for the killings. Yet even though this sequence of events is not – could not be – in dispute, the preferred interpretation in Tulle is that no causal link be made among the three days. Understanding June 9 through what happened before is at the limit of acceptability. And if bringing up the hangings meant bringing up the *maquis*, perhaps it was better to avoid the subject altogether.

Early on the morning of June 7, 1944, a contingent of four hundred Resistance fighters attacked the German garrison at Tulle. It was one day after the Normandy landings, France was still occupied and Tulle was hundreds of miles from the front. The town's Germans, in fact, were particularly quiescent. But the clandestine French Communist Party had decided, months before D-day, that the national fight should be moved from country to city, and that attempts should be made to seize apparently vulnerable provincial capitals outright. The Resistance leader in nearby Limoges thought the idea was madness and refused to countenance it.[1] Five days before the attack, the chief of the *maquis* in Tulle, a schoolteacher named Chapou ('Kléber' was his dashing nom de guerre, after a hero of the French Revolution), still did not know how many German troops he would be up against and, four days before, was unclear about the exact state of his own forces.[2] Nonetheless, the attack went ahead, despite his serious reservations. Sure enough, soon after the firing began, some of the barely trained *résistants*, lacking adequate ammunition and quickly wearying of the fighting, fled to the countryside.

But for a few brief hours on the afternoon of June 8, the Germans were kept at bay, and there was uneasy euphoria in the town. Tulle had been miraculously 'liberated', the first prefecture in France to be so. 'Tulle is jubilant,' a young lawyer wrote in a memoir of those days. The ragged Resistance men strutted in the cafés by the river; the bodies of the forty Germans they had killed littered the narrow streets and alleyways.[3] 'Our men roamed the town, and the population acclaimed them with great warmth and enthusiasm,' one of the *résistants* wrote later. 'Women and young girls reached into their meagre food stocks and offered us nourishment.'[4]

Then, at around 8:30 P.M., the low growl of massed engines could be heard throughout Tulle. A heavily armoured reconnaissance unit of the Das Reich division was advancing toward town. Tulle's 'liberation' was over; the SS had come to deliver the beleaguered German garrison. Its larger mission was to stamp out the Resistance on its way from the south to Normandy, a job it was well prepared for, the division's officers having fought brutally for years on the eastern front.

The Resistance men faded away into the wooded hills. In Tulle, some thought the engine noises meant the arrival of the Americans. That hope lasted no more than a few minutes.

Six days later, after the hangings, Chapou was to write, 'Political considerations supplanted military ones.'[5] The following month, Chapou-Kléber was killed in a mysterious ambush. He was thirty-five.

At the Resistance museum in Tulle, a thick book is on sale, an oral history of the local *maquis*, published by a collective of old *résistants* under the direction of one of their own, M. Montagnac, the former deputy mayor. It enshrines the official memory of the Communist Resistance in the area (M. Montagnac is a party member), and it contains heroic tales of bombings, confrontations with Germans and this unmitigated judgement of the attack on Tulle: 'It remained a unique accomplishment in France: a German garrison was taken by force, and that, two months before the Liberation.'[6]

The hefty volume has a few quotations from the reports of Chapou, but it does not include his assessment of the Tulle attack, written on the night of June 8: 'The attack on Tulle has taken place. It has failed.' Nor does it include this bitter observation of June 14: 'The population of Tulle has risen up solidly against us, making us shoulder the entire responsibility for the Nazi repression.' A glimpse of an anguished Chapou by another *résistant*, from the days after the hangings – a sentence that found its way into an edition of the oral history published in the 1970s – is also missing: 'At the La Bonde command post, Kléber was in a foul mood.'[7]

I met M. Montagnac at the modest Resistance museum. He had known Chapou in 1944, when he himself was twenty-four. The old man said indignantly, 'We hadn't done months of resistance to wait lead-footed for them to come and liberate us. We had to do whatever we could.' Six years before, when M. Montagnac was still at city hall, stacks of a booklet with various accounts of those three days in June, not all of them favourable to the *maquis*, disappeared overnight from the town's book fair. The booklets were returned only after angry protests to the mayor.

'There has been a stranglehold on the memory of these events,' said M. Beaubatie, a high school history teacher, the Corrèze associate of the national Institut d'Histoire du Temps Présent (Institute of Contemporary History). 'This memory was confiscated,' he said. 'One couldn't do with it just anything one pleased.' He complained that the pallid local newspaper always quoted M. Montagnac and his comrades on the events of June 9. 'This militates against the assumption of real responsibilities,' he said.

Criticism of the *maquis* was rare in Tulle. 'It is, it is, I find it's taking it out of context,' said the municipal employee whose father had died at Dachau. Oradour, resented *sotto voce* because it obscured Tulle, is nonetheless cited to excuse the *maquis*. 'And it is true that with hindsight, when one thinks of Oradour, there was no attack, and that didn't stop them from making martyrs of six hundred,' a woman said. 'At Oradour, they didn't even have an excuse. No excuse,' said a man who survived that day. In the documentary film that stirred such emotions, old *résistants* are interviewed, but there is no hint that the attack on the garrison might have been a mistake – a point of view that certainly existed but was rarely voiced openly. I suggested it to a bourgeois lady, in her apartment overlooking the cathedral. 'A mistake?' she cried. 'I would say it was a sin!' At the annual commemorative procession, ancient *résistants* are well represented, family members of victims less so. I asked a man whose father was hanged why he never went. 'Because of the idiocy of some people!' he spat out.

The word 'martyrs', so widely used in Tulle – the long, winding street alongside the factory on which the first group was hanged was renamed rue des Martyrs after the war – was in its own way a deformation of history, since, with perhaps two exceptions, the men who died were not in the Resistance at all. They had made what, at that stage, was a more or less deliberate choice not to join the *maquis* but to stay home and take care of their families. The men could be said to have died *because* of the Resistance, not *for* the Resistance.

It was significant that the voice of their privileged witness had been muffled over the years. But not because the man who had seen more than anybody else that day did not want to talk; quite the contrary. In fact, this man's eagerness to testify only seemed to reinforce the conviction that he should not be heard from.

Sometime between June 9 and July 3, 1944, the priest Espinasse wrote his account of what he had seen that day, which contains these words: 'I am the only Frenchman on the rue du Pont-Neuf, in front of the Allary-Vaujour store, lost in the middle of the SS soldiers who stroll about, talk and laugh, insensible to this terrible spectacle.'

The singularity of his position was apparent to the *abbé* Espinasse immediately, as it was in the decades that followed. He had been rounded up with the other men of Tulle and been forced to wait, like them, while others were picked to die. And then he had been allowed to step away from them. He had accompanied the men to their deaths. He was the unique witness, because he alone had seen their faces. He spoke with them, sometimes one on one, as they waited to be hanged. To him they gave their wallets, watches and last notes to their families. Because of all this, he quickly went about setting down his testimony.

Espinasse was present at each stage in the events of June 9. Months later, after the Germans had left and the victims could be dug up, the priest assisted in the excruciating task of identifying their remains. Every historian who wrote about the events of Tulle paid him a visit over the years. His own brief account has been republished several times, most recently in 1994. Yet until the day of his death, nearly a half-century after June 9, and to his dismay, Tulle maintained a distinct distance from the priest.

15

The Privileged Witness

The Ninth of June

LOOKING OUT his window at nine o'clock on the morning of June 9, 1944, Jean Espinasse saw a column of perhaps five hundred men walking silently in the morning sun along the narrow quai de Valon on the other side of the Corrèze River. The men were surrounded by armed soldiers. The roundup was under way; his turn was coming. Soon he and his brother heard a harsh '*Raus! Raus!*' echoing up the stairwell. The SS men had been at work since six, banging on doors, rousting from their beds every male they could find. By ten, some three thousand men had been herded onto the service road inside the gates of the arms factory.

An officer of the German security police, known to the inhabitants as Lieutenant Walter (his real name was Walter Schmald), methodically paced up and down the ranks of the hostages. Many were released, those the French authorities said were essential to the town: doctors, postal clerks, municipal employees. Most remained, scrutinised by Lieutenant Walter. He was not in a good mood. He had been stationed in Tulle for five months now and had barely escaped death during the Resistance siege of the town in the preceding days. Tall, thin, blond, he was dressed in a threadbare cape the battered state of which made an impression on everyone who saw him. He spoke good French; he had been born in Belgium.

'He made the oddest, most unexpected observations, as if he were some part-time reserve officer at loose ends: "You certainly didn't shave very carefully. Your shoes need a shine. Where on earth did you get that old coat? You could have had it dyed. Would you kindly get rid of that cigarette?"[1]

The men stood in the heat, wondering about the meaning of this incessant sorting and scrutinising. 'They sorted us over and over and over,' said Jacques Martinie, who was seventeen at the time. 'Every time he went away we said, "*Ouf!* We're saved!" But he would come back. We weren't proud. It was terrible, a real torture.' Still, anxiety was quieted somewhat by German assurances early in the day that there would be no executions.

Soon the hostages on either side of the road noticed that the small group slowly forming in the centre, next to building 54 of the factory, shared certain characteristics. An old man I met remembered: 'There weren't many of them. And we told ourselves, "Oh, they're sort of dark-complected, they're badly dressed." They gave one the impression of being North African.' With two exceptions, they were not. The sorting was methodical and senseless. 'The victims were chosen without any investigation, without even any questioning,' the prefect wrote in his report to Vichy. 'Jumbled together were workers, students, teachers, businessmen, artisans.'[2] The men in the central group looked, according to the Germans' crude criteria, as though they might have spent the night with the *maquis*. One man who by chance had been released remembered passing an acquaintance in this group on his way out of the factory. 'This is not good here,' the acquaintance, Auguste Pierre, thirty-seven, an executive at the arms factory and a father of two, said quietly.

When sixty had been picked out, they were marched away from the mass of men and led to the superintendent's lodge at the factory entrance. By 12:30 a second group of sixty had been formed. Among them were Henri-Julien Mons, thirty-three, a sandblaster; Pierre Reginensi, twenty-eight, an instructor at the arms factory's apprentice school; Maurice-Roger

Broustassoux, thirty-six, a grocery store employee; Jean-Simon Curabet, eighteen, an apprentice at the factory; Marcel Demaux, thirty, a philosophy teacher at the local lycée; an insurance agent; a bicycle shop owner; a baker; and others.[3]

The Germans went to lunch, leaving the men guarded by sentries. They stood in the heat and waited. Nobody spoke and nobody moved. The priest read his breviary.[4] They didn't know that the SS had spent the morning combing the town for rope and ladders.

Several miles away, at the prefecture, a nineteenth-century red-brick pile crowning the main street, Major Kowatch of the SS entered the offices of the prefect of the Corrèze *département*, Pierre Trouillé. Seating himself, he announced that in reprisal for the killing of Germans the day before, 120 citizens of Tulle, 'accomplices of the *maquis*', were to be hanged. Trouillé recorded the subsequent exchange in his memoirs, twenty years later: 'As he was getting up, I said to him in a toneless voice, "Don't hang them, it's too awful!"' Major Kowatch replied, 'I'm sorry, in Russia we got used to hanging, we hanged more than 100,000 at Kharkov and Kiev, this is nothing for us here.'[5]

At 3 P.M. the German officers came back to the arms factory. The mayor of Tulle arrived. An elderly, tired man, he had been appointed by Vichy. He addressed the men assembled inside the iron gates, the ones not picked out earlier: 'I have some very painful news. You are about to witness an execution. I ask that you maintain the greatest possible calm. Do not make the slightest gesture, do not say a word, it would only make things worse.' These men, several hundred of them now, were marched out the factory gates to the little square opposite, which was lined with German tanks and armoured vehicles.

Inside the gates, the priest Espinasse walked alone toward the superintendent's lodge. An officer started calling names from a list in a strangely formal tone: 'M. Godillon, M. Mestre, M. Druliolle . . .'

A platoon of soldiers surrounded ten of the condemned men. The priest said, 'My friends, you are about to appear before God.' Eight dropped to their knees to receive absolution; the two Algerians among them began sobbing. With their hands tied behind their backs and the priest walking alongside them, praying, the men were marched to the corner of the rue du Pont-Neuf and the rue du Quatre-Septembre. There, for the first time, they saw the ropes, suspended from balconies, telephone and electricity poles and lampposts. The priest was stunned. He didn't notice that the ropes hung all the way to the train station.

An SS officer, his sleeves rolled up in the heat, took the first man by the arms and helped him ascend a ladder. Another officer climbed a second ladder, placed next to the first and put the noose around the man's neck. Abruptly the first ladder was pulled away.

'Ten times, the same painful scene repeats itself before my eyes. I can attest that the hanged men had no reaction: they fell like dead weight and did not move, which leads me to think that death is instantaneous, or at least loss of consciousness sudden and complete,' the priest wrote. When the tenth man was hanged, the priest thought the executions were finished. Then he saw another group of ten advancing, hurried along by the soldiers. The same sequence was repeated, and then again, and again.[6]

Possessed by the Story

IF YOU HAD left the provincial capital of Tulle in, say, 1944 and returned in the late 1970s, you might have had a difficult time finding your way around. You would notice that the map was no longer quite the same. Street names would be different;

street after street now bore names that would, in all probability, be unfamiliar to you: Gamblin, Caquot, Souletie, Gazin, Abbé Lair – men hanged on the Ninth of June or deported the next day, or *résistants* shot by the Germans in the years before – nearly two dozen such streets in all. Souilhac is now known as the Quartier des Martyrs, and there is an ugly monument, an upright slab of stone and granite in the middle of a parking lot, announcing this. Tulle, severely marked by the war, has memorialised its victims and its heroes. In the suburb of Cueille, where the bodies were dumped, there is another monument, a fifty-yard esplanade of stone and gravel by the side of the national highway. A sign exhorts motorists, strangely, to maintain a respectful silence as they pass by. On the monument itself, in low relief, a woman – a mother or housewife of Tulle – permanently grieves, her hand on her forehead in a stylised socialist realism redolent of the 1930s. Inscribed on bronze plaques are the names of all two hundred men, those who were hanged and those who did not return from the camps.

Tulle did not memorialise Jean Espinasse. No street is named after him, and no plaque commemorates the priest whose account, still in print, continues to inform the rest of France about what happened there. When the memorial at Cueille was unveiled in the 1950s, the priest was not invited to the ceremony. He was not even invited to say the solemn Mass that day at Tulle's cathedral. 'Never, at Tulle, was I asked to talk in public about those who were hanged,' he wrote in his autobiography, published in 1979.[7] In the late 1990s several members of the city council, not on the left, had considered naming a street after him. Knowing the idea would not pass, they gave up.

Espinasse felt his neglect keenly. In 1970 he wrote a letter to M. Soulier, who was president of the Comité des Martyrs, summing up a quarter-century of bitterness: 'My testimony, objective but incomplete, could have been expanded on and sharpened. After the Liberation, who asked this of me? Nobody. Not even your committee. Wasn't it to them especially that I could have said everything?' In his letter, preserved in the archives of the Corrèze, he goes on to talk of the victims. 'By reducing to silence their principal, not to say only, witness, they have been willed to oblivion. Never have I received a single word from the committee, not even a word of thanks or satisfaction . . . This silence for twenty-five years was a trial, and finally has seemed to me an injustice. I want to know the reasons. And if I am shortly to receive the Legion of Honour, it is because some people considered it scandalous that nobody at Tulle saw fit to take the initiative to propose me.'[8] President Jacques Chirac himself, then a young government minister in Paris who had got his political start in the Corrèze, decorated the priest.

It is a workers' town, governed by French Communist Party mayors for considerable stretches after the war, and a traditional anti-clericalism, of the sort with roots going back at least to the Revolution, comes naturally to it. It was easy to dismiss the priest who had been so intent on seeking the spiritual salvation of 'martyrs' to a cause not his at all. He had filled their last moments with talk of God, when really the men had been heroic victims of the struggle against fascism. 'They are representatives of a world of submission,' a local Resistance magazine, after the war, mockingly commented about Espinasse and the Chantiers de Jeunesse, the Vichy youth group whose local members had gathered up the bodies afterward.[9] 'Since he was Catholic, he fudges things up a bit,' a retired armaments factory worker, a hostage that day, said to me. M. Montagnac remembered with satisfaction his own lively confrontations with the priest over the memory of June 9, intimating that Espinasse's capacities had diminished sharply in old age. M. Beaubatie, the high school history teacher, recalled that he himself was fiercely attacked as a 'revisionist' – assimilated to Robert Faurisson – for having defended Espinasse at the book fair.

There were people in Tulle who could not forgive the priest for having come to the defence, after the war, of Lieutenant Walter. In 1970 he gave a speech in Paris in which he said the German officer, during the afternoon of the Ninth, had spoken of his unease at having to carry out 'barbarous' orders. The speech provoked a small uproar around Tulle. In his memoirs, written nine years later, Espinasse even writes, 'A sort of complicity had established itself between us . . . We were in this hell . . . we knew each other to be Christians.'[10] At the Resistance museum M. Montagnac snorted, 'Look, when he describes Walter, the man who picked the hostages, as a seminarian . . . Look, Walter was as much a seminarian as I am the pope.'

I suggested to the priest's brother and sister-in-law, a gentle old couple, that the *abbé* Espinasse had been subjected to a kind of rejection. Georges Espinasse, his brother, replied, 'It's right what you say. He wasn't appreciated by everybody. It's very curious.'

Tulle resented him for reasons that were not just political. True, he had been born in the town, and his father was the churchgoing manager of a hotel on the rue Nationale, a place now dark and seedy with age. But the thin, pale cleric had violated a code, one established at the start. 'So look, when you encountered people, you didn't know if they were directly affected by the tragedy,' Georges Espinasse remembered. 'So you were under a kind of constraint, almost as if you were at a funeral.' In the low-relief carving on the memorial at Cueille, the grieving woman looks down, her lips pursed in silence. She incarnates the suffering town, and she is mute. Jean Espinasse wrote in his letter to M. Soulier of having been reduced involuntarily to silence. Of all the witnesses, he alone, from the very beginning, wanted to communicate, and to a large audience. In a town that had collectively witnessed a tragedy, he had seen more than anyone. And he was the first, and remained nearly the only, witness to arrange the events into a coherent narrative with the sole objective of recounting what he had seen. A version of his 'testimony' was published as early as the autumn of 1944, in newspapers. M. Soulier's little book remained locally printed, but it is less a narrative than a combination of martyrology and polemic, containing annotated lists of the victims uneasily juxtaposed with hallucinated visions of *la chienne* and disconnected, grief-struck reminiscences. The emotion of the father works against clarity.

Before the war, Jean Espinasse was considered 'somebody who was rather insignificant', his cousin Pierre Roubinet remembered. He was 'sickly'. A retired university professor, the cousin was amused that the 'rather flat' young man he recalled from his own youth should have ended his life with a kind of stature (Mme Roubinet, Pierre Roubinet's wife, snorted with incredulity at the idea). Not everybody in the family had had such conventional beginnings: Pierre Roubinet had read modern poetry with Tulle's bohemians and was a teenage *résistant*, while his father, a founder of the Resistance in Tulle, was arrested by the Gestapo as early as January 1943 and had survived Mauthausen (and has a street named for him). In short, the priest was a pious young man who was delighted to have become, thanks to the Vichy regime's clericalism, the state-paid chaplain at the lycée in Tulle. In Espinasse's autobiography, the war years before June 1944 pass in a pleasant haze of reading, discussions with colleagues and summer vacations with students in the Basque country. 'If one remembers that all this took place during the Occupation or immediately after the war, you have to admit that it wasn't so bad at all,' he comments.[11]

Then came June 9. Espinasse was transformed by the story. By Monday, June 12, three days after the hangings, he was attempting a summary of what he had seen, in a letter to his uncle the *abbé* Bouillac. It may be the first written description of what had happened. The letter is scribbled on fragile note paper and punctuated with repeated ellipses. He was in a hurry. This is the embryo of his writing of the next three weeks, and the next fifty years, though it contains a harsh judgement of the *maquis* attack ('this sinister farce') that was later to be dropped, perhaps out of prudence:

> I give up on telling you everything, I'm too exhausted and I've got too much to do. I was the only one arrested in the quai de Rigny house, and providence willed that I be there, the lone priest helping those condemned to die.
>
> For four hours I led to execution about a hundred young men (I can't give the exact number ... the order stated 120 ... and it seems that only 99 were executed).
>
> They were hanged from the balconies, the electric pylons etc.... of Souilhac, from the Vaujour grocery store, past the main bridge, the level crossing, all the way to the Hôtel La Trémoliere.[12]

He was not someone with a gift for description and detail. It was not the act of communicating that was apparently important to him, but the communication itself. Espinasse had given contradictory explanations as to why he went on to write much more than was in the letter to his uncle. In 1953 he said it was simply to avoid repeating himself 'a hundred times over' to the families and others; in 1979, that the prefect had asked him to write a 'testimony' that was to be sent to the government in Vichy.[13]

But the recollections of his sister-in-law and brother, with whom he was living at the time of the hangings, suggest a more personal motivation. Mme Espinasse, who greeted him when he returned that night, said, 'He wanted to write, right away. Because afterward, you run the risk of ornamenting things like that.' Georges Espinasse recalled the frozen look on his older brother's face the night of June 9. The priest had been able, oddly, to share a meal with them, but it was hardly a convivial occasion. He spoke very little. 'He really had this concern to give an exact account, and he said that as the days passed one risked being influenced by one thing or another,' Georges Espinasse said. 'He wanted it to be *exact*.'

In these memories the priest was seen to have felt some urgency. In the text itself there are hints of this. His account is written in the present tense, as if the scene is unfolding around him as he writes. Again and again he uses the personal pronoun 'I'. This is not a vehicle for emotion. Rather, it emphasizes that in this short narrative, the recounter, Espinasse, is at the centre. This is an episode that he didn't simply observe, but one that he lived (continued to live) and that affected him. It is an account evidently written for others, and yet it is full of 'I'. It is thus an acknowledgement that in any future recountings, he will always be present. A view current in the town interprets this involvement somewhat unfavourably. 'He was an egotist,' said the arts centre director. The film about June 9, an important document for the people of Tulle, ignores Espinasse.

The priest was possessed by the story. His personal papers at the departmental archives are crammed full of multiple examples of his 'testimony', copy after copy carefully kept over the years. And for fifty years the priest also preserved every note he received having to do with the events of June 9, from politicians prominent and obscure, ordinary citizens and fellow ecclesiastics. On many of these papers the letters 'JE' are scribbled, the priest's initials, but also, as he half-humorously points out in his autobiography, the French word for 'I'. In a tape recording from the early 1980s he delivers the narrative in a measured, unhesitating rhythm, confident of every moment.

'I knew him very well,' M. Diederichs said. 'He didn't hesitate to put himself forward, to talk, which might have irritated some . . . He was someone who liked to have contact with people,' he said. 'He wasn't, if you will, fearful to put himself just a little bit forward, to put himself at the centre.

This might have irritated people,' the teacher repeated, hesitating slightly. 'So, ah, perhaps this is precisely what some, at bottom, reproached him for, not having played the game of silence. He was not, in fact, someone who wanted to cover the past with a film of silence.'

16

Living Memory

The Memory of a Dream

IF THE STORY of what had happened in Tulle was blocked, if people felt constrained in evoking among themselves why the men had died, and how, there remained a problem. How was the Ninth of June to be remembered by individuals? How were people to tell this story to themselves? These questions appeared to be all the more pertinent because the memory of that day had been forced inside by the 'game of silence', as M. Diederichs had put it. Unfortunately, they were also questions that appeared to be, on their face, beyond the reach of an outsider like myself. I was unavoidably clouding the picture, going to the town and focusing on this portion of memory. Many of the citizens had agreed to see me, although, sitting across from me, some looked as if they would rather be anywhere but just there. I was eliciting words where none might ordinarily have existed.

Yet it was clear that the question of individual remembrance had to have been confronted. It seemed possible that simply by listening to people talk about that day, you could get some insight into the form it assumed in their consciousness – in effect, how they lived with it.

In the papers of Jean Espinasse there is an old typescript of several pages containing the testimony of M. Lajugie, the chief road engineer for the Corrèze *département*. (It is also reproduced in M. Soulier's book.) On the afternoon of June 9, M. Lajugie climbed into a German vehicle and was driven from the centre of Tulle toward the Souilhac district. He did not know what was taking place there except that there were hostages, and some had been released. The car entered the avenue Victor Hugo, slowly making its way up the long street. His surprise at seeing soldiers lining both sides was quickly replaced by something else: 'I then saw on the pavements men who were climbing on wooden folding ladders and, a little farther along, men who had already mounted them. I was surprised by this unusual scene and by the number of men who, or so it seemed to me, were occupying themselves thus, among the soldiers, in laying out or repairing telephone or electricity lines.'

The car carrying M. Lajugie drives closer, proceeding into the avenue de la Gare. He can now see exactly what is happening: 'Two soldiers, their sleeves rolled up, one on the right, the other on the left, took the victims by the arms, to make them climb, while a third stood behind, bayonet fixed. When the noose had been put in place, one of the executioners, kicking or pushing the ladder, sent tumbling the victim, who, though the fall was not great, was immobilised immediately in death.

'I asked myself if I wasn't the victim of a hallucination, remembering the assurances that had been given that morning.'[1]

Among the few published eyewitness testimonies, these words, dated October 3, 1944, have the distinction of representing an impression gathered from a distance. In that way, they could reflect the experience of a great many of the citizens. They also faithfully – and courageously – record the scene purely in visual terms. They record, too, the attempt, made on the scene, to extract a meaning from what was witnessed – a credible memory, since it was transcribed only four months after the event.

But the scene is literally incredible, both from a distance and up close. It makes no sense that all those men would be repairing utility cables. This erroneous interpretation is replaced by something equally far-fetched. What is before M. Lajugie, in its strangeness, is so disconnected from his expectations that it cannot be assimilated. He appears to see something that cannot, in all probability, be there.

Often, when I met with someone who had been present on that day – as a teenager, a young adult or even a child – there would be a pause in the encounter. After the pause, the person would suggest the particular kind of incredulity that had afflicted him all those years before, much like the one M. Lajugie describes. In many cases it was the same, and this sameness seemed to be a clue. Perhaps, even though these witnesses were discussing the memory of long-ago events, they might actually be saying something about their present-day relation to them.

Mme Vaux said, 'But how should I describe it? You don't believe what you are seeing. It's surreal. It's not true. I'm not seeing this. It's not possible'; Mme Brugeaud said, 'This is something . . . we were in a trance. We lived a little as though we were in a dream'; M. Clair said, 'Trance. We were nearly unconscious'; and M. Martinie said, 'We had trouble taking it all in, it was going so fast. You're in a nightmare.'

You could take these characterisations as casual figures of speech: the word 'dream' and its equivalents are in such common use it would be easy to ignore them. Or – and given the frequency with which they recurred, this seemed to me more plausible – you could accept them. You could suppose that these people had imagined themselves to be in a dream – or even that immediately, as the event was unfolding, they had been shocked into a kind of dream state. One thing seemed clear: many years later, this was the way they remembered their mental state at the time.

As a defensive strategy in the face of unassimilable events, it had a certain logic. Figuring the Ninth of June as a terrible dream seemed to make sense as insurance against a too long memory. Events that had occurred in a dream could be thought of, in some inner recess, as not having occurred at all. Consider, for instance, some of the dream's characteristics as enumerated by Freud. The dream is 'pushed aside as something foreign' in the waking state; a dream's contents are deliberately obscure and difficult to interpret, in order to hide the thoughts that underlie them. Dreams are inherently predisposed to being forgotten: 'There is, however, no possible doubt that a dream is progressively forgotten on waking,' says Freud. And forgetting the dream is part of the will to repress its underlying meaning: 'The forgetting of the dream is not innocent of hostile intention.'[2]

In Freud, the 'psychic intensity' of certain ideas is transposed in the dream into vivid sensory images. The dream is inhabited by these images. It was striking that in the accounts the people of Tulle gave of that day, strong images, visual and aural, crowded out what might have been the most coherent recounting, a chronological one. Nearly all the people I interviewed, for example – even those who had been small children – brought up the cherry trees. They remembered the SS men, in their dark uniforms, gorging themselves amid the bright red fruit and green leaves of the verdant trees. 'They carried off the cherries, laughing and yelling,' Mme Picard said; 'three-quarters of them were in the cherry trees,' M. Martinie said, 'everybody in Tulle will tell you exactly the same thing.' Such images dominated their memories, and in conversation they insisted on them, giving their recountings almost the character of a dream.

I met Mme Brugeaud in the low-rise apartment block where the Tivoli café once stood, overlooking what used to be the square where the men had waited and watched on the Ninth of June. She had been telling me about those few days of her adolescence: the arrival of the Germans on the night of the eighth, an officer's arm raised to give the signal, and the blast of their heavy artillery.

Immediately she jumped forward a full day. 'Look, there's something else I haven't forgotten. You see, it's in the hearing. I've got the memory of sounds,' Mme Brugeaud said slowly. 'It's the noise when they cut down the bodies. They came with a . . . and I can still hear the noise of that, falling, there, right in front . . .'

I asked, 'They cut the ropes?'

Mme Brugeaud said, 'They cut the ropes, and then . . . oh, they weren't too unhappy about it, you know.'

Then she told me about approaching the bodies lying on the pavement, to verify that, as she suspected, her schoolmate was among them. And then she jumped back to the night of the Germans' arrival.

Later, she told me about looking through the cracks in the shutters of her parents' house, and seeing, in one of the groups of ten, someone who resembled her schoolmate.

I asked her whether she remembered seeing the faces of the young men. She replied, 'And then I heard . . . I must have better auditory than visual memory. Because . . .'

'What did you hear?'

'I heard, when they were climbing, there was one who called out for his mother. Who called out. So I don't know. When they say, when they say that they died courageously, I don't know. But they weren't singing the "Marseillaise", you know. Ah, no. There was one who begged for mercy, you know.'

It wasn't as if Mme Brugeaud had only *heard* that day and not *seen*. For instance, she was able to say that, through the shutters, she had glimpsed men being hanged. But here her language became like the published accounts, what might have been read subsequently. The vivid memories were aural. The one strong visual image she reported came partly from someone else: her father, who had been rounded up with the other men, though his relatively advanced age saved him from death. Twice, she said, he had had to push aside the bodies hanging from their own balcony in order to enter the front door; twice, she informed me, his face had gone all white.

On the morning of the Ninth of June, Mme Vaux saw a woman running up her street, crying and gesticulating. They're looking for rope in the attics. Rope and ladders,' the woman screamed. 'They're going to hang them, they're going to hang them!' Mme Vaux, barely twenty-one at the time, thought the woman had lost her mind. (It was Mme Nuñez; her husband, a Spanish republican refugee working at the arms factory, was among those killed.)

Later, curiosity overtook her. Mme Vaux climbed to a plateau above her parents' house, carrying a pair of binoculars. At that distance, the events unfolding below her were hardly decipherable, difficult to see distinctly: a confusing game of ladders being manipulated. 'What I remember, right, they were raising a ladder, that's it,' she said. Her strongest memory wasn't visual. 'What I also remember was the accordion music. Because it was to the sound of accordion music that it took place.' She brought up *la chienne*, whom she had not seen. Then she said, 'I heard the accordion, that's it. But at what time it all finished, I don't remember at all, good gracious.'

Another sound had not left Mme Vaux. She was a large, expressive woman, theatrical in a way others I had met in Tulle were not, and the memory of this sound agitated her. It was connected to the cherry trees. In the afternoon, she had seen, to her indignation, two young girls, pretty teenagers from her building, giving baskets of cherries to a couple of smiling SS men. That night, the night of the hangings, she was awakened. 'All of a sudden we heard real screams. The screams came from an apartment in the building. So, right. We got up. We got up.'

The reason for the screams soon became evident. One of the two smiling SS men had come back, revolver in hand. He had forced the mothers of the girls to leave the building. 'You know what happened next,' Mme Vaux said.

The images were disconnected from one another; the form

was like a dream. And they were disconnected from the experience of the days before and the days after. In that sense, they could appear to the person, in memory, as being part of a dream. But unlike the enigmatic and disjointed images of a dream, these referred unmistakably back to what was known to have actually happened.

Here was an acute dilemma for individual memories. It was underlined by the fact that not only the women who had observed, but also the men forced to participate, recollected a dream-like state. M. Clair had been a hostage on the square that day. I asked him whether he remembered seeing the faces of the people being led off.

'But we weren't *looking* at all,' he insisted. 'We didn't know what we were seeing. We were completely . . . I don't know how to say it. We were in a trance. We didn't understand why it was them and not us. So much so that we didn't look at the faces.' He saw without really seeing, or without understanding what he was seeing, a difficult state to describe but reminiscent of those dreams in which events are clearly occurring yet are still incomprehensible.

A man who had just finished recounting his experience of being held hostage said, 'It unfolded like a film. The images remain in my head.' Mme Raze's sister began, 'It's the same film. I almost see the faces passing in front of my eyes.' It was as though I were being allowed a glimpse of a series of images that were continually present. Mme Raze's sister was telling me about the memory of seeing her father for the last time, before he was deported on June 10. At their house in Souilhac, a neighbour had breathlessly told them that the remaining hostages were being loaded onto trucks, to be taken to an unknown destination. 'First of all, we run, run. And my mother says, "Don't look, don't look!" Because still, from some balconies, there were bits of rope hanging. So she told me not to look. But you know, at six years old, when you are told

"Don't look," I looked.' With its few simple, repetitive actions, the memory was like a child's dream.

A decade after Freud, the poet Paul Valéry wrote: 'The dream is the phenomenon we observe only during its absence. The verb "to dream" has practically no present tense.' It was the corollary of Freud's observation about the progressive forgetting of dreams upon waking: a dream exists only in memory. 'We only know the dream by its memory,' wrote Valéry, whose obsessive preoccupation with the structure of dreams led him to fill notebook after notebook with observations about them. 'It is above all a memory.'[3] If it was true that these people had experienced the events of June 9 as a dream, it would mean that these events had continued, since the dream's existence begins in memory. Their real existence, their true meaning, had come *after*. This present-day existence was thus comparable to what it had been from the earliest days.

A 'Lack' That Was Not an 'Emptiness'

A DOCTOR RECORDED in his diary the look of Tulle on Sunday, June 11, 1944: 'The town is deserted. Shops and shutters are shut tight. There is no sign of life.'[4]

I asked Mme Brugeaud how it had been possible to carry on afterward. 'I still wonder about it,' she said. But there had been school, daily chores, her ageing parents to take care of. Almost apologetically, she said, 'As for us, we were young. Life picked up.' Then, as if she wanted to override the importance of this statement, she looked at me fixedly. Life had indeed picked up, but the statement needed qualifying. 'But you see, this is something that . . . that I can't forget.' She was staring at me, perhaps wanting me to sense – without being provided an explicit explanation – the precise weight that day continued to have for her.

June 9 was still present for certain people in Tulle, people who would be influential in the town's consciousness. It seemed that if these events continued to exist in some form, the town would be forced to live among them. That is, if some people – people who were demonstrably not unbalanced – remained substantially haunted by the events, then many others, to a greater or lesser degree, would have to be as well. Living among people who exist in both the present and the past, you would inevitably be co-opted into this dual reality.

There were people who might have a reason to resist this. These people wouldn't have seen anything to speak of and might have few specific memories. They would have some connection – like so many in the town – yet could, in the interest of equilibrium, be expected to have put as much distance as possible between themselves and June 9. I wanted to see if this was so – or whether, instead, any aspect of their comportment might betray a lingering presence.

Mme Raze had been two years old that day. Yet she said, 'Because, finally, those who died under such circumstances, that is weightier than any present life.' It was a statement severe in its implications. She was fifty-eight years old, a life-long schoolteacher who had known professional satisfaction, a married woman with children whose husband sat attentively by her side in a house above Souilhac – attributes of a life that wasn't to be pitied. She was insisting nonetheless on their relative lack of importance in the face of events over half a century old. As if to make sure I understood, she added, 'And I would say that humanity has no interest in forgetting.' This was said dismissively – so much so that the whole idea of forgetting could only be considered absurd, or something worse. What personal impulse could so entirely rule it out of the question? 'As I've grown older, over the years, I don't think a year passes when I am not more appalled . . . by the horror of, ah . . . let's say the events of Tulle.' She felt that her connection with these events, instead of diminishing, actually increased, to the extent of impinging on present-day existence.

She mentioned with approval the philosopher Vladimir Janké-lévitch, and her words called to mind his notion of the meaninglessness of present circumstances in the face of the catastrophic occurrences of the war.[5]

For more than two hours I was locked into Mme Raze's monologue, a torrent of words that rose and fell in intensity as she recounted the stages in the satisfaction or frustration of memory: a half-memory of her own, the only one she possessed, of her father's 'informal manner when he took his lunch'; her wait as a child for his return; the silences of sister, family and town; and the fragmentary testimony of those who had last seen 'Ricou', her father, in Tulle and in the concentration camp. An apparently unrealisable preoccupation revealed itself: 'This is where we are at Tulle: we don't know precisely where some of them were hanged.' Later, she returned to this idea, which seemed strange to me: 'I haven't stopped pestering people in these last years. We don't know precisely where the different martyrs were. For some we know, but it hasn't even been clearly established. This hasn't been done. I've been after everybody about this: the facts, minute by minute, and the precise spots haven't been established.'

She wanted a closer connection, barely articulated, to these events. 'The years pass, all the loves are fused,' she said, explaining that she could now feel not only filial love for her absent father, but also, because of her age, maternal love as well. There was a yearning for a sort of immersion, so that when she left her house and descended the hill to Souilhac, she might, on driving through the streets, be able to assign historical significance to each bit of terrain, even though the 'precise spots', in many cases, didn't exist any more, as she pointed out. Still, what had occurred on these spots was a reality more 'real' than anything that might exist in the present, like the vacant lot that had replaced the house where the first men were hanged. Jankélévitch had written, 'Where one can't actually "do" anything, one can at least feel, inexhaustibly.'6

Halfway through the afternoon she made an enigmatic statement that was intelligible only in the context of other discussions I had in Tulle. She had been complaining about the persisting pockets of silence and the consequent ignorance of her students, some of them grandchildren of the victims. She said: 'And so I think that when you wipe out a town's history, or when you wipe out a sorrow – when you don't take into account the *fullness* of people – there is a lack. And this lack is not an emptiness.'

If it wasn't an 'emptiness', as she put it, it had to be its opposite. In other words, it was all very well to have tacitly agreed long before on a sort of collective silence. But this was no guarantee against a gnawing in people like Mme Raze. The 'lack' wasn't an 'emptiness'. But it remained no more defined than that.

Standing in the back room of Charles Godillon's newsstand in Souilhac, I had a window into this incoherence. 'Go ahead, ask me some questions. I'll answer you if I can,' he said. Edgily moving back and forth in the bare room, muscular and compact, he didn't invite me to sit down. He had been born several months after his father was hanged; with his siblings he had gone to school 'dressed as best we could, because we were destitute.' He never read anything about the war, never talked about the Ninth of June, turned off the television when war appeared on the screen. 'It's just the same old thing all over again. All over again,' he said. 'They let people be killed, they let people be murdered. Nothing is ever done unless there are thousands, thousands of dead.'

The interview seemed to have ended almost as soon as it began. I thanked him and started to leave. But there were things he still needed to tell me. He was angry – at the 'big shots', at the 'financial interests' who sponsored wars and exploited misery, at the prefect, at families who had given up

going to the yearly ceremony, at the schoolmasters who had
snubbed the poor boy. An officious envoy of the prefect had
once tried telling him, Charlie Godillon, where to stand in the
June 9 parade. 'I stopped the prefect. I said, "Families, step to
the front." Ah, no. No no. It was unacceptable. These big shots
who think . . . Unacceptable. And I'm telling you, they talked
about Godillon after that.'

When he ran out of things to say, and had offered me and
another visitor a drink, there was relief in the small room.
Afterward, I thought about the remark he made at the
beginning: 'Every day. I think about it every day.' That may
have been an understatement, or at least a self-assessment that
didn't quite capture the depth of his preoccupation. Here was
something that never really left him. In every exchange, every
encounter, some corner would always be reserved for what had
happened on the Ninth of June. He had admitted, 'I feel anger
about every thing.' The 'lack' in Charlie Godillon had been
filled with undifferentiated anger. Later, his wife told me how
surprised she had been to hear that her husband had expressed
his 'hatred', general and diffused, to an interviewer.

In others, what the 'lack' had become might not be so
evident. The retired schoolteacher Pierre Diederichs was four
and a half when his father was deported; Noël Diederichs, a
garage owner, scout leader and devout Catholic, died of
typhoid fever at the camp of Hersbrück, in Germany, five
months later. Pierre Diederichs had retained few specific
memories: his father's face, a kindly German officer at the
garrison, gunfire on the night of June 8, the SS men who
appeared at his grandparents' house the next day to tie rope to
the balcony (it remained unused). One day in November or
December 1945 the family's cleaning lady came to fetch him at
nursery school. She said, 'Right, it's me that's come for you
today, because your father, he's seriously . . . wounded.' When
he arrived back home, he found the whole family gathered
there, weeping. Evoking this particular memory, he said

briskly, was somewhat 'painful'. Then he quickly said, 'But still, there is a distance, which means that I am able to speak about it with serenity.'

He repeated variations of this notion several times. 'I speak of this, if you will, without difficulty, because ... I am of a generation after all that can evoke this serenely,' he said, speaking of his father's death. 'It has never bothered me to talk about all this,' he said a little later. 'This isn't really that painful for me, though I feel it fairly strongly,' he said in connection with something else.

It was true that he remained calm throughout our encounter in a dark little café by the cathedral. Yet he insisted, in ever so restrained a fashion, that speaking of all this didn't upset his equilibrium. So he appeared to be quite conscious of his own demeanour. It made me think that some inner effort of discipline must have been required for him to achieve this calm. At the end, he thanked me for having listened to him. He smiled and looked relieved.

The past had been present in these exchanges. Mme Raze had spoken of a 'lack' that was not an 'emptiness'. She had suggested that what was missing for her and others had been filled with something else, something related to the Ninth of June. It turned out to be a sentiment that was, in its own way, insistent. For her, the 'lack' was transformed into an inchoate wish for a closer, more detailed connection to the events; for Charlie Godillon, into undefined anger; and for Pierre Diederichs, into a kind of studied serenity.

17

Woven History

DISQUIET hovered over encounters in Tulle. Troubling visions had been forced to the surface that were not going to dissipate the moment I left. I was leaving my interlocutors to reckon with them, alone.

There had never been any sort of relief. Of the five hundred-odd SS men who entered Tulle on the night of June 8, only two were brought to justice. At their trial in Bordeaux in July 1951, Officer Wulf and Sergeant Hoff were sentenced to ten years and life, respectively; they were free by the following year. Both of them, still smooth-faced young men, denied any responsibility for the hangings of June 9. Hoff, in particular, insisted mutely on the unimportance of his role. 'His gestures are evasive, he doesn't remember,' the *Le Monde* reporter observed on the first of the trial's two days. But a younger recruit, an Alsatian who was to entertain a frenetic correspondence with several in Tulle (including Jean Espinasse and M. Beaubatie), had succinct memories of Hoff, later that same day: 'He erected the ladders,' ex-Private Schneid recalled. 'He had been in Russia. He knew the score.'[1]

Lammerding died in his bed in January 1971 (his wife blamed the harassing phone calls for hastening his death); Kowatch was never found.[2] Lieutenant Walter had been hastily shot by *maquisards* in August 1944 at a local château. An old *résistant* I met in the countryside who saw Lieutenant Walter die recalled a haggard German who 'knew his goose was cooked' and who would only repeat dumbly, 'I was under orders.' The old man scoffed at this memory. He was impatient to move on to something more important, insisting on the ludicrous juxtaposition of Walter's 'miserable end', so 'thoroughly insignificant', with his role in the history of Tulle.

More diligent retribution might have resulted in a collective satisfaction, a basis for shared memory. Unfortunately, this element of consensus had been denied. There had been no common vindication. Mme Raze had spoken of a process of remembering, mysterious to her, that sometimes unfolded in the high school classes she taught. Occasionally the students would recite passed-on memories of the Ninth of June: 'And when these testimonies are spoken out loud, and exchanged, you can see history being woven – the uncle of so-and-so was locked up with the grandfather of so-and-so ... All of a sudden, something is *woven* in the class. It's hard to explain. This history, which seems thoroughly individual, in fact is truly collective. All of a sudden the children weave a single thread between these buried things. It creates a remarkable unity for these children, who suddenly rediscover the unity that existed before.'

These classroom episodes bore the unmistakeable stamp of Tulle and what had occurred there: a disaster in common. They were salutary; Mme Raze told of them with pleased bemusement. But in the town, they were not the norm.

Maurice Halbwachs, the French sociologist who pioneered the exploration of the societal background to memory, suggested that memory's natural setting was collective. Even memories that seem thoroughly individual never exist in a vacuum; all remembering is informed by shared experiences.[3] In Tulle, collective memory might indeed exist in the abstract, at a level that was undetectable. Occasionally, it might take shape under artificial conditions – in the classroom, for instance. Halbwachs's idea might describe an ideal. But what was most apparent in the town, even to the people there, was the isolation of memory. June 9, 1944, had been experienced in public, and in common, yet over the course of years its memory had been kept inside, to haunt individuals alone.

Where there was no collective remembering, there was, inevitably, no dialogue. Mostly, there was silence, or what seemed to me its surrogates, like the story of *la chienne*. The silence was sometimes broken, in the presence of an inquisitive outsider like myself. This keeping inside had made the remembered experience and its descendants all the more vivid, or so it seemed to me. Silence had fuelled preoccupation. It was perhaps no wonder that people in Tulle were still 'profoundly sick' from June 9, as Mme Roubinet had put it: they were still physically inhabited by that day. Unsustained by a common memory, they seemed haunted by something else: the fugitive nature of their relation to the past.

At the end of an afternoon of inconsequential rambling, in his house high above the arms factory, M. Druliolle, the son of a victim, unexpectedly said, 'It's present all the time. I don't just think about it on the Ninth of June. It's omnipresent. It sure is.' The statement had the character of an assertion; after what had come before, M. Druliolle seemed to be lunging in order to reassure himself. In a café on the river, on the morning of a recent June 8, a jolly stout man quaffing a beer asked, 'It's tomorrow, then? You'll see, they'll be putting up the garlands.' He hesitated. 'Is that today or tomorrow?' The man made a remark about the music that was to be played on June 9. 'Lugubrious,' he said. 'It really grabs you, right here.' He put down his beer and clutched his throat. He had no plans to attend the ceremony.

The next morning I was walking in the town cemetery, on a barren hill at the top of the town. It is visible from most points in Tulle; many of the victims of June 9, 1944, were reburied here. The cemetery was deserted on this particular June 9. I spotted a middle-aged lady walking slowly up the central path carrying a bouquet and a jug. She was going to her father's grave on the anniversary of his death. She had been five that day, and she started to tell me about a memory. Then she interrupted herself. She was doubtful. It probably wasn't a memory at all, she said, just something that had been passed on to her. (Later, I found the incident in M. Soulier's book: 'You mustn't take father,' the little girl was supposed to have said, clutching the German soldier. 'I have two little brothers, and Mama is sick.')[4] She was a purposeful woman, a retired Air France employee, with a son living in Canada and a voluble admiration for what she considered American 'efficiency'. Although she had recently had an operation, her pace picked up as she neared her goal. Along the way, she filled up her watering jug at a spigot.

We arrived at the black granite stele of Adolphe-Pierre Mestre, forty-one, father of three, a salesman, who had provided a comfortable living for his family. She placed the bouquet on the stone and stooped to water a pot of flowers. She looked down at her father's grave. She thought back to the dreadful days in the autumn of 1944 when the remains of the men were dug up. A sceptical half-smile flashed across her face. 'To tell you the truth, there wasn't much left of them. It was more or less to comfort the families,' she said.

Conclusion

A YEAR AFTER the Papon trial ended, I went back to Bordeaux. The Hotel de Saige, the old prefecture building where Papon worked during the war, was being converted into luxury apartments. I walked through the huge glass doors with their ancient panes, up the sweeping stone staircase, past stone ornaments of garlands and cherubs, to a spacious high-cei-linged ante-room. A mythological stone youth languished in an alcove; some of the architectural details had faint traces of gold paint. There was a feeling of gravity and stateliness.

The property entrepreneur who met me was persuasive. He was keen to sell apartments: 'I know that in the United States you are used to extremely large surfaces. I can assure you, in the French scheme these will be very big indeed.' It was all still on the drawing boards; huge amounts of work remained. 'Everything has to be redone,' he said. 'The plumbing, the painting, everything.' He launched into detailed explanations: the fancier apartments would have two bathrooms, immense sitting rooms, here were the plans and prospectuses.

I couldn't listen to this patter. I left, relieved to be back out on the Cours du Chapeau-Rouge. In Paris, in December 1999, I went to the funeral of Maurice Couve de Murville, the patrician diplomat who had been de Gaulle's foreign minister and his last prime minister. It was a dignified, crowded affair, in an austere Protestant church in the heart of the city. The wife of the president of the French Republic was in attendance, as were the president of the French senate and various Gaullist dignitaries. Couve de Murville, before joining de Gaulle in March 1943, had spent nearly three years going back and forth between Paris and the Hotel Carlton in Vichy, as director of foreign exchange in the Finance Ministry of the État Français. As the delegate for financial affairs to the Franco-German Armistice Commission in Wiesbaden, he had had the vital job of watching over the transfer of French assets to the German war economy, including assets of Jews. He had given approval, for instance, of the takeover of a French firm's German branch in January 1941 – so long as the stock that was ceded 'was taken from shares held by Israelite stockholders, in such a way as to diminish the Israelite influence on your company,' as he had put it, months before the enactment of the French government's 'Aryanisation' laws.[1] At the time of his death at the age of ninety-two, Couve de Murville was in all likelihood the highest-ranking surviving member of the Vichy government.

At the funeral, the man delivering his eulogy, a longtime faithful subordinate, spoke of having known the haughty Couve before the war. Then he said, 'Our acquaintance was renewed in Algiers in 1943.' The years in between had disappeared. He didn't mention them, nor did anybody else.

In Vichy, Mme Léger had announced the imperative of forgetting a 'deplorable' past. It was an understandable goal, even if, after three years, it seemed to me unattainable. You could feel reasonably confident in the act of repression, but in the end you might be left – and this seemed to be the case with my interlocutors – with what you had repressed. I had met people enveloped in omissions, distortions or silence. They had helped me to understand that living with the past did not take place outside, at sunny commemorative celebrations. It was not a peaceful relation. I could see that what persisted might be all the more obsessive for hardly emerging at the surface at all.

Papon himself had made a last, wilful effort to push away

the past, in the autumn of 1999. With the help of some former *résistants* he fled to Switzerland, declaring that he wanted to 'defend the truth'. The unlikely flight of the eighty-nine-year-old convict mesmerised France's media; at his recapture, in a fashionable skiing resort, the French prime minister said he was 'profoundly satisfied'.

From Paris I called M. Edier, the old *légionnaire* in Vichy. Paris made him think of an encounter, in a luxurious hotel in Spain after the war, with General von Choltitz, the German officer who had surrendered the city in August 1944. 'He was a perfectly charming man,' M. Edier recalled with pleasure. I asked him about the detail he had left out during our long afternoon together: his imprisonment at the Concours Hippique. The old man laughed. As if we had suddenly resumed our dialogue of the year before, he said, 'Oh, it wasn't so bad. We wandered around in the courtyard a good bit. And when we were freed, at the end, the judge said, "We are giving you back not only your liberty, but your honour as well."'

NOTES
BIBLIOGRAPHY
ACKNOWLEDGEMENTS

. . . .

Notes

Introduction

1. Silverman, *Gyp: La Dernière des Mirabeau*, 9, 175, 243, 252, 256; Sicard, 'Thierry de Martel', 99; Maurois, *Destins exemplaires*, 79. Silverman ascribes his death to an overdose of phenobarbital.
2. See, for example, Morgan, *An Uncertain Hour*, 29, and Weber, *The Hollow Years*, 278.
3. *Washington Post*, May 1, 1966; *Dartmouth Alumni Magazine*, November, 1966.
4. *Washington Post*, May 1, 1966.
5. Rousso, *The Vichy Syndrome*, 82.
6. *New York World-Telegram*, April 17, 1954.
7. 'Histoire et justice: Débat entre Serge Klarsfeld et Henry Rousso.' Esprit, May 1992, 21, 23.
8. Rousso, 'L'Épuration en France', 93, 102; Paxton, *Vichy France*, 333. For the minor exceptions, see Rousso's 'Une Justice impossible', 745–70.
9. Slama, 'Les Yeux d'Abetz'.
10. Paxton, *Vichy France*, 20.
11. Fishman et al., *France at War*, 25.
12. Reprinted in ibid., 286.
13. Judt, 'Betrayal in France', 31.

The Stain on the Stone

1. Reproduced in Violet, *Le Dossier Papon*, 252.

1. Papon's Wager

1. Rousso, 'L'Épuration en France,' 97.
2. *Le Monde*, February 28, 1998.
3. National Archives, RG84, Entry 2490.
4. Laurens, 'La Femme au turban', 155f.
5. *Libération*, March 24, 1998. Another poll, taken eight months later, had opposite results: 59 per cent judged the trial 'more or less' or 'absolutely' necessary. *Le Monde*, November 27, 1998.

2. The Missing Context

1. Brutel, *Les Dynasties bordelaises*, 395.
2. Terrisse, *Bordeaux*, 94.
3. *Le Monde*, December 25, 1997.
4. Favreau, *Georges Mandel*, 272.
5. Bergès et al., *Les Néo-Socialistes girondins*, 119.
6. Sarrazin, *Adrien Marquet*, 25.
7. Coustet et al., *Bordeaux et l'Aquitaine*, 157.
8. Delvaille, *Bordeaux*, 66.
9. Terrisse, *Bordeaux*, 99.
10. Sollers, *Vision à New York*, 48.
11. 'Emperor': Mothe, *Toutes hontes bues*, 38; 'idol': Chastenet, *Chaban*, 157.
12. Interviews with Jean-Henri Schÿler, Jean-Philippe Larrosse.
13. Dufourg, *Adrien Marquet*, 71.
14. Archives Nationales, 3W, 245.
15. Chastenet, *Chaban*, 157.
16. De Gaulle, *Mémoires de guerre*, vol. 3, 23.
17. In Ophuls, *Le Chagrin et la pitié*, 42.
18. 'Stuntman': Marcel Déat, 'Mémoires'. In Bergès et al., *Les Néo-Socialistes girondins*, 118; 'dandy': Blum, *Le Prison, le procès, la déportation*, 100.
19. Terrisse, *Bordeaux*, 18.
20. Loiseau, *Souvenirs et temoignages*, 134.
21. *Les Néo-Socialistes girondins*, 64.
22. Dufourg, *Marquet*, 38.
23. *Sud-Ouest*, December 13, 1947.

24. Dufourg, *Marquet*, 167, 241.
25. *Sud-Ouest*, December 17, 1947.
26. Chastenet, *Chaban*, 157, 160–65.
27. Butel, *Les Dynasties bordelaises*, 337.
28. Mothe, *Toutes hontes bues*, 84.
29. 9.57 million: ibid., 162; 144 million: Azéma, *From Munich to the Liberation*, 130.
30. *Sud-Ouest*, September 26, 1997.
31. Butel, *Les Dynasties bordelaises*, 368.
32. *Sud-Ouest*, November 10, 1945.
33. Mothe, *Toutes hontes bues*, 161.
34. *Sud-Ouest*, September 26, 1997.
35. Ibid.

3. The Exigencies of Memory

1. Mauriac and Suffran, *Bordeaux*, 80.
2. Archives Nationales, 3W, 245.
3. Loiseau, 'Souvenirs et temoignages', 136.
4. *Sud-Ouest*, June 22, 1945; July 20, 1945; August 7, 1945.

4. The Judgement of Papon: History's Revenge

1. Conan, *Le Procès Papon*, 128; *Libération*, January 16, 1998.

Bordeaux–Vichy

1. *Esprit Public* (weekly public affairs programme on the France Culture radio station), July 12, 1998; *Le Monde*, October 14, 1997, and April 7, 1998.
2. *Le Procès du Maréchal Pétain*, 68 (testimony of Paul Reynaud, July 24, 1945).

5. The Past Effaced

1. Marrus and Paxton, *Vichy France and the Jews*, vii.
2. Azéma, *From Munich to the Liberation*, 45–46; Pétain, *La France nouvelle*, 24.

3. Cointet, *Vichy capitale*, 17–18; Baudoin, *Neuf Mois au gouvernement*, 226; Bullitt, *For the President*, 482.

4. Cointet, *Vichy capitale*, 19.

5. I am indebted to Jean Faye for the use of the journal of Robert Maes; Blum, *Le Prison, le procès, la déportation*, 65; Noguères, *Vichy, juillet 40*, 21.

6. Pétain, *La France nouvelle*, 51, 61, 65, 111, 156.

7. Bove, *Le Piège*, 77–78.

8. Noguères, *Vichy, juillet 40*, 27.

9. Aron, *Chroniques de guerre*, 36, 77.

10. Cremieux-Brilhac, *Les Voix de la liberté*, 23 (broadcast of July 18, 1940).

11. *Nouveau Mémorial de Vichy*, 13.

12. Paxton, *Vichy France*, 199, 265, 335; Paxton in *L'Amérique dans les têtes*, 72–87.

13. Rougeron, *L'Épuration en Allier*, 18; Rousso, *L'Épuration en France*, 102.

14. Bove, *Le Piège*, 60.

15. Archives Départementales de l'Allier, 778, W15.

16. Aron, *Histoire de l'épuration*, 577.

17. Ibid.

18. Archives Départementales de l'Allier, 654, W12.

6. Reimagining the Past

1. See Gelin, 'Eclectisme de l'architecture a Vichy', vol. 1, 93.

2. Larbaud, *Enfantines*, 60.

3. Gelin, 'Eclectisme de l'architecture à Vichy', vol. 1, 94.

4. Constantin-Weyer, *Vichy et son histoire*, 110.

5. Simenon, *Maigret à Vichy*, 149, 158.

6. Archives Départementales de l'Allier, 654, W12; 778, W15.

7. Gelin, 'Eclectisme de l'architecture à Vichy', vol. 1, 104.

8. Pierre Péan, *Une Jeunesse française*, 188.

9. Rebatet, *Les Décombres*, 480; Du Moulin de Labarthète, *Le Temps des illusions*, 168.

10. Archives Municipales de la Ville de Vichy, sessions of the municipal council.

11. Archives Municipales de la Ville de Vichy, sessions of the municipal council, January 15, 1941; May 10, 1941.
12. Sérézat, *Et les bourbonnais se levèrent*, 271.
13. Baruch, *Servir l'État Français*, 220.
14. See *The Economist*, May 1, 1999.
15. All quotations from Sjöberg, *Hors-saison à Vichy*.
16. National Archives, RG84, Entry 2489.
17. Archives Municipales de la Ville de Vichy, sessions of the municipal council.
18. *Le Progrès de l'Allier*, January 27, 1942.
19. Archives Départementales de l'Allier, 972, W61.
20. Baruch, *Servir l'État Français*, 84, 563.
21. Bouthillier, *Le Drame de Vichy*, 22.
22. Anecdote related by Robert-Louis Liris.
23. Archives Départementales de l'Allier, 654, W12.
24. Rougeron, *Quand Vichy était capitale*, 340.
25. Rougeron, *Mémoires d'autre temps en Allier*, 47; Cointet, *Vichy capitale*, 258.
26. Nicolle, *Cinquante Mois d'armistice*, 483.

7. Interlude: Escape from Vichy

1. Du Moulin de Labarthète, *Le Temps des illusions*, 165.
2. Bidault, *Souvenirs de guerre et d'occupation*, 133.
3. Vulliez, *Vichy*, 8.
4. Martin du Gard, *Chronique de Vichy*, 144.
5. Bidault, *Souvenirs de guerre et d'occupation*, 116.
6. Vulliez, *Vichy*, 60.
7. Loiseau, *Souvenirs et temoignages*, 213.
8. Leahy, *I Was There*, 75.
9. Dallek, *Franklin Roosevelt and American Foreign Policy*, 251.
10. Langer, *Our Vichy Gamble*, 382.
11. National Archives, RG84, Entry 2491.
12. Leahy, *I Was There*, 41, 53, 68, 85.
13. National Archives, RG84, Entry 2489.
14. Leahy, *I Was There*, 14.
15. Ibid., 43, 45, 51.
16. Ibid., 28.

17. Langer, *Our Vichy Gamble*, 194.
18. National Archives, RG84, Entry 2489.
19. *New York Times*, July 21, 1959.
20. Débordes, *Vichy*, 156; *New York Times*, April 23, 1967.
21. National Archives, RG84, Entry 2491; *New York Times*, April 23, 1967.
22. US Department of State, *Foreign Relations*, 1942, vol. 2, 710–14.
23. US Department of State, *Foreign Relations*, 1942, vol. 1, 464.
24. In Paxton and Marrus, *Vichy France and the Jews*, 228.
25. Boegner, *Carnets du Pasteur Boegner*, 212.
26. Ellsworth (Maine) *American*, January 10, 1985.
27. Du Moulin de Labarthète, *Le Temps des illusions*, 44.
28. Bochurberg, *Entretiens avec Serge Klarsfeld*, 76; Pryce-Jones, *Paris in the Third Reich*, 213.
29. *La Patrie de l'Allier*, November 6, 1944.
30. National Archives, RG84, Entry 2491. Letter of November 9, 1942, from Pinkney Tuck.
31. Ibid., Entry 2490. Letter of September 30, 1942, from Pinkney Tuck.
32. Leahy, *I Was There*, 70.
33. Boissieu, 'Souvenirs du pays retrouvé', 20. I am indebted to Anne-Marie Pathé of the Institut d'Histoire du Temps Présent for allowing me to read this unpublished manuscript.
34. *The Nation*, July 25, 1942.
35. Grafton: Cited in Langer, *Our Vichy Gamble*, 173; Root: *The Nation*, January 17, 1942; Liberal groups: *New York Times*, July 14, 1941. Root and the *New York Times* also cited in Langer, 174, 224.
36. Weil, *A Pretty Good Club*, 123, 125.
37. National Archives, RG84, Entry 2490; RG84, Entry 2489.
38. Du Moulin de Labarthète, *Le Temps des illusions*, 91; Paxton and Marrus, *Vichy France and the Jews*, 137.
39. Courtesy of Mme Colette Faus.
40. Du Moulin de Labarthète, *Le Temps des illusions*, 241.

8. Vichy and the Jews

1. Simenon, *Maigret à Vichy*, 9; *Ellsworth* (Maine) *American*, January 10, 1985; Fry, *Surrender on Demand*, 125.
2. The figure is cited in a report prepared by the Vichy synagogue in May 1941, preserved at the Centre de Documentation Juive Contemporaine, Paris.
3. Municipal records of Vichy, Register 107, no. 98–183.
4. Archives Nationales, AJ38, 983.
5. Ibid, AJ38, 195, 6292, 6302.
6. Marrus and Paxton, *Vichy France and the Jews*, 104.
7. Ibid., 130.
8. *Le Procès de Xavier Vallat*, 63.
9. Madeleine Lespinasse in *Xavier Vallat, 1891–1972*, 34, 35.
10. Archives Nationales, AJ38, 195.
11. Vallat, *Feuilles de Fresnes*, 11.
12. *Xavier Vallat, 1891–1972*, 22.
13. *Aspects de la France*, July 7, 1966.
14. *Xavier Vallat, 1891–1972*, 11, 34.
15. Débordes, *Vichy*, 9, 228.
16. Archives Nationales, AJ38, 237–45.
17. Marrus and Paxton, *Vichy France and the Jews*, 105.
18. Débordes, *Vichy*, 231; Archives Départementales de l'Allier, 778, W15.
19. Ibid.
20. Ibid.
21. Ibid.
22. Ibid.
23. See Winock, 'La Gauche et les juifs'. In *Nationalisme, antisémitisme, et fascisme en France*.
24. Faurisson has told this story before; it is quoted by Florent Brayard, who describes it as 'hallucinated confidings', in *Comment l'idée vint à M. Rassinier*, 421, 437.
25. Louis Harris poll for the prime minister's Commission Nationale Consultative des Droits de l'Homme. *Le Monde*, March 16, 2000.

9. Vichy Lives

1. Sjöberg, *Hors-saison à Vichy*, 56.
2. Vulliez, *Vichy*, 109.
3. Paxton, *Vichy France*, 165.
4. Henri Amouroux, 'Joies et douleurs du peuple libéré', 751.
5. Stücki, *La Fin du régime de Vichy*, 108–14.

10. Postscript: Xavier Vallat at the Parc

1. Vallat, *Feuilles de Fresnes*, 9.

11. Its Normal Life

1. Verynaud, *Histoire de Tulle*, 71.
2. Maureille, 'Vivre à Tulle', 3.
3. Mérimée, *Notes d'un voyage en Auvergne*, 69.

12. Unavoidable Past

1. Published in *Le Crapouillot* 11 (1950), 67.
2. Archives Départementales de la Corrèze, 487, W25.
3. White, *Three Rivers of France*, 33.
4. See Farmer, *Martyred Village*.
5. *New York Times*, October 12, 1944.
6. *Tulle et ses environs*, 69.
7. Soulier, *Le Drame de Tulle*, 22.
8. Ibid., 126.
9. Pierrette Troyes in Beaubatie, 'Le Drame de Tulle, Une Evocation', 208.
10. Archives de la Haute-Vienne (courtesy of the Musée Départementale de la Résistance et de la Déportation, Tulle).
11. Archives Départementales de la Corrèze, 487, W20–21.

13. Measuring Silence

1. Tillinac, *Spleen en Corrèze*, 85, 127.
2. *Le Droit de vivre*, December 1970; *Le Populaire du centre*, November 30, 1970.

3. *Le Monde*, September 26, 1978.
4. Soulier, *Le Drame de Tulle*, 23–24.
5. *Centre-Presse*, September 24, 1978.
6. *Vendredi, Samedi, Dimanche*, no. 56.
7. *La Mémoire des vivants*, Revfilms, 1994.
8. Amouroux, 'Joies et douleurs du peuple libéré', 528.
9. *Vendredi, Samedi, Dimanche*, no. 56.
10. Postel, '*Un fils de Tulle*', 176.

14. A Difficult Story

1. Beaubatie, 'Le Drame de Tulle: Une Évocation', 25, 26, 33. I am indebted to M. Beaubatie, the Corrèze correspondent of the Institut d'Histoire du Temps Présent, for the use of this unpublished paper. See also Musée Départementale de la Résistance et de la Déportation, *Maquis de Corrèze*, 497; and Hastings, *Das Reich*, 101–12.
2. Beaubatie, 'Le Drame de Tulle: Une Évocation', 43, 59.
3. Bourdelle, *Départs*, 19.
4. Musée Départementale de la Résistance et de la Déportation, *Maquis de Corrèze*, 562.
5. Beaubatie, 'Le Drame de Tulle: Une Évocation', 68, 81; Musée Départementale de la Résistance et de la Déportation, *Maquis de Corrèze*, 593; Laborie, 'Sur J. J. Chapou et sa mort', 13.
6. Musée Départementale de la Résistance et de la Déportation, *Maquis de Corrèze*, 594.
7. Laborie, 'Sur J. J. Chapou et sa mort', 13.

15. The Privileged Witness

1. Soulier, *Le Drame de Tulle*, 14.
2. Archives de la Haute-Vienne (courtesy of the Musée Départemental de la Résistance et de la Déportation, Tulle).
3. Soulier, *Le Drame de Tulle*, 26–53.
4. Espinasse, *Prêtre en Corrèze*, 62.
5. Trouillé, *Journal d'un préfet pendant l'occupation*, 134.
6. Espinasse, *Prêtre en Corrèze*, 61–64.
7. Ibid., 88.

8. Archives Départementales de la Corrèze, 47, J5.

9. Espinasse, *Prêtre en Corrèze,* 91.

10. *Centre-Presse,* March 17, 1970; Espinasse, *Prêtre en Corrèze,* 69.

11. Ibid., 53.

12. Archives Départementales de la Corrèze, 47, J5.

13. Espinasse, *Tulle,* 20; Espinasse, *Prêtre en Corrèze,* 59.

16. Living Memory

1. Archives Départementales de la Corrèze, 47, J5; Soulier, *Le Drame de Tulle,* 138.

2. Freud, *Sur le rêve,* 46, 113; *The Interpretation of Dreams,* 375.

3. Valéry, *Cahiers,* vol. 2, 75; Valéry, *Notes sur le rêve,* 15.

4. Diary of Dr Alfred Pouget in *Centre-Presse,* January 28, 1960.

5. See Finkielkraut, *Une Voix vient de l'autre rive,* 12–16.

6. Ibid., 42.

17. Woven History

1. Hastings, *Das Reich,* 227; *Le Monde,* July 6–7, 1951; *Sud-Ouest,* July 5, 1951.

2. Hastings, *Das Reich,* 227; *France-Soir,* January 15, 1971.

3. Halbwachs, *La Mémoire collective,* 53.

4. Soulier, *Le Drame de Tulle,* 47.

Conclusion

1. Verheyde, *Les Mauvaises Comptes de Vichy,* 355.

Bibliography

Archives

Archives Départementales de l'Allier, Moulins
Archives Départementales de la Corrèze, Tulle
Archives Départementales de la Gironde, Bordeaux
Archives du Ministère des Affaires Étrangères, Paris
Archives Municipales de la Ville de Vichy
Archives Nationales, Paris
Centre de Documentation Juive Contemporaine, Paris
National Archives, College Park, Maryland

Books and Articles

Abribat, Jean-Paul, and Maurice David Matisson. *Psychanalyse de la collaboration, le syndrome de Bordeaux:* 1940–1945. Marseille: Hommes et Perspectives, 1991.
Agulhon, Maurice. *La République.* Vol. 2, *1932 à nos jours.* Paris: Hachette, 1990.
Amouroux, Henri. 'Joies et douleurs du peuple libéré'. In *La Grande Histoire des français sous l'occupation,* vol. 8. Paris: Robert Laffont, 1999.
— 'Les Reglements de comptes'. In *La Grande Histoire des français après l'occupation.* Paris: Robert Laffont, 1999.
Annales. Économies, sociétés, civilizations. Special issue on the Holocaust and memory in France, May–June 1993.
Archives Départementales de la Corrèze. *Tulle: Mémoire en images.* Joué-lès-Tours: Alan Sutton, 1998.

Arendt, Hannah. *Eichmann in Jerusalem: A Report on the Banality of Evil*. New York: Penguin, 1978.

Aron, Raymond. *Chroniques de guerre: La France libre, 1940–1945*. Paris: Gallimard, 1945, 1990.

Aron, Robert. *Histoire de l'épuration*, vol. 2. Paris: Fayard, 1967.

Assouline, Pierre. *Une eminence grise*. Paris: Balland, 1986.

— *Le Fleuve Combelle*. Paris: Calmann-Lévy, 1997.

Azéma, Jean-Pierre. *From Munich to the Liberation, 1938–1944*. Cambridge,: Cambridge University Press, 1990.

— and François Bédarida, eds. *La Régime de Vichy et les français*. Paris: Fayard, 1992.

Bartov, Omer. *The Eastern Front, 1941–1945: German Troops and the Barbarisation of Warfare*. London: Macmillan, 1985.

Baruch, Marc-Olivier. *Le Régime de Vichy*. Paris: La Découverte, 1996.

— *Servir l'État Français*. Paris: Fayard, 1997.

Baudoin, Paul. *Neuf Mois au gouvernement*. Paris: La Table Ronde, 1948.

Beau, Georges, and Léopold Gaubusseau. *R5: Les SS en Limousin, Périgord, Quercy*. Paris: Presses de la Cité, 1969.

Beaubatie, Gilbert. 'Le Drame de Tulle: Des Sources pour une histoire'. *Revue des lettres, sciences et arts de la Corrèze* 102 (1999) (Société des Lettres, Sciences et Arts de la Corrèze, Tulle).

— 'Le Drame de Tulle: Une Evocation'. Unpublished paper.

Beevor, Antony, and Artemis Cooper. *Paris After the Liberation*. New York: Doubleday, 1994.

Benoist-Méchin, Jacques. *À l'épreuve du temps*. Paris: Julliard, 1989.

Bergès, Brana, et al. *Les Néo-Socialistes girondins*. Bordeaux: Institut Aquitaine d'Études Sociales, 1988.

Bidault, Suzanne. *Souvenirs de guerre et d'occupation*. Paris: La Table Ronde, 1973.

Billig, Joseph. *Le Commissariat générale aux questions juives*. Paris: Editions du Centre, 1955.

Bloch, Marc. *Strange Defeat*. New York: Norton, 1968.

Bloch-Lainé, François, and Claude Gruson. *Hauts Fonctionnaires sous l'occupation*. Paris: Odile Jacob, 1996.

Blum, Léon. *Le Prison, le procès, la déportation*. Paris: Albin Michel, 1955.

Bochurberg, Claude. *Entretiens avec Serge Klarsfeld*. Paris: Stock, 1997.

Boegner, Marc. *Carnets du Pasteur Boegner*. Paris: Fayard, 1992.

Boissieu, Françoise de. 'Souvenirs du pays retrouvé, 1940–1944'.) Unpublished manuscript, Institut d'Histoire du Temps Present, Paris.

Boulanger, Gérard. *Maurice Papon: Un Technocrate français dans la collaboration*. Paris: Seuil, 1994.

— *Papon: Un Intrus dans la république*. Paris: Seuil, 1997.

Bourdelle, J. L. *Départs: Souvenirs de l'année 1944*. Limoges: Rougerie, 1953.

Bouthillier, Yves. *Le Drame de Vichy*, vol. 1. Paris: Plon, 1951.

Bove, Emmanuel. *Le Piège*. Paris: Gallimard, 1945, 1991.

Brayard, Florent. *Comment l'idée vint à M. Rassinier*. Paris: Fayard, 1996.

Brossat, Alain, ed. *Libération: Fête folle*. Paris: Autrement, 1994.

Bruno, Jean, and Frédéric de Monicault. *L'Affaire Papon: Bordeaux, 1942–1944*. Paris: Tallandier, 1997.

Bullitt, Orville H., ed. *For the President, Personal and Secret: Correspondence Between Franklin D. Roosevelt and William C. Bullitt*. Boston: Houghton Mifflin, 1972.

Burrin, Philippe. *La Dérive fasciste*. Paris: Seuil, 1986.

— *La France à l'heure allemande*. Paris: Seuil, 1995.

Butel, Paul. *Les Dynasties bordelaises*. Paris: Perrin, 1991.

Carcopino, Jérôme. *Souvenirs de sept ans*. Paris: Flammarion, 1953.

Chaix, Marie. *Les Lauriers du lac de Constance: Chronique d'une collaboration*. Paris: Seuil, 1974.

Chambrun, René de. *Mes Combats pour Pierre Laval*. Paris: Perrin, 1990.

Chastenet, Patrick and Philippe. *Chaban*. Paris: Seuil, 1991.

Cobb, Richard. *French and Germans, Germans and French: A Personal Interpretation of France Under Two Occupations, 1914–18, 1940–44*. Hanover, NH: University Press of New England, 1983.

Cointet, Jean-Paul. *La Légion française des combattants, 1940–1944*. Paris: Albin Michel, 1995.

Cointet, Michèle. *Le Conseil national de Vichy*. Paris: Aux Amateurs de Livre, 1989.

— *Vichy capitale, 1940–1944.* Paris: Perrin, 1993.

Conan, Eric. *Le Procès Papon: Un Journal d'audience.* Paris: Gallimard, 1998.

— and Henry Rousso. *Vichy: Un Passé qui ne passe pas.* Paris: Fayard, 1994.

Constantin-Weyer, Maurice. *Vichy et son histoire.* Vichy: Szabo, 1947.

Cornut-Gentille, Gilles, and Philippe Michel-Thiriet. *Florence Gould.* Paris: Mercure de France, 1989.

Coustet, R., et al. *Bordeaux et l'Aquitaine, 1920–1940:* Urbanisme et architecture. Paris: Techniques and Architecture / Regirex-France, 1988.

Cremieux-Brilhac, Jean-Louis, ed. *Les Voix de la liberté: Ici Londres, 1940–1944.* Paris: La Documentation Française, 1975.

Dallek, Robert. *Franklin Roosevelt and American Foreign Policy, 1932–1945.* New York: Oxford University Press, 1979, 1995.

Dauzier, Pierre, and Denis Tillinac. *Les Corrèziens.* Paris: Robert Laffont, 1991.

Débordes, Jean. *Pierre Coulon.* Moulins: Éditions les Cahiers du Bourbonnais, 1991.

— *Vichy: Capitale à l'heure allemande.* Paris: Godefroy de Bouillon, 1998.

De Gaulle, Charles. *Mémoires de guerre.* Vol. I, *L'Appel.* Vol. 2, *L'Unité.*

  Vol. 3, *Le Salut.* Paris: Plon, 1959.

Delarue, Jacques. *Trafics et crimes sous l'occupation.* Paris: Fayard, 1968.

Delvaille, Bernard. *Bordeaux.* Seyssel: Champ Vallon, 1985.

Desgraves, Louis. *Évocation du vieux Bordeaux.* Bordeaux: Vivisques, 1989.

— *Voyageurs à Bordeaux.* Bordeaux: Mollat, 1991.

Dufourg, Robert. *Adrien Marquet.* Paris: Janmaray, 1948.

Dumay, Jean-Michel. *Le Procès de Maurice Papon.* Paris: Fayard, 1998.

Du Moulin de Labarthète, Henri. *Le Temps des illusions.* Geneva: Le Cheval Ailé, 1946.

Duroselle, Jean-Baptiste. *Politique étrangère de la France: L'Abîme 1939–1944.* Paris: Seuil, 1990.

Dutourd, Jean. *Au bon beurre*. Paris: Gallimard, 1952, 1995.

Erlanger, Philippe. *La France sans étoile*. Paris: Plon, 1974.

Espinasse, Jean. *Prêtre en Corrèze*. Paris: Robert Laffont, 1979.

— *Tulle: 9 Juin 1944*. Paris: La Table Ronde, 1994.

Fabre, Marc-André. *Dans les prisons de la Milice*. Vichy: Wallon, 1945.

Farmer, Sarah. *Martyred Village: Commemorating the 1944 Massacre at Oradour-sur-Glane*. Berkeley: University of California Press, 1999.

Favreau, Bertrand. *Georges Mandel*. Paris: Fayard, 1996.

Finkielkraut, Alain. *Remembering in Vain: The Klaus Barbie Trial and Crimes Against Humanity*. New York: Columbia University Press, 1989.

— *Une Voix vient de l'autre rive*. Paris: Gallimard, 2000.

Fishman, Sarah, et al., eds. *France at War: Vichy and the Historians*. Oxford and New York: Berg, 2000.

Frasnetti, Pascal. 'La Mémoire de la ville de Vichy'. Thesis. Maîtrise d'Histoire Contemporaine, Université Charles de Gaulle, Lille, 1997–98.

Frélastre, Georges. *Les Complexes de Vichy*. Paris: France-Empire, 1975.

Frenay, Henri. *The Night Will End: Memoirs of a Revolutionary*. New York: McGraw-Hill, 1976.

Freud, Sigmund. *The Interpretation of Dreams*. Translated by A. A. Brill. New York: Modern Library, 1950.

— *Sur le rêve* (On Dreams). Paris: Gallimard, 1988.

Froment, Pascale. *René Bousquet*. Paris: Stock, 1994.

Fry, Varian. *Surrender on Demand*. Boulder, Colo.: Johnson Books, 1945, reprint 1997.

Galtier-Boissière. Jean. *Journal, 1940–1950*. Paris: Quai Voltaire, 1992.

Gelin, Fabienne. 'Éclectisme de l'architecture à Vichy: Les Architectes et les villas, 1890–1914', vols. 1 and 2. Thesis, Université Blaise Pascal, Clermont-Ferrand, 1998.

Gildea, Robert. *France Since 1945*. Oxford: Oxford University Press, 1996.

Gillouin, René. *J'Étais l'ami du Maréchal Pétain*. Paris: Plon, 1966.

Giolitto, Pierre. *Histoire de la Milice*. Paris: Perrin, 1997.

Golsan, Richard J., ed. *Memory, the Holocaust, and French Justice.* Hanover, NH: University Press of New England, 1996.

— ed. *The Papon Affair: Memory and Justice on Trial.* New York: Routledge, 2000.

Greilsamer, Laurent, and Daniel Schneidermann. *Un Certain Monsieur Paul: L'Affaire Touvier.* Paris: Fayard, 1989.

Guéhenno, Jean. *Journal des années noires, 1940–1944.* Paris: Gallimard, 1947, 1973.

Halbwachs, Maurice. *La Mémoire collective.* Paris: Albin Michel, 1950, 1997.

Harté, Yves, and Alain Béguerie. *Le Parc Lescure.* Bordeaux: Confluences, 1998.

Hastings, Max. *Das Reich: Resistance and the March of the 2nd SS Panzer Division Through France.* New York: Holt, Rinehart, and Winston, 1982.

Hoffmann, Stanley. *Decline or Renewal? France Since the 1930s.* New York: Viking, 1974.

Hoover Institution, Stanford University. *La Vie de la France sous l'Occupation.* Statements assembled by Mr and Mrs René de Chambrun. Paris: Plon, 1957.

Hurstfield, Julian G. *America and the French Nation, 1939–1945.* Chapel Hill: University of North Carolina Press, 1986.

Igounet, Valérie. *Histoire du négationnisme en France.* Paris: Seuil, 2000.

Isorni, Jacques. *Souffrance et mort du Maréchal.* Paris: Flammarion, 1951.

Jaeckel, Eberhard. *La France dans l'Europe de Hitler.* Paris: Fayard, 1968.

Jardin, Pascal. *La Guerre à neuf ans.* Paris: Grasset, 1971.

Judt, Tony. *The Burden of Responsibility. Blum, Camus, Aron, and the French Twentieth Century.* Chicago: University of Chicago Press, 1998.

— 'Betrayal in France'. *New York Review of Books*, August 12, 1993.

Jünger, Ernst. *Journal de guerre et d'occupation.* Paris: Julliard, 1965.

Kaplan, Alice. *The Collaborator: The Trial and Execution of Robert Brasillach.* Chicago: University of Chicago Press, 2000.

Kedward, H. R. *In Search of the Maquis: Rural Resistance in*

Southern France, 1942–1944. Oxford: Oxford University Press, 1993.

— and Nancy Wood, eds. *The Liberation of France: Image and Event.* Oxford and Washington, DC: Berg, 1995.

Klarsfeld, Arno. *La Cour, les nains, et le bouffon.* Paris: Robert Laffont, 1998.

Klarsfeld, Serge. *Vichy-Auschwitz: Le Rôle de Vichy dans la solution finale de la question juive en France.* Paris: Fayard, 1983.

Laborie, Pierre. 'Sur J. J. Chapou et sa mort: Essai de bilan'. *Quercy recherche*, September-December 1984 (Comité de Diffusion de la Recherche Quercynoise, Cahors).

Lacorne, Denis, Jacques Rupnik, and Marie-France Toinet, eds. *L'Amérique dans les têtes: Un Siècle de fascinations et d'aversions.* Paris: Hachette, 1986.

Lacouture, Jean. *De Gaulle.* Vol. I, *The Rebel, 1890–1944.* Vol. 2, *The Ruler, 1945–1970.* New York: Norton, 1993.

Lajugie, Joseph, ed. *Histoire de Bordeaux.* Vol. 7, *Bordeaux au XXeme siècle.* Bordeaux: Fédération Historique du Sud-Ouest, 1972.

Lambron, Marc. *1941.* Paris: Grasset, 1997.

Langer, William L. *Our Vichy Gamble.* New York: Knopf, 1947.

Larbaud, Valery. *Enfantines.* Paris: Gallimard, 1917, 1950, 1977.

Laurens, Corran. '"La Femme au turban": Les Femmes tondues'. In *The Liberation of France: Image and Event*, edited by H. R. Kedward and Nancy Wood. Oxford and Washington, DC: Berg, 1995.

Leahy, William D. *I Was There.* New York: McGraw-Hill, 1951.

Levendel, Isaac. *Not the Germans Alone.* Evanston, Ill.: Northwestern University Press, 1997.

Limagne, Pierre. *Éphémérides de quatres années tragiques.* Paris: La Bonne Presse, 1946.

Loiseau, Ivan. *Souvenirs et temoignages.* Moulins: Éditions des Cahiers Bourbonnais, 1974.

Lowrie, Donald A. *The Hunted Children.* New York: Norton, 1963.

Maier, Charles. *The Unmasterable Past: History, Holocaust, and German National Identity.* Cambridge: Harvard University Press, 1988.

Marrus, Michael R., and Robert O. Paxton. *Vichy France and the Jews.* Stanford, Cal.: Stanford University Press, 1995.

Martin du Gard, Maurice. *Chronique de Vichy*. Paris: Flammarion, 1948.

Maureille, Paul. 'Vivre à Tulle, 1920–1925'. In *Lemouzi*. Tulle: École Limousine Félibréenes, 1990.

Mauriac, François. *Préséances*. Paris: Flammarion, 1962.

— and Michel Suffran. *Bordeaux: Une Enfance*. Bordeaux: L'Esprit du Temps, 1990.

Maurois, André. *Destins exemplaires*. Paris: Plon, 1952.

Mendès France, Pierre. *The Pursuit of Freedom*. London: Longmans, Green, 1956.

Mérimée, Prosper. *Notes d'un voyage en Auvergne, 1838*. Paris: A. Biro, 1989.

Meyssignac, Marcel. *Comment Tulle ne fut pas Oradour*. Brive: Chastrusse, 1994.

Michel, Henri. *Paris allemande*. Paris: Albin Michel, 1981.

Miller, Gérard. *Les Pousse-au-jouir du Maréchal Pétain*. Paris: Livre de Poche, 1988.

Morgan, Ted. *An Uncertain Hour: The French, the Germans, the Jews, the Barbie Trial, and the City of Lyon, 1940–1945*. New York: Morrow, 1990.

Mothe, Florence. *Toutes hontes hues: Un Siècle de vin et de négoce à Bordeaux*. Paris: Albin Michel, 1992.

Murphy, Robert. *Diplomat Among Warriors*. New York: Doubleday, 1964.

Musée Départemental de la Résistance et de la Déportation. *Maquis de Corrèze*, 5th ed. Tulle: Collectif 'Maquis de Corrèze', 1995.

Nicolle, Pierre. *Cinquante Mois d'armistice: Vichy, 2 juillet 1940–26 aout 1944*. Paris: André Bonne, 1947.

Noguères, Louis. *Vichy, juillet 40*. Paris: Fayard, 2000.

Nouveau Mémorial de Vichy. Vichy: Montagnes Bleus, 1946.

Novick, Peter. *L'Épuration française*. Paris: Balland, 1985. Translation of *The Resistance Versus Vichy: The Purge of Collaborators in Liberated France*. New York: Columbia University Press, 1968.

Odin, Jean. *Les Quatre-vingts*. Bordeaux: La Presqu'île, 1946, reprint 1997.

Ophuls, Marcel. *Le Chagrin et la pitié*. Film script. Paris: Alain Moreau, 1980.

Ory, Pascal. *La France allemande: Paroles du collaborationisme français*. Paris: Gallimard, 1995.

— ed. *La France allemande, 1933–1945: Paroles françaises*. Paris: Gallimard, 1995.

Paxton, Robert O. *Vichy France: Old Guard and New Order, 1940–1944*. New York: Columbia University Press, 1972, 1982.

— 'The Trial of Maurice Papon' *New York Review of Books*, December 16, 1999.

— and Nicholas Wahl, eds. *De Gaulle and the United States: A Centennial Reappraisal*. Oxford and Providence, R.I.: Berg, 1994.

Péan, Pierre. *Une Jeunesse française: François Mitterrand, 1934–1947*. Paris: Fayard, 1994.

Pétain, Maréchal. *La France nouvelle: Principes de la communauté, suivis des appels et messages, 17 juin 1940–17 juin 1941*. Paris: Fasquelle, 1941.

Poirot-Delpech, Bertrand. *Papon: Un Crime de bureau*. Paris: Stock, 1998.

Postel, Alain. 'Un fils de Tulle'. *Revue des lettres, sciences et arts de la Corrèze* 101 (1998) (Société des Lettres, Sciences et Arts de la Corrèze, Tulle).

Poznanski, Renée. *Être juif en France pendant la Seconde Guerre Mondiale*. Paris: Hachette, 1994.

Le Procès du Maréchal Pétain: Compte rendu stenographique. Paris: Albin Michel, 1945.

Le Procès de Xavier Vallat: Présenté par ses amis. Paris: Éditions du Conquidstador, 1948.

Pryce-Jones, David. *Paris in the Third Reich: A History of the German Occupation, 1940–1944*. London: Collins, 1981.

Que Faire de Vichy? Special edition of *Esprit*, May 1992. Edited by Olivier Mongin.

Rebatet, Lucien. *Les Décombres*. Paris: Denoël, 1942.

Rémy [Gilbert Renault]. *Les Balcons de Tulle*. Paris: Perrin, 1962.

Rist, Charles. *Une Saision gâtée: Journal de la guerre et de l'occupation, 1939–1945*. Paris: Fayard, 1983.

Rougeron, Georges. *L'Épuration en Allier, 1943–1946*. Moulins: Conseil Général de l'Allier, 1982.

— *Mémoires d'autre temps en Allier.* Moulins: Conseil Général de l'Allier, 1984.

— *Quand Vichy était capitale, 1940–1944.* Le Coteau: Horvat, 1983.

Rousso, Henry. *La Hantise du passé.* Paris: Textuel, 1998.

— *Pétain et la fin de la collaboration.* Brussels: Complexe, 1994.

— *The Vichy Syndrome.* Cambridge: Harvard University Press, 1991.

— 'L'Épuration en France: Une Histoire inachevée'. *Vingtième Siècle, revue d'histoire* 33 (January-March 1992).

— 'Une Justice impossible: L'Épuration et la politique antijuive de Vichy'. *Annales économies sociétés civilisations,* May-June 1993.

Roy, Jules. *The Trial of Marshal Pétain.* New York: Harper & Row, 1967.

Saint-Bonnet, Georges. *Vichy capitale: Ce que j'ai vu et entendu à Vichy.* Clermont-Ferrand: Montlouis, 1941.

Sarrazin, Hélène. *Adrien Marquet.* Montreuil-Bellay: Éditions CMD, 1999.

Sérézat, André. *Et les bourbonnais se levèrent.* Nonette: Créer, 1985.

Sicard, André. 'Thierry de Martel, seigneur de la chirurgie et homme d'honneur'. *Histoire des sciences medicales* 26, no. 2 (1992).

Silverman, Willa Z. *The Notorious Life of Gyp, Right-Wing Anarchist in Fin-de-Siècle France.* New York: Oxford University Press, 1995 (*Gyp: La Dernière des mirabeau.* Paris: Perrin, 1998).

Simenon, Georges. *Maigret à Vichy.* Paris: Presses de la Cité, 1968.

Sjöberg, Henri. *Hors-saison à Vichy.* Paris: Seuil, 1945.

Slama, Alain-Gérard. 'Les Yeux d'Abetz'. *Contrepoint,* April 1973.

Slitinsky, Michel. *Procès Papon.* Paris: L'Aube, 1997.

Sollers, Philippe. *Vision à New York.* Paris: Gallimard, 1981, 1998.

Soulier, Antoine. *Le Drame de Tulle.* Tulle: Maugein, 1971.

Soulier, Régis. *La Vie politique locale: Le Cas de Tulle.* Tulle: Maugein, 1979.

Stendahl. *Bordeaux, 1838.* Paris: Proverbe, 1995.

Sternhell, Zeev. *Ni droite ni gauche: L'Idéologie fasciste en France.* Brussels: Complexe, 1992.

Stücki, Walter. *La Fin du régime de Vichy.* Neuchâtel, Switzerland: La Baconnière, 1947.

Sweets, John. *Choices in Vichy France.* Oxford: Oxford University Press, 1986.

Taylor, Telford. *The Anatomy of the Nuremberg Trials*. New York: Knopf, 1992.

Terrisse, René. *Bordeaux, 1940–44*. Paris: Perrin, 1993.

Théolleyre, Jean-Marc. *Procès d'après-guerre*. Paris: La Découverte, 1985.

Tillinac, Denis. *Spleen en Corrèze*. Paris: La Table Ronde, 1984, 1997.

Tracou, Jean. *Le Maréchal aux liens*. Paris: André Bonne, 1948.

Trouillé, Pierre. *Journal d'un préfet pendant L'occupation*. Paris: Gallimard, 1964.

Tulle et ses environs. Guidebook. Martel: Éditions du Laquet, 1997.

Tulle: Résistance et déportation par la mémoire des rues, 1940–1945. Collective, Collège Clemenceau, 1995–96. Naves: Imprimerie du Corrèzien, 1996.

US Department of State. *Foreign Relations of the United States*, 1942, vols. 1 and 2. Washington, DC: GPO, 1962.

Valéry, Paul. *Cahiers*, vol 2. Paris: Gallimard / Éditions de la Pléiade, 1974.

— *Cahiers Paul Valéry* 3: Questions du rêve. Paris: Gallimard, 1979.

— *Notes sur le rêve* (from the notebook *Somnia*, 1911). Paris: Les Cahiers de la Pléiade, 1949.

Vallat, Xavier. *Feuilles de Fresnes, 1944–1948*. Annonay: privately printed by the author, 1971.

Xavier Vallat, 1891–1972. Paris: Les Amis de Xavier Vallat, 1977.

Veillon, Dominique, ed. *La Collaboration: Textes et débats*. Paris: Le Livre de Poche, 1984.

Verheyde, Philippe. *Les Mauvaises Comptes de Vichy*. Paris: Perrin, 1999.

Verynaud, Georges. *Histoire de Tulle*. Limoges: CRDP, 1976.

Violet, Bernard. *Le Dossier Papon*. Paris: Fayard, 1997.

Vulliez, Wanda. *Vichy: La Fin d'un époque*. Paris: France-Empire, 1986.

Weber, Eugene. *The Hollow Years: France in the 1930s*. New York: Norton, 1994, 1996.

Weil, Martin. *A Pretty Good Club: The Founding Fathers of the U.S. Foreign Service*. New York: Norton, 1978.

Werth, Léon. *Impressions d'audience: Le Procès Pétain*. Paris: Viviane Hamy, 1995.

White, Freda. *Three Rivers of France*. London: Faber, 1952, 1986.

Wieviorka, Annette. *Déportation et génocide: Entre la mémoire et l'oubli*. Paris: Plon, 1992.

Winock, Michel. *Nationalisme, antisémitisme, et fascisme en France*. Paris: Seuil, 1990.

Wyman, David S. *The Abandonment of the Jews: America and the Holocaust, 1941–1945*. New York: New Press, 1984, 1998.

Zaretsky, Robert. *Nîmes at War: Religion, Politics, and Public Opinion in the Department of the Gard, 1938–1944*. University Park: Pennsylvania State University Press, 1995.

Zuccotti, Susan. *The Holocaust, the French, and the Jews*. New York: Basic Books, 1993.

Periodicals

Aspects de la France
Libération
Le Monde
La Montagne
The New York Times
La Petite Gironde
Le Progrès de l'Allier
Le Progrès de Bordeaux
La Semaine de Vichy-Cusset
Sud-Ouest

Film

La Mémoire des vivants (Tulle). Directed by Jean Pradinas. Revfilms (Paris) and France 3 (Limoges), 1994.

Acknowledgements

My greatest thanks go to my wife, Sharon, without whose support, patience and wisdom this book would not have been possible. I would also like to thank my editor, Eric Chinski, whose insights were essential. He is a model editor, and this book would have been very different without his contribution. My agent, Gloria Loomis, sustained this project from the beginning, and I am deeply grateful to her. I benefited greatly from the careful reading of Laurence Cooper, senior manuscript editor at Houghton Mifflin. I also want to thank my brothers, Joshua and Jonathan Nossiter, for their attention to the manuscript of this book.

In France, I would especially like to thank Joan and Michel Mendès France. Their friendship and counsel were precious and deeply valued. I would also like to give special thanks to Gilbert Beaubatie and Robert-Louis Liris; their thoughtfulness and wisdom inform this book.

I also want to thank the following people for their help:

In Bordeaux: Marilyn August, Jean-Michel Dumay, José-Alain Fralon, Lee Yanowitch, Nicolas Weil, Denis Demonpion, Anne-Marie Dignac, Denis Dignac, Hugues Lawton, Pierre Lawton, Claire Cruse, Robert Ducos-Ader*, Benoît Ducos-Ader, Maurice-David Matisson*, Michel Slitinsky, Yves Harté, Dominique Richard, Gilbert Gauthier, Odile Touzet,

* Deceased

Michel Touzet, Gerard Boulanger, Bertrand Favreau, Patrick Chastenet, Suzanne Fribourg*, Martine Navarri, Marie-Laurence Navarri, Pierre Agrelli, Jean-Philippe Larrose, Michael and Colette Scott.

In Vichy/Allier: Jean Débordes, Robert Edier, Jacques Lacarin, Virginie Gonnat, Jean Faye, Maurice Benhamou*, Suzanne de la Maisonneuve, Denis Tranchard, Guy Maingonat, Henri Maingonat*, Jean Pagnat, Stephen Burke, Pierre des Ligneries, Pierre Corniou, Paul Aletti, Marguerite Pougnié, Georges Frelastre, André Touret, Roger Cléry, Sophie Caracciolo, Jacques Chervet, Jean-Michel Belorgey, Georges Rougeron, Lucienne Bernard, Jacques Rivière, Jean-Louis Bourdier, Michel Hilleret, Charles Desausse, Nicolas Guillot, Isabelle Guillot, Georges Tixier, M. and Mme Jacques-Pierre Léger, Monique Léger, Pierre Saurou, André Boaziz, Max Seror, Samuel Mechoulan, Pierre Broustine, Bernard Broustine, Georges Fleury, Henri Sjöberg*, Yves Billard, Simonne d'Escrivan, Anne Bourge, Fabienne Gelin, Fabrice Dubusset, Michel Arnaud, Michelle London, Jean Corre, René Galant, Thierry Malard, M. and Mme de Chassat, Henri Bardiaux, Jacques Pegand and Jean Giraud*.

In Tulle: Pierre Diederichs, Patrick Teyssandier, Jacques Dauzier, Pierre-Henri Drelon, Jacques Spindler, Charles Godillon, Marie-Louise Godillon, Christian Cueille, Jean-Marc Laurent, Charles Clair, M. and Mme Georges Espinasse, Jean Charoux, Philippe Feydeau, Hélène Say, Pierre Barbazanges, Mme M. J. Brugeaud, Paul Capredon, Monique Gamblin, Mme S. Sainmont, Mme Marius Raze, Janine Picard, M. and Mme Louis Vaux, M. and Mme Pierre Roubinet, Charles Montagnac, Jacques Martinie, Jean Dautrement, Bruno Ledée, Mme Maurice Neyrat and Jacques Druliolle.

In Paris: Colette Faus, Sarah Farmer, Didier Rioux, Nicole Bernheim, Anne-Marie Pathé, Marc-Olivier Baruch, Michel

* Deceased

and Françoise de Boissieu, Agnès Bos, Philippe Luyt, John Fredenberger, Thelma Agopian, Jean Vaujour, Dominique Schneider, Serge Klarsfeld, Sonia Kronlund and Anne Bagamery.

In the United States: Tyler Thompson, Peter Travers, Polly Saltonstall, Lawrence N. Powell, Paul Haskins, Stanley Hoffmann, Milton O. Gustafson and William J. Walsh.